John F. Kennedy

A lively, concise and cutting-edge biography of one of the towering figures of twentieth-century history. Of all the US presidents of the post-Second World War period, John F. Kennedy is the most idolized. There is a well-documented gulf between the public's largely positive appraisal of this glamorous historical figure and professional historians' skeptical and mixed evaluation of a president who had only one foreshortened term in which to make his mark.

What made JFK the man he was? How does he fit into the politics of his time? What were his policy goals, how did they shift, and how far did he manage to advance them? What was the Kennedy style of governance? Why was he killed and how can we explain the unprecedented outpouring of grief at his death? How have perceptions of him evolved since 1963?

Acclaimed biographer Peter J. Ling explores all of these important questions, sifting and synthesizing the prodigious mass of Kennedy scholarship to provide readers with a fresh and strongly contextualized portrait of the man and his presidency.

John F. Kennedy is essential reading for students of modern American history and anyone else seeking to understand the political and private life of America's best known president.

Peter J. Ling is Professor of American Studies in the Department of American and Canadian Studies at the University of Nottingham, UK. He has been Visiting Professor of African American Studies at Emory University and Visiting Professor in Political Science at Georgia State University, Atlanta. His previous works include a highly regarded biography of Martin Luther King, Jr. (2002) and a history of the Democratic Party (2004).

Routledge Historical Biographies

Series Editor: Robert Pearce

Routledge Historical Biographies provide engaging, readable and academically credible biographies written from an explicitly historical perspective. These concise and accessible accounts will bring important historical figures to life for students and general readers alike.

In the same series:

John F. Kennedy

Peter J. Ling

Best Wishes

Peter J Ling

Routledge
Taylor & Francis Group

LONDON AND NEW YORK

First published 2013
by Routledge
2 Park Square, Milton Park, Abingdon, Oxon OX14 4RN

and by Routledge
711 Third Avenue, New York, NY 10017

Routledge is an imprint of the Taylor & Francis Group, an informa business

British Library Cataloguing in Publication Data
A catalogue record for this book is available from the British
Library

Library of Congress Cataloging in Publication Data
Ling, Peter J. (Peter John), 1956–
John F. Kennedy / Peter J. Ling.
pages cm. – (Routledge historical biographies)
Includes bibliographical references.
1. Kennedy, John F. (John Fitzgerald), 1917–63. 2. Presidents –
United States – Biography. 3. United States – Politics and
government—1961–1963. I. Title.
E842.L55 2013
973.922092 – dc23
[B]
2013017516

ISBN: 978-0-415-52885-6 (hbk)
ISBN: 978-0-415-52886-3 (pbk)
ISBN: 978-1-315-88168-3 (ebk)

Typeset in Garamond
by Taylor and Francis Books

MIX
Paper from
responsible sources
FSC
www.fsc.org   FSC® C013056

Printed and bound in Great Britain by
TJ International Ltd, Padstow, Cornwall

Contents

List of plates

Plates (between pages 144 and 145)

1   President Dwight D. Eisenhower and President-elect John F. Kennedy stand before reporters, December 6, 1960

2   Dinner at Mount Vernon in honor of Muhammad Ayub Khan, president of Pakistan, July 11, 1960

3   President John F. Kennedy with Attorney General Robert F. Kennedy, October 3, 1962

4   President John F. Kennedy and First Lady Jacqueline Kennedy greet Cuban Invasion brigade members, December 29, 1962

5   The Reverend Thich Quang Duc burns to death in front of thousands of onlookers in Saigon, Vietnam, June 11, 1963

6   President John F. Kennedy speaks in Rudolph Wilde Platz, June 26, 1963

7   President John F. Kennedy and his son, John Junior, 1963

8   President John F. Kennedy and First Lady Jacqueline Kennedy arrive in Dallas, November 22, 1963

Chronology of the Kennedy presidency

Date	Personal events	National events	International events
1960	(Jan) JFK announces candidacy for Presidency.		(Jan) Civil war in former Belgian Congo, bringing UN troops by June. (Mar 27) Sharpeville massacre in South Africa.
	(Apr) Wins first contested primary v. Hubert Humphrey in Wisconsin.	(Feb) Greensboro sit-ins mark new phase in civil rights protests.	
	(May) JFK wins in West Virginia, proving he is not just a Catholic candidate.	(May) Paris summit meeting breaks up over spy scandal.	(May 9) USSR publicizes capture of downed U-2 spy plane's pilot.
	(Jul 15) JFK wins nomination on first ballot and chooses Lyndon Johnson as his running mate.	(Jul 11) Democratic National Convention opens in Los Angeles. (Jul 25) Republicans meet in Chicago. Nixon chooses Cabot Lodge as his running mate. (Aug 24) Ike's press gaffe minimizing Nixon's role as his vice president.	
	(Sept 12) JFK addresses Houston ministers on Catholic question. (Sept 26) JFK outshines Nixon in first ever televised presidential debate.	(Sept) Nixon hospitalized until 12th with knee infection.	(Sept) Castro nationalizes US banks in Cuba.
	(Oct) LBJ campaigns for JFK in the South.	(Oct 19) Martin Luther King arrested.	
	(Oct 26) JFK phones Mrs. King to express concern about her imprisoned husband, Martin Luther King.		
	(Nov) JFK wins election narrowly.	(Nov 9) Nixon concedes election despite reported voting irregularities.	(Dec) Civil war intensifies in Laos. Ex-premier Lumumba of the Congo is detained by UN forces. He is murdered in custody. France tests nuclear weapon. East German (DDR) government limits movement from east to west Berlin.
	(Nov 25) John Junior born.	(Dec 3) Musical *Camelot* premieres.	
	(Dec 15) Secret Service arrest potential assassin Richard Pavlick in Palm Beach.		

Date	Personal events	National events	International events
1961	(Jan 20) JFK inaugurated and gives a brief, eloquent and memorable speech.		(Jan 6) Khrushchev addresses Communist international conference and predicts victory via small wars of liberation.
	(Jan 25) First live press conference.	(Jan 17) Eisenhower gives Farewell Address warning of the perils of a "military–industrial complex."	
	(Jan 30) State of the Union warns of perils abroad and recession at home.		
	(Mar 1) Executive order establishes the Peace Corps. (Mar 11) JFK offers Latin America an Alliance for Progress.	(Mar 8) Unemployment highest in 20 years—5.7 million.	(Mar 11) Fighting intensifies in Laos.
	(Apr 16) Bay of Pigs operation begins.		(Apr 12) Soviet cosmonaut Yuri Gagarin becomes first man in space.
	(Apr 24) JFK takes sole responsibility for the failure of Bay of Pigs operation.		(Apr 20) International press speculates about US involvement in failed Cuban invasion.
	(Apr 29) National Security Council (NSC) discusses US involvement in Laos and Vietnam.		
	(May 1) JFK signs Area Redevelopment Act to aid Appalachia and other areas of high unemployment.	(May 5) Alan Shepherd orbits the Earth.	
		(May 14) Freedom Ride firebombed by segregationists in Alabama.	
	(May 25) JFK sets goal of man on the Moon by end of decade.	(May 20–21) Freedom Riders besieged in Montgomery before RFK ensures safe passage to Mississippi, where they are arrested.	
	(May 31) JFK in Paris with Jackie.		(May 30) Dictator Rafael Trujillo of the Dominican Republic assassinated.

(continued)

Date	Personal events	National events	International events
	(Jun 3) Vienna summit sharpens US–Soviet tensions over Berlin.	(June 26) National port strike stopped by Taft Hartley cooling off provisions after 11 days.	(Jun 9) Vietnamese premier Ngo Dinh Diem asks for additional US troops.
	(Jul 20) JFK announces expanded civilian defense with national fallout shelter program.	(Jul 10) State banquet for Pakistan's Prime Minister Ayub Khan at Mount Vernon.	(Jul 9) Khrushchev reverses defense cuts to match US expansion.
	(Jul 25) Presidential address on the Berlin crisis.	(Aug 17) Defense Act approves $46 billion increase.	(Aug 13) Construction of the Berlin Wall begins.
		(Aug 18) 1500 US troops and Vice President Johnson in Berlin.	(Aug 30) USSR resume nuclear testing.
	(Sept 25) JFK challenges USSR to a "peace race" rather than an "arms race" in his UN speech.	(Sept 5) Resumption of US nuclear tests to match USSR's.	
		(Sept 22) Federal ban on segregation in interstate travel.	(Oct) Soviets explode largest bomb (50 megatons) at Arctic test site. JFK advisors Rostow and Taylor visit South Vietnam.
		(Oct 28) Standoff between US and Soviet tanks at Berlin Wall.	(Nov) US military advisors and helicopters dispatched to train and assist South Vietnamese in fight with Viet Cong.
	(Dec 19) JFK's father, Joseph, suffers major stroke that leaves him paralyzed on right side and unable to speak.	(Nov 13) Cellist Pablo Casals plays at the White House.	(Dec) Venezuelans warmly welcome JFK and first lady, in contrast to their heckling of Nixon in 1958.
		(Dec) Albany, Georgia civil rights protests escalate with arrival of Martin Luther King.	

(continued)

Date	Personal events	National events	International events
1962	(Jan 5) *Time* magazine names JFK its man of the year.		(Jan 10) Cuba announces extended trade agreement with USSR.
	(Jan 11) Second State of the Union deals with economic issues as well as defense.		(Jan 22) Organization of American States suspends Cuba's membership.
	(Feb 7) JFK imposes embargo on exports to Cuba (except food and drugs).	(Feb 8) US military command set up in Saigon under General Harkin to coordinate efforts.	
	(Feb 20) Edward Lansdale, head of Operation Mongoose, outlines escalating program of measures against Castro.	(Feb 14) 50 million Americans tune in to enjoy Jackie Kennedy's televised tour of the White House.	
		(Mar 8) Jackie Kennedy begins visit to India and Pakistan.	(Mar 23) US bans all Cuban imports.
	(Apr 11) JFK denounces steel industry leaders for raising prices.	(Apr 13) Steel companies rescind price increases.	
	(May 19) 15,000 people attend a birthday gala for JFK and see Marilyn Monroe sing "Happy Birthday" in a sultry tone.	(Apr–May) US resumes atmospheric testing of nuclear weapons.	
	(Jun 11) JFK explains his economic policy in a commencement speech at Yale.	(May 28) New York stock exchange loses $20 billion in value, the biggest one-day loss since 1929.	
	(Jul 11) JFK increases tax depreciation allowances for businesses.	(Jul 10) Martin Luther King arrested in Albany.	(Jul 1) The Kennedys are greeted by 1.5 million cheering Mexicans.
	(Jul 20) Maxwell Taylor made head of the Joint Chiefs of Staff.		(Jul 2) Castro visits Moscow.
			(Jul 23) Laos neutrality settlement.

(continued)

Date	Personal events	National events	International events
		(Aug 4) Marilyn Monroe found dead from apparent overdose.	(Aug 15) Military junta takes control in Peru and unrest grows in Argentina.
	(Sept 4) JFK warns about Soviet arms build-up in Cuba.	(Aug 27) Congress passes 24th Amendment outlawing use of poll tax to limit voting.	(Sept 11) Soviets complain about US troop call-ups and warn that attacking Cuba could result in nuclear war. (Sept 20) Armed clashes in Buenos Aires. (Sept 22) Soviet minister Gromyko warns UN that a US attack on Cuba could mean nuclear war.
	(Sept 30) JFK's televised address calls for calm at the University of Mississippi where James Meredith has enrolled as the first African American student.	(Sept 28) Defense Secretary McNamara says that the US is willing to use nuclear weapons to defend Berlin.	
	(Oct 16) JFK shown photos of missile sites in Cuba. Forms Ex-Comm. His generals urge air strikes and plan for an invasion. (Oct 18) JFK meets with Soviet foreign minister Gromyko who falsely claims that all arms in Cuba are defensive. (Oct 20) JFK decides to blockade Cuba but not attack.	(Oct 11) Passage of the Trade Expansion Act. (Oct 21) *New York Times and Washington Post* editors agree to hold stories about the missiles.	(Oct 11) Second Vatican Council begins under liberal Pope John XXIII. (Oct 12) Fighting on the India–China border.
	(Oct 23) Bobby Kennedy meets secretly with Soviet Ambassador Dobrynin. (Oct 24) Rusk says the other side "just blinked."	(Oct 22) Kennedy confers with Congressional leaders who favor an immediate attack on the missile sites. He later goes on national television to call for the missiles' removal and to announce the "quarantine." (Oct 25) At the UN, Adlai Stevenson shows photos of the Soviet missiles.	(Oct 23) Soviets denounce US aggression. They and Castro insist that the nuclear missiles are intended to defend Cuba. The OAS backs the blockade.
	(Oct 26) Khrushchev's first letter urging concessions arrives.		(Oct 26) Privately, Khrushchev writes to Kennedy warning about the "knot of war." (Oct 27) A second Soviet letter demands removal of missiles in Turkey and a UN-brokered settlement. Moscow receives Castro's
	(Oct 27) Ex-Comm is dismayed by second letter but decides to respond to the first. Privately Bobby tells Dobrynin time is running out.	(Oct 26) Defense Department announces that its review of nuclear shelters reveals room for only one-third of the population. (Oct 27) A U-2 plane is shot down by a SAM missile site in Cuba. Another US plane flies off course into Soviet airspace, where fighters scramble.	letter urging a first nuclear strike to preempt a US invasion of his country. (Oct 28) Khrushchev announces the missile bases will be demolished and the missiles withdrawn under UN supervision.
	(Oct 28) JFK accepts Soviet withdrawal in return for pledge that US will not invade Cuba.		

Date	Personal events	National events	International events
	(Nov 20) JFK signs an executive order banning racial discrimination in federally funded housing. He announces that all missiles have been removed from Cuba and so the quarantine is lifted.	(Nov 6) Midterm elections see only six House seats lost to the Republicans and four Democrat gains in the Senate, including Edward Kennedy of Massachusetts. Richard Nixon is defeated in California governor's race.	(Nov 21) Sino-Indian ceasefire.
			(Dec 15) Cancellation of US Skybolt missile project provokes political crisis in Britain.
	(Dec 29) JFK accepts flag of Cuban brigades and promises the flag will one day fly in a free Havana.	(Dec 26) National Maritime Union refuses to work in ports picketed by striking longshoremen.	(Dec 24) Cuba releases 1113 Bay of Pigs prisoners in return for $53 million in food and drugs.
1963	(Jan 14) Third State of the Union stresses need for tax cuts. Half of the federal budget is for defense.	(Jan 11) Newly installed Alabama Governor George Wallace declares he will defend "segregation forever."	(Jan 3) US-backed South Vietnamese forces defeated at Ap Bac.
	(Jan 20) JFK releases letter to Khrushchev regarding nuclear test ban talks. (Jan 27) He ends atmospheric tests to signal his good faith.	(Jan 25) Hilsman-Forrestal report: US efforts in Vietnam are hindered by the unpopular Diem regime.	(Jan 14) Despite US objections, de Gaulle vetoes UK entry into the EU.
		(Feb 12) Civil Rights Commission warns of widespread racial discrimination in the North.	
	(Mar 22) JFK urges states to ratify the anti-poll tax (24th) Amendment.	(Mar 16) Congress votes to extend draft law or selective service act.	(Mar 21) Central American leaders hear JFK praise their unity in the fight against Communism, including Castro.

(continued)

Date	Personal events	National events	International events
	(Apr 15) JFK tells Mrs. King he has checked on her husband's safety in prison.	(Apr 10) Nuclear submarine Thresher sinks with the loss of 129 crewmembers. Lee Harvey Oswald secretly fires at right-wing figure, Major-General Edwin Walker, but misses.	
		(Apr 12) Martin Luther King imprisoned in Birmingham jail.	(Apr 22) Reacting to instability in Laos and Southeast Asia more generally, US sends 22 naval vessels to the area.
	(May 4) JFK describes images of police violence against young demonstrators in Birmingham as a "terrible picture."	(May 10) Birmingham accord agreed.	(May 9) South Vietnamese troops attack Buddhist protesters.
		(May 24) Bobby Kennedy meets angry black intellectuals at a private meeting in New York.	
	(Jun 9) JFK gives American University address urging nuclear disarmament.		(Jun 5) UK defense minister John Profumo resigns due to a sex scandal.
	(Jun 11) JFK's civil rights address. (Jun 19) JFK sends civil rights bill to Congress. (Jun 21) JFK meets civil rights leaders at the White House. He reluctantly accepts the March on Washington will go ahead.	(Jun 11) Alabama National Guard federalized to guarantee safe enrolment of two black students at the University in Tuscaloosa.	(Jun 12) Buddhist monk Thich Quang Duc sets himself on fire in protest against Diem regime's treatment of dissenters.
	(Jun 26) "Ich bin ein Berliner" speech in Berlin.		(Jun 24) JFK assures Germans that US commitment to their defense is assured.
	(Jun 27) JFK visits family's ancestral home in County Wexford, Ireland.		(Jun 30) UK premier Macmillan and JFK issue joint appeal for a test ban treaty with the USSR.

(continued)

Date	Personal events	National events	International events
	(Jul 27) JFK addresses the nation in support of the test ban treaty.	(July 28) Black leaders list the deficiencies in the Kennedy civil rights bill.	(Aug 12) Henry Cabot Lodge sworn in as US Ambassador to South Vietnam. (Aug 26) Voice of America bluntly blames Diem's brother Nhu for pagoda raids, thus revealing US coup plans.
	(Aug 7) JFK's newborn son, Patrick, dies in a Boston hospital.	(Aug 10) Justice Department announces it will prosecute the "Albany Nine", causing outrage among civil rights supporters.	
	(Aug 24) Hilsman and Harriman draft telegram to embassy in Saigon recommending removal of Diem. (Aug 28) JFK tells Lodge to judge whether a coup will be successful and to proceed only if success is assured.	(Aug 28) March on Washington passes off peacefully with King's "I Have a Dream" speech.	
	(Sept 4) JFK tells Walter Kronkite on TV that the Vietnamese people must win the war, even though he argues against withdrawal.		(Sept 7) Fidel Castro warns the Kennedys about plotting to kill foreign leaders.
	(Sept 10) NSC listens to contradictory reports of Major General Krulak and State Department's William Mendenhall.	(Sept 15) Sixteenth Street Baptist Church bombed in Birmingham, Alabama, killing four girls in Sunday school class.	
		(Sept 24) US Senate ratifies the test ban treaty.	(Sept 27) Lee Harvey Oswald visits Cuban and Soviet consulates in Mexico City.
	(Oct 2) NSC receives McNamara–Taylor report which foresees military gains but a need for reform by Diem.	(Oct 24) UN Ambassador Adlai Stevenson is attacked after a speech in Dallas.	(Oct 9) British premier Macmillan resigns in aftermath of the Profumo scandal.
		(Nov 10) Texans reject poll tax repeal and elect conservative councilmen in Dallas.	

(continued)

Date	Personal events	National events	International events
	(Nov 21) JFK and Jacqueline Kennedy rapturously received in San Antonio, Texas.	(Nov 21) Richard Nixon tells Dallas audience that JFK has excelled only at public relations. Lee Harvey Oswald makes an unexpected call on his estranged wife Marina, giving her $170 in cash and leaving his wedding ring.	(Nov 1) Military coup topples Diem in South Vietnam. He and his brother Nhu are murdered.
	(Nov 22) JFK addresses breakfast reception in Fort Worth and then flies to Love Field in Dallas.	(Nov 22) Oswald gets lift into work with coworker, who asks about a package Oswald is carrying and is told it is curtain rods.	
	(11:40, Central Time) Motorcade leaves Love Field		
	(12:29) Motorcade reaches corner of Houston and begins slow turn past Book Depository.	(c. 12:35, Central Time) Oswald stopped by Officer Baker in the Book Depository lunchroom.	
	(12:30) Assassination. Texas Governor Connally also wounded.		
	(12:38) Parkland Hospital logs JFK's arrival.	(c. 13:00) Oswald seen by landlady at his rented room. (c. 13:15) Oswald shoots and kills Officer Tippitt. (c. 13:50) Oswald arrested in the Texas Theater. (14:30) Lyndon Johnson sworn in as President aboard Air Force One.	(Nov 22) Widespread mourning erupts in cities across the world at the news of Kennedy's murder.
	(13:00) Doctors end attempts to "save" JFK.		
	(13:38) JFK's death announced.		
	(14:14) JFK's body arrives at Love Field.		
	(20:00–midnight) Autopsy performed at Bethesda Naval Hospital, Maryland.		
	(Nov 23) JFK's body lies in the East Room of the White House.	(Nov 24, 11:20) Oswald is shot by Jack Ruby in the basement garage of the Dallas police headquarters.	
	(Nov 24) The flag-draped coffin lies in state in the Capitol.		
	(Nov 25) Burial at Arlington after requiem mass at St Matthew's cathedral.		

Acknowledgments

I would like to thank my Nottingham colleagues, and students in my American Presidency class. My intellectual debts are enumerated in the bibliography, although the failings that remain are mine alone. I am grateful to my editor Robert Pearce, and to Laura Mothersole and the team at Routledge UK. This book is dedicated to Gualtiero Coslovi and family for their many kindnesses.

Introduction

The death defined the life. The bullets fired in Dealey Plaza not only took President John F. Kennedy's life, they also wrapped themselves magically around his memory. Even individuals who cannot name a single achievement of Kennedy's time in office may nevertheless know the gruesome details of his death, via the Zapruder film footage. They may even ponder, were there shots from the "grassy knoll"? The gap between the popular rating of JFK as one of the greatest American presidents and the common historical judgment that he was good, but only potentially great, is bridged best by the still disputed and shocking facts of his death. No one reading this book will need to be told how Kennedy's life ended.

The assassination was a national trauma seen upon a global stage, and the depth of public grief and scale of public interest remain crucial to understanding the significance of the Kennedy presidency. They incline his biographers to follow narrative paths that lead to tragedy, eulogy, and the complex process of debunking (complex not least because it can launch its own myths, even as it overturns others). In the pages that follow, there is sufficient praise for the president John F. Kennedy seemed to be becoming to justify the sense of loss that his murder prompted. There is also due acknowledgement of his failings and errors. The many conspiracy theories that identify his murderers as (among other things) domestic conservative radicals, organized crime, political rivals, anti-Castro Cubans, Castro's agents, the Soviet Union, or vengeful agents of the murdered South Vietnamese leader Ngo Dinh Diem, testify to the reality that the man so lauded in death was widely loathed in life.

While he was the first to be murdered, Jack Kennedy was the third of his father's children to die violently—his older brother Joe and younger sister Kathleen both died in air crashes. With his younger brother Bobby's assassination in 1968 and his son John Junior's death in a plane crash in 1999, the morbid fascination with the seemingly cursed Kennedy dynasty grew. Like most biographies, this one seeks to understand JFK as a product of his family upbringing, acknowledging the influence of his fiercely ambitious millionaire father Joseph and his equally driven, devout mother Rose, and of the remarkable household over which they presided. Kennedy's personal political ascent is inseparable from the impact of the Kennedys, as the nation's preeminent Catholic family, on the campaign trail and in the media more generally.

The prominence of image in Kennedy's rise to the presidency has sharpened the debunkers' knives. They have revealed that the presidential candidate, who was seen on television in 1960 as visually so much more healthy and glamorous and trustworthy than his opponent Richard Nixon, was actually beset with deep-seated health problems. Despite his lovely young wife and family, Jack Kennedy was also so accustomed to sexual promiscuity that he declared that if he did not get "tail" at least once a day, he felt ill. The personal and the political intertwine powerfully in the Kennedy story. As we will see, they explain his success and the pattern of his remembrance.

As a historical biography, this book makes a concerted attempt to situate Kennedy in his times, particularly in relation to the early Cold War. Locating JFK within Cold War politics presents him as a candidate who courted a frightened nation. By the late 1950s, American public life was arguably dominated by fear: of a missile gap in the Soviet Union's favor, of the onward march of Communism and anti-Americanism around the world, of a sluggish domestic economy and a society that seemed already torn by internal divisions between races, regions, and generations. Arguably, Kennedy's success as president rested on his ability to raise the nation's confidence, while maintaining the unity that fear appeared to foster. He came to office with a clarion call for action and spent his first year warning the American people of the perils they faced. In 1962, the Cuban Missile Crisis seemed to offer the climax of those fears and resolve them in Kennedy's favor, enabling him apparently to change course towards disarmament and détente in the summer of 1963.

Over the same period, Kennedy struggled to respond to the challenge of racial injustice as the civil rights movement's actions forced the reality of inequality into the nation's consciousness. Yet it appeared to some observers in the summer of 1963 that Kennedy shared Martin Luther King's "dream" of an America that lived up to the full meaning of its creed, and that he was at last prepared to act. The nature and extent of Kennedy's commitment to racial equality are explored in this book, in ways that set them firmly in the context of competing priorities, including his desire to restore economic growth and extend social welfare. While the prolonged recession of the late 1950s abated during Kennedy's term in office, his proposals for reflationary measures and the expansion of federal efforts in terms of aid for schools, medical care for the elderly, or assistance for the poor remained for the most part stalled in a Congress dominated by conservative elements, both Republican and Democrat. In these pages we consider the claims that Kennedy shifted his position over the course of his foreshortened term. Kennedy's successor, Lyndon Johnson, eulogized him as a champion of liberal measures, but was this an accurate portrait or a calculated misrepresentation?

Kennedy's theme in the 1960 election contest was renewal. His central criticism was that the Eisenhower administration had grown tired and ineffectual, allowing the economy to stay in recession and the Soviet Union to seize the initiative internationally. In a very close contest, Kennedy won narrowly by promising voters that he would fight the Cold War more vigorously. Although many of the changes that he brought to the White House were more symbolic and cosmetic than substantive, there were some that directly affected the conduct of government. Some of these related to the organization of the Executive in terms of policy meetings and staffing. Others related to policy in terms of Eisenhower's persistent efforts to cap defense spending.

Eisenhower had used his military background to establish an elaborate committee structure with reporting procedures to both the National Security Council and the Cabinet that ensured full and informed discussion and, in general, efficient oversight of policies and their development. Eisenhower's secretary of state,

John Foster Dulles, was so prominent in the presentation of policy that journalists mistakenly believed that he set foreign policy as much as the president. Similarly, Ike's Chief of Staff, Sherman Adams, was highly visible in his role, while the president was pictured playing golf. The impression created was of Eisenhower as a genial figurehead, apt to delegate and allow others to govern.

In marked contrast, Kennedy was conspicuously in charge with his Secretary of State Dean Rusk apt to be listened to less closely than National Security Advisor McGeorge Bundy or Secretary of Defense Robert McNamara. While this change sharpened the image of the activist president, we will ask whether it ensured careful policy formulation and implementation. Where it did not, it can be argued that Kennedy left the presidency weaker than he found it.

Kennedy also warned in the 1960 campaign that Americans were threatened by the prospect of the Soviet Union's gaining an advantage in nuclear missile technology. In office, he rapidly learned that this was not so, but he also came to grasp that the established practice of nuclear deterrence ran the risk of lowering the threshold at which the use of nuclear weapons had to be considered. Developing what was known as a more flexible response and avoiding pressure from his military advisors to use nuclear weapons to deal with the Communist threat became key aspects of Kennedy's presidency, and thus crucial to gauging his success. In what follows, we look at the measures he took to revitalize US conventional capabilities and assess whether this made the nation safer, or in some sense made war more likely.

"Style" and "image" have always been key terms in discussions of the Kennedy years, and much of this impression sprang from the deliberate contrast between the oldest man ever to be president (Eisenhower) and the youngest (JFK). Kennedy won the 1960 election so narrowly that some attributed his victory to the positive image he conveyed during the first ever televised debate. Even more striking was the growth in his popularity once in office. Less than 50 percent of Americans voted for Kennedy, yet opinion polls found that his approval rating never dipped below fifty and averaged 70 percent. Understanding the significance of the Kennedy presidency entails an exploration of the way in which his strategy of photo opportunities and media management set the model for future presidents to follow. So potent was the Kennedy media style that leaders across the world tried to emulate it.

At the same time, the impact of Kennedy on the imagery of the presidency was compounded by the glamor associated with his first lady, Jacqueline, as a young mother—just thirty-one when her husband became president—and by the photogenic appeal of the other Kennedys. We remember Kennedy in a different way because of Jackie's sunglasses, the games of touch football, the banter in live press conferences, and the picture of John Junior peeping out from under his father's desk in the Oval Office. This aspect of the Kennedy presidency is considered specifically in Chapter 9.

The images that many readers may bring to these pages may come from the day of the assassination and the four days that followed, culminating in the funeral and the picture of John Junior saluting his father's casket. No biography of Kennedy can escape the assassination and historians have even been criticized for their reticence to enter into the heated discussions that circulate around that event. This book provides a summary of the major conspiracy theories, but it also places the conduct of government agencies in the context of the time, to explain why mistakes were made and why information was provided that is no longer credible.

Other biographies have followed the conventional path of ending their story at Arlington, with a grave marked by an eternal flame. This one very deliberately extends its scope into the posthumous period, in which a president who was still a politician became a president who was overwhelmingly a symbol and a hero. The process by which Kennedy is remembered is a vital part of his biography; his afterlife in the media commemorations is so conspicuous a part of the figure he has become. While the Kennedy family played an important role in framing that remembrance in positive terms, the media were vital to the development of the Kennedy legend as not simply a slain president but a vindicator of the media as a social force. In the shock of the assassination, what bound the nation, and some would claim the world, together was the mass media. By the 1980s, commemorations were as much about the newscasters and reporters who covered the event as about the murdered man and his bereaved family.

Historians mistrust biography. No single person can causally determine the course of history. Yet at the same time each person plays a part. A biography of John F. Kennedy inevitably involves consideration of an extraordinary individual: possibly the sickest man ever to be president, yet one who left the office with an enhanced image of physical glamor and intellectual vitality. It also entails an examination of his extraordinary family: parents, spouse, and siblings. They too shaped his presidency—in the case of Bobby Kennedy very directly, and far beyond the assumed juris-diction of an attorney general. His formidable father was struck down by a debilitating stroke in late 1961 so the influence he clearly had on JFK's rise did not continue in the period of the presidency itself.

Some writers have ascribed Kennedy's narrow victory in 1960 largely to the prejudice aroused by the fact that he was an Irish-American Catholic. Others ascribe it to his performance in the first televised debate or to his shrewd intervention in the Martin Luther King arrest. In each case, his victory marked an important watershed: a sign that the "immigrants" of the late nineteenth century had reached a stage where their representative could lead the nation; a sign that American politics was now vitally shaped by television, with all of its implications for image-making and campaign finance; and a sign that the African American vote in key electoral college states would go to the candidate who acted, rather than simply leaving it to the courts to act. This biography seeks to assess the significance of each of these trends.

But biography does not fully explain the substance of the Kennedy presidency in terms of what it tried to achieve and what it failed to do. Kennedy's tough Cold War line coming into the presidency reflected a broader anxiety in public and policy circles; an anxiety born of perceived setbacks, notably in Cuba, and increased risks in terms of defections to the Soviet side from across the decolonizing world and of advances in Soviet technological capabilities, sym-bolized by the space race. As we shall see, these contextual pres-sures explain Kennedy's approval of the disastrous Bay of Pigs event, his demand for increased defense spending, his commit-ment to a Moon landing, and his fascination with counter-insurgency as a means of expanding his options beyond capitulation or nuclear war.

Writing a biography is perhaps easier when one likes one's subject; it is a position that may involve slightly fewer perils than writing about a personality one loathes. As a synoptic work, this biography is informed by early studies written by men such as Ted Sorenson, and others in the Kennedy inner circle, who quite clearly loved JFK. They loved his wit, his abiding curiosity, and his extraordinary grace under pressure. It has equally found insight in revisionist accounts animated by anger at JFK, as a liar, a cheat, an egomaniac, a privileged and indulged figure of decidedly suspect character. Few of the more recent postrevisionist accounts can match the flair that these apologists and critics brought to the Kennedy story. Yet a balanced account is needed to accommodate the contradictions of the man. In a brief compass, that is what this book tries to provide: an assessment of Kennedy in life and in death.

1 The second son

Family background

John Fitzgerald Kennedy's birth on May 29, 1917 brought him not just into a family, but into a clan that was amassing wealth and seeking political power: in short, into a dynasty. His mother Rose Fitzgerald's family had enjoyed local political success. Her father John Francis Fitzgerald, an Irish-American charmer nicknamed "Honey Fitz," had been a star of the Boston political scene since the early 1890s, first as a city councilman, then as a congressman, and notably as mayor from 1906 until 1913, when the threat of a sex scandal brought his political ascent to a premature end. He went on to contest Massachusetts' first popularly elected US Senate seat against incumbent Senator Henry Cabot Lodge in 1916, giving the patrician Republican a stern test, but thereafter Fitzgerald was destined to be a political "also-ran." His grandsons, boosted by financial resources from the Kennedy side of the family, would surpass Honey Fitz's local political eminence, but the fusion of families did not come easily.

A maverick rather than a loyalist, Fitzgerald's electoral successes had occurred despite the efforts of fellow Irish-American Patrick Kennedy, a mainstay of Boston's Democratic Party machine. This naturally made Mayor Fitzgerald hostile to his teenage daughter's romantic attachment to Kennedy's eldest son, Joseph. Fitzgerald tried to end the relationship through foreign travel and well-connected rival suitors. He even went so far as to send Rose to not one but two nunneries, at home and abroad—but the marriage of warring parties can help dynasties grow. Relenting after seven years, Fitzgerald announced publicly in the summer of 1914 that his daughter would marry the twenty-five-year-old Joseph P. Kennedy, who—as a sign of his considerable business prowess—had recently become an unusually youthful bank president at the Columbia Trust Company.

Within a year of marriage, Joseph and Rose had their first child, Joseph Patrick Kennedy Jr. An exuberant Honey Fitz announced that his first grandson was destined by birth to be not just Boston's mayor and Massachusetts' governor, but US president as well. Less than two years later, he made no such pronouncements on the birth of grandson number two, his namesake. JFK was, in the terminology of the English aristocracy, not the heir but the spare. More importantly, whereas Joe Junior was to prove the epitome of health and fitness, Jack, as he was always called, had health problems almost from birth. He did not feed well as an infant and contracted scarlet fever at the age of three. He would get nearly all the childhood illnesses severely, and subsequently develop an adrenal condition, a type of Addison's disease. He would also damage his back, aggravate that injury during his naval service and eventually have several unsuccessful spinal operations. Pain became a defining feature of JFK's life and a vital shaper of his character. His political courage was sometimes questioned, but his fortitude in the face of personal suffering was undeniable, and makes his relaxed public persona all the more remarkable. Had Americans known how ill Jack Kennedy was in 1960, in one of America's closest elections, it is doubtful they would have chosen him as their president. Ironically, the vitality and dynamism he so embodied as both candidate and president, setting the standard for the television age, were prompted by a need to show (even at home, where his parents prized vigor) that he was no invalid, and by a realization that death was always near. Friends remember him asking them how they would want to die. His hope was that it would be quick.

Over a span of seventeen years, Rose Kennedy gave birth to nine children—Joe, Jack, Rosemary, Kathleen, Eunice, Patricia, Robert, Jean and Edward. By the time Edward was born in 1932, his father Joe Kennedy was a multi-millionaire. In the unregulated stock market boom of the 1920s, Kennedy had amassed his fortune using tactics that would later be seen as "insider trading."

His personal wealth was estimated at $4 million in 1929, and through shrewd and ruthless investment decisions made during the Great Crash and the Great Depression that followed, it grew far larger. By 1935, it was over $180 million, making Kennedy Senior a billionaire by modern standards. The rumor has persisted that Joe Kennedy was a bootlegger, illegally distributing alcohol during Prohibition, a supplier to Al Capone and other gangsters, but the reality is that he made a lot of money as the sole legal importer of Haig's and Dewar's Scotch whiskies and Gordon's gin, which he and Franklin Roosevelt's son, James, had stockpiled in anticipation of the new administration's repeal of the Prohibition laws in December 1933.

Kennedy also reaped large profits from the merger and refinancing of Hollywood studios, most notably RKO, and from property investments in New York, Chicago, and Florida. These investments frequently took him away from Boston, and his flagrant infidelity to Rose was common knowledge. In addition to bedding a succession of movie starlets, Joe had a lengthy affair with Hollywood legend Gloria Swanson. In general, he offered his sons a model of sexual promiscuity that they largely adopted, notoriously so in the case of Marilyn Monroe, despite the political risks such liaisons entailed. With wealth came public prominence, and links to important political figures like Franklin Roosevelt, who eventually made Joe Senior the first head of the Securities and Exchange Commission. This was a classic case of "poacher turned gamekeeper," since Kennedy had himself profited from the financial maneuvers that the new agency was set to eliminate.

In 1927 the Kennedy family moved to Riverdale, New York, and two years later they moved still further up the Hudson, to Bronxville. By that stage, a pattern of seasonal travels had begun. Summers were spent in what became the Kennedy Compound at Hyannis Port, Cape Cod, and Christmas, Easter and other breaks were taken at their winter home in Palm Beach, Florida. By the time Jack entered his teens, his father's wealth had taken the family a long way from a simple Boston-Irish experience. Rose Kennedy took pains to Americanize her children, and, stung by his experience of social exclusion in the notoriously snobbish city of Boston, Joe was also determined to give his children every chance to advance. Winning had always been what mattered to him. At the age of fifteen he had organized a neighborhood baseball team. His drive made him its business manager, coach, and first baseman, and his management style gave his teammates no say in anything. Joe's philosophy, he told his sister, was: "If you can't be captain, don't play." A basic lesson for all his children was that you were in it to win it (Dallek 2003: 15).

In most respects, Joe and Rose Kennedy were more eager to show how American their family was than to show how Irish it remained. Prejudice against Irish newcomers to America had been particularly strong in the 1850s and it persisted for the rest of the century, especially in relation to complaints about the Irish role in the corrupt politics of America's big cities. In Boston especially, the older Anglo-Saxon families, known as Brahmins, looked down on the Irish no matter how successful they were, and Joe Kennedy felt their condescension keenly. The Irish had also faced discrimination because of widespread anti-Catholic feeling among the largely Protestant American population. The depth of this anti-Papist sentiment was demonstrated in the 1928 presidential election, when the Democratic nominee Alfred E. Smith of New York was soundly defeated by Herbert Hoover, in large part because he was Catholic. Thereafter the conventional wisdom was that no Catholic would ever be elected president, and one of Joe Kennedy's main objectives was to overturn this belief.

Being married to Joe was difficult. The devoutly religious Rose had to endure his absences and his infidelities, as well as childbirth nine times in seventeen years. She accepted the Catholic Church's teaching that sex had been ordained by God for procreation, but beyond that she seems to have taken little pleasure in it. According to one family friend, after Edward's birth she told Joe flatly, "No more sex," and moved into a separate bedroom (Dallek 2003: 22). She also seems to have established her right to travel independently as a means of escaping the ceaseless demands of a large household, even one that boasted a retinue of servants. During Jack's illness-prone adolescence, Rose was frequently away. She made seventeen trips to Europe in the mid-1930s, but never once visited Choate, the elite Connecticut boarding school that Jack went to from 1931. Looking back on his childhood, Jack told a close friend that he had cried every time his mother left, until he realized that his tears irritated her and made her like him less.

Then, he decided that he had "better take it in stride" (Dallek 2003: 69).

Rose, like Joe, played a part in toughening up her children for life's challenges. Her undemonstrative parenting came more from science than from her religion, however. She read Dr. L. Emmett Holt's *The Care and Feeding of Children* and closely followed its advice against displays of affection, particularly its warning against hugging a crying child. She also closely monitored her children's diet, allocating food in medicinal doses, adding more to the sickly Jack's plate and taking it away from the robust Joe Junior. Decades later, Jack revealed that his older brother had sometimes bullied him, but this did not stop Jack idolizing Joe, who steadily acquired a formidable reputation as a sportsman, first at Choate school and then at Harvard, in a way that Jack could not equal. When he graduated in 1933, Choate awarded Joe its top prize, as the student who best combined scholarship and athletics.

In sharp contrast, Jack failed to make the football team, had many spells in the infirmary, and was the leader of a small group of troublemakers—the "Muckers"—who enraged the school's headmaster, George St. John. Teachers complained that Jack daydreamed in class, and although he read a great deal in his sickbed, especially works of history and knightly tales of derring-do, his academic record was disappointing. He finished with a ranking of 65 out of a class of 110, and the school's letter to prospective colleges was hardly glowing. Kennedy's "rather superior mental ability," it noted, was offset by a lack of interest in academic study and an immaturity that made him unable to give "his best effort all the time." The best Choate tutors would say was that Jack "can be relied upon to do enough to pass" (Leamer 2001: 92).

The various pranks associated with the "Muckers" not only prompted the headmaster to summon Jack's father, but also to send Jack himself to a psychologist. The consultant reported that a "good deal of his trouble is due to comparison with his older brother." If Joe Junior "were not so efficient," he reported Jack as saying, "it would be easier for me." Instead, Jack was living up to his contrasting reputation for "thoughtlessness, sloppiness, and inefficiency." Whatever his standing with his tutors, what was also apparent during JFK's last year at Choate was his popularity, not just with his fellow "Muckers" like LeMoyne Billings and Ralph

Horton, both of whom remained his lifelong friends, but across his year. Classmates signaled their appreciation in their yearbook, voting him the boy most likely to succeed (Leamer 2001: 92–93).

Nevertheless, sickness, as much as charm, seemed the most notable thing about the adolescent Kennedy, as his poor health continued. His anxious father sent him to the world-famed Mayo Clinic. Jack's letters from there detail his symptoms graphically and list the many tests he had to endure. He wrote Lem Billings about how they "gave me 5 enemas until I was white as snow" and on the side of another letter, he scribbled: "The reason I'm here is that they may have to cut out my stomach!" Historian Robert Dallek notes that a Boston gastroenterologist reported the clinic's diagnosis as "diffuse duodenitis and severe spastic colitis." He surmises that Kennedy, even at this early stage, may have begun to take corticosteroids in the form of pellets implanted under the skin. An expensive experimental treatment, this relieved his inflammatory problems, but at the expense of long-term damage. Chronic use of such drugs can produce spinal osteoporosis and a suppression of normal adrenal function. Thus the remedy prescribed may have spawned Jack's major medical problems in adulthood: acute degeneration of the spine and Addison's disease (Dallek 2003: 74–75).

Politics: The New Deal and intervention in World War II

While the young Kennedy was struggling with ill health and adolescent rebellion, most Americans were facing a grim period of deepening economic depression and political change. Herbert Hoover, the third successive Republican occupant of the White House since 1921, was succeeded in 1933 by the most successful Democratic president of all, Franklin Delano Roosevelt, the only man to be elected to the office four times. FDR emboldened the nation with his self-confidence, declaring in his morale-boosting inaugural address that the nation "had nothing to fear, but fear itself." He pushed through a remarkable range of measures in his first "Hundred Days," and by the time of his re-election in 1936 he had persuaded many Americans that his New Deal was creating a new kind of America in which the government provided a safety net in hard times and acted as a countervailing force against corporate greed.

Joseph Kennedy Senior was an early backer of FDR in 1932, and had become close to the latter's son. He raised substantial amounts for the campaign and used his influence with press magnate William Randolph Hearst to swing vital party convention votes behind FDR. However, the two men were not friends. The most bizarre expression of this animosity was recorded by FDR's son, James, who arranged for Joe to visit the president to ask him outright for the London ambassadorial post. FDR astonished his two visitors by asking Joe to step away from the desk into the open space of the room and to drop his pants. Having first checked that he had not misheard FDR's order, Joe slipped off his suspenders and let his trousers fall. "Just look at your legs," Roosevelt declared, and went on to remind Kennedy that the induction ceremony for ambassadors to the Court of St. James required a formal dress of knee britches and silk stockings. With his bow legs, Roosevelt declared, Kennedy would be a laughing-stock, adding with emphasis, "You're not right for the job, Joe" (Schwartz 2003: 6).

Swallowing his pride at this humiliation, Joe asked the president for two weeks to induce the British to change their practice and permit the wearing of a cutaway coat and striped pants. Believing that the British would resist such a change, FDR consented. Two weeks later, however, the White House announced the appointment of Ambassador Joseph P. Kennedy, the first American of Irish stock to hold the post. While Kennedy did not have the legs for the role he certainly had the wealth, a key concern since the official allowance for the London embassy had never come close to covering its real cost. He also had experience in international trade, and had recently moved from the Securities and Exchange Commission to the newly created Maritime Commission. Events proved that what he lacked for the diplomatic post was tact, and more importantly a willingness to fulfill FDR's idea of the ambassadorial role, which was to relay accurate information back to Washington and obey orders. Being ambassador to the Court of St. James did confirm the family's celebrity status in the magazines of the late 1930s, however, and gave young Jack the chance to observe the major political players on the international scene in the critical period from Munich to Dunkirk.

According to some reports, Joe's priority was raising his family's prestige, particularly if this boosted Joe Junior's political prospects. Leading liberals in the Roosevelt administration, such as Harold Ickes, felt that Kennedy was a poor choice. In his diary, Ickes described Joe as "untrained in diplomacy, unlearned in history and politics." A publicity-seeker, Joe seemed to Ickes to be maneuvering for a presidential run himself. He was also alleged to have given the German ambassador to Britain, Herbert von Dirksen, the impression that the US admired the Fuehrer's achievements and was largely sympathetic to the Nazis' approach to the "Jewish question." Joe's anti-Semitism almost certainly did not go so far as to endorse Hitler's final solution, but it was sufficiently well known to remain a problem for JFK later. Worries about Joe Kennedy's appointment deepened when the newly appointed ambassador responded to Hitler's takeover of Austria by telling the press bluntly that he was "unable to see that the central European developments affect our country or my job" (Schwartz 2003: 238–40). Many in the US and Britain shared Joe's neutralist position, but it played better with anti-FDR elements than with Roosevelt's inner circle. Despite these misgivings about his ambassador, FDR concluded that Joe Kennedy could be an even bigger nuisance at home, where he might use his isolationist opinions to contest Roosevelt's bid for an unprecedented third presidential nomination in 1940.

Kennedy wealth gave Joe's sons a blinkered view of the United States during the Depression decade, but it also enabled them to see the world, particularly the world of high politics on the eve of a second global conflict. In the summer of 1937, Jack traveled through Europe with his friend Lem Billings, from the Franco–Spanish border to Berlin, as a gap break before college. When Ambassador Joseph Kennedy arrived in London in March 1938, neither of his two older sons was with him, since they were at Harvard, but by June Joe Junior had graduated and through his father's contacts was able to travel to Paris, Prague, Warsaw, Leningrad and Copenhagen, despite the deepening international crisis. Like his father, Joe expressed admiration for Hitler's Germany, and was equally sympathetic to Franco's regime in Spain. With remarkable bravado and resourcefulness, he managed to get into Madrid even before it fell to Franco's Nationalists.

Following in Joe's footsteps at Harvard, Jack enjoyed the social scene, living in a suite at Winthrop House and taking dinner at the Spee Sailing Club, but his health problems persisted. His stomach troubles saw him hospitalized in Boston twice in 1938. The following spring, he joined his father in England, ostensibly to research his senior honors thesis on recent British foreign policy. Jack was beginning to develop a genuine interest in his studies and his father's position ensured that he was able to meet ambassadors and other high officials as he journeyed across Europe and even visited Palestine. His letters to Lem Billings mixed tales of diplomatic receptions with salacious stories of sexual encounters. He was vacationing near Cannes on the Riviera with the rest of the family when the Nazi–Soviet pact signaled ominously that the Anglo–German Munich agreement had certainly not ensured "peace for our time."

By September 1, 1939, when the Germans invaded Poland, the Kennedys were back in London. The ambassador had become close friends with Prime Minister Neville Chamberlain and was with him as he prepared to address the nation and announce that Britain was at war. An almost hysterical Joe Kennedy rang his president, awakening him at four in the morning. In Joe's view, Britain was doomed and a new dark age was set to descend on Europe. "It's the end of the world," he cried, "The end of everything." America remained neutral but quickly faced its first losses. A German torpedo sank the British liner *Athena*, with three hundred Americans among its fourteen hundred passengers. The ambassador dispatched his son Jack to offer comfort to the American survivors. He did so skillfully and wrote a memo urging that a US ship with naval protection should be sent to Glasgow to ensure their safe return. While the survivors waited, Jack, the billionaire's son, took the ferry to Ireland and then flew home to complete his studies at Harvard (Leamer 2001: 140).

During his first two years at Harvard, Jack had remained the unimpressive scholar that Choate had judged him to be. His energies had gone mainly into extracurricular activities. He served on the Annual Show committee as a freshman and on the business board of the Harvard *Crimson* newspaper the following year. An intercollegiate sailing trophy was the one glittering prize of his early college years. He also gained a "playboy" reputation, in which he reveled. He boasted of his sexual conquests in letters to Lem. "I can now get my tail as often and as free as I want which is a step in the right direction," he declared (Dallek 2003: 46). In this respect, he had overtaken his older brother Joe, whose athletic prowess and political ambitions continued to overshadow him. According to one of Jack's tutors, Payson Wild, only when Joe left for law school did Jack begin to make his mark academically.

From Harvard, Jack wrote to his father to report that being an ambassador's son gave him some cachet with the girls. So "before resigning," he joked, "give my social career a bit of consideration" (Dallek 2003: 60). Joe Kennedy's ambassadorship to London was becoming more difficult as the British position deteriorated. He had become notorious for his stark views, alienating British people by telling them they were doomed and dismaying Roosevelt by his overt support for American isolationism, which was strengthening as the 1940 election approached. Fueling FDR's mistrust, Joe hosted Henry Luce, the *Time-Life* publisher, and his wife Clara, who were known to be strong supporters of the Republican presidential hope, Wendell Wilkie. There was even talk that if Joe Kennedy, the most prominent Catholic in the administration, abandoned Roosevelt as an interventionist and endorsed Wilkie as a true defender of American neutrality, thousands of Catholic voters would follow his example. Underlining his father's opposition to American involvement in the war, Joe Junior vociferously opposed US aid to Britain in the summer of 1940, telling Boston audiences "convoys mean war." As a delegate to the Democratic National Convention in July, the younger Kennedy even went so far as to vote against FDR's nomination (Leamer 2001: 152). At the same time, Joe Senior was pressing to be relieved of his post so that he could return to America before the November election. With the Luces, he had hatched a plot to thwart FDR's dreams of an unprecedented third term.

FDR was easily Joe's equal when it came to political scheming, however. He ensured that Joe was chaperoned directly to Washington along with his wife Rose, who had shown evident delight in her role as America's first lady in London. As expected, she warned Joe that he risked not just his own but the entire family's reputation by coming out against the president. At the White House, FDR listened with apparent sympathy to Joe's denunciation of State Department officials who had contacted British officials behind his back and even assured him that after the election he would have "a real housecleaning." FDR's master-stroke, however, was to underline the implications of Joe's choice for his sons' political future. Years later, Joe told Clara Luce that FDR offered him a deal whereby the president would repay the 1940 endorsement with an endorsement of his own: namely of Joe Junior for governor of Massachusetts in 1942. Others recalled the president's offer in less specific terms: he would do what he could to help should Joe's boys run for political office (Leamer 2001: 155).

The offer was simultaneously a promise and a threat. FDR would work for the young Kennedys if Joe cooperated, but equally he would work against them if Joe's plotting produced a Repub-lican victory. A few days later, Ambassador Kennedy gave a CBS Radio address to the nation in which he declared that the charge that the president was leading America into war was false. He admitted that he and the president had disagreements, but encouraged his listeners to trust his honest judgment. "After all, I have a great stake in this country. My wife and I have given nine hostages to fortune," he reminded the audience. "Our children and your children are more important than anything else in the world" (Leamer 2001: 156).

The speech was welcomed by Democrats, and FDR's landslide victory seemed to set the stage for the Kennedy boys to cash in on their father's diplomatic U-turn. The Luces and others who had expected Joe Senior to aid their cause would subsequently regard all Kennedy promises with skepticism. Yet only days after the election, Joe forfeited all that he had gained. In conversation with journalists he foolishly said that democracy was "all finished in England" and "it may be here" as well (Leamer 2001: 157). His blindly inappropriate comments lambasted both the new Churchill government in Britain and Eleanor Roosevelt, FDR's often out-spoken and ultraliberal first lady. Once the story appeared on November 10, 1940, even Joe realized that he must resign.

It was in this unfolding context that Jack Kennedy wrote his undergraduate dissertation, entitled "Appeasement at Munich."

He argued that Britain's failure to rearm in the 1930s had given Chamberlain no alternative but to appease Hitler, and that this failure flowed from the strength of public opinion, which subjected democratic politicians to greater accountability than was the case for the European dictators. It is easy to read the thesis as a defense of his father's pro-Chamberlain position at the time of Munich, but there are other aspects that would be central to JFK's politics for most of his life. First, the piece embodied a fear that democracies could not mobilize their resources as readily as authoritarian regimes. Second, it articulated Kennedy's conviction that the strongest protection against aggression was an adequate arsenal of weapons. In order to move a democratic nation to action, Kennedy believed, its leaders had to make a compelling case for sacrifice, a belief that would be echoed in his inaugural address just over two decades later. Equally, the Kennedy who decried what proved to be an imaginary missile gap in the late 1950s and who presided over a significant expansion of defense spending in his first two years in office, but who then made significant moves towards détente and disarmament in the closing months of his life, is also evident in his undergraduate thesis.

Ever supportive of his sons' pursuits, Joe Kennedy felt that Jack's work deserved a wider audience than four Harvard tutors. He used his considerable influence to have it published. Both Harpers and Harcourt Brace turned it down, as a publication whose potential readership might soon be overtaken by events. But publishing house Wilfred Funk took it on. With the able assistance of *New York Times* columnist Arthur Krock, the thesis was swiftly revised, and *Why England Slept* appeared to positive reviews. At the age of twenty-three, Jack was uncertain of his future but felt that journalism might be his chosen field. The book had put him ahead of Joe Junior in that respect, but the international situation it analyzed represented a challenge to them both, and to all young men of the time. Ill health dogged Jack still, as he wrestled with abdominal pain, a spastic colon and weight loss. While playing tennis in the later part of 1940, he reported a sensation of sudden pain in the lower right of his back, as if "something had slipped." This may well have been the first significant sign that the adrenal extracts he had been given to ease his colitis had produced spinal osteoporosis. Nevertheless, his health problems did not prevent him accompanying his mother and sister Eunice on a tour of Latin America in the spring of 1941 (Dallek 2003: 81).

Early in 1941, Joe Junior wrote to his father explaining his predicament, as a critic of intervention who still wanted to be seen as a patriot. "I think in that Jack is not doing anything," he noted rather harshly, "and with your stand on the war, that people wonder what the devil I am doing back at school with everyone else working for the national defense" (Leamer 2001: 162–63). To prepare himself, Joe began taking private flying lessons from a family friend and in June he enlisted in the Naval Aviation Cadet Program. A prime specimen, he sailed through the medical examination, but both the army and the navy physicals flunked his brother Jack when he applied. Only the former ambassador's string-pulling secured Jack admission to Naval Intelligence in October 1941. He became one of six officers assigned to condense news of international developments, a task that acquired a new intensity after Japan's December 7 attack on Pearl Harbor.

Jack's sister Kathleen, known affectionately as "Kick," was also in Washington working for the conservative *Times-Herald* newspaper, and through her JFK met the first sexual companion of his whose background drew the attention of the Federal Bureau of Investigation. Inga Arvad was a stunning Danish blonde who wrote a regular *T-H* column. Four years older than Jack, she was going through a second divorce when they met, a situation that made her unacceptable as a serious marital prospect for the son of one of America's most prominent Catholic families. Of greater interest to the FBI was her previous contact with high-ranking Nazis, including Hitler himself, while working in Germany. Her affair with Jack, an officer in the intelligence service, set alarm bells ringing, and the navy tried to put some distance between Jack and the girl he called "Inga-Binga" by transferring him to the Charleston Navy Yard in South Carolina. FBI wiretaps confirmed that the passionate and stormy relationship continued, with the two spending long weekends together in Charleston. The FBI also caught, and probably shared, JFK's condemnation of "stinking New Dealism" (Leamer 2001: 177). Under pressure from his father and with Inga's consent, Kennedy eventually ended the relationship in March.

Jack's liaison with a suspected Nazi spy was not the only threat of scandal which Joseph Kennedy felt obliged to deal with in 1942. His eldest daughter Rosemary had been kept in the family home despite a growing recognition that she was mentally impaired. As she reached maturity, she was moved to a convent home, but her carers struggled to control her. The nuns reported instances where she had sneaked out at night and returned in the early morning with her clothes disheveled. Just as in Jack's case, Joe sought the latest medical advice, and tragically he arranged for Rosemary to have a prefrontal lobotomy. More shockingly, he did so without his wife's knowledge. The surgery was disastrous, leaving Rosemary capable of speaking only a few words and with none of the gentle warmth that her siblings remembered. She was kept in private care, away from the family, for the rest of her life.

In the aftermath of his affair with Inga, Jack was once more beset by health problems, particularly back pain. From March to June 1942 he was ferried between doctors, who debated the need for surgery, a move that might end his naval career. Historian Robert Dallek reports that during this period Jack considered renouncing his Catholicism in retaliation for his parents' pressurizing him to end his affair with Inga. His sarcastic denunciation, in a letter to his mother, of the Church as "a completely ritualistic, formalistic, hierarchical structure in which the Word, the truth, must only come down from the very top" certainly smacks of anger but whether it sprang solely from the loss of Inga, or from despair at his unending health problems, or anger at his sister's mutilation is unclear (Dallek 2003: 86–87). What is certain is that he now pressed for an active service role. With characteristically anti-Semitic comments, his father explained Jack's admission to midshipman's school to Joe Junior on June 20: "[Jack] has become disgusted with desk jobs and all the Jews, and as an awful lot of the fellows he knows are in active service, and particularly with you in the fleet service, he feels that at least he ought to be trying to do something. I quite understand his position, but I know his stomach and his back are real deterrents—but we'll see what we can do" (O'Brien 2005: 125).

Jack's martial ambitions focused on becoming a torpedo boat commander. These small, high-speed craft known as "PT" (patrol torpedo) boats or "PTs" had attracted extensive press coverage, with Lieutenant Commander John Bulkeley winning one of the early Congressional Medals of Honor of the war for his role in evacuating General MacArthur's forces from the besieged beaches at Bataan. Against his better judgment, Joe went to see Bulkeley on Jack's behalf and argued that having his son among the first fifty new PT commanders would generate powerful publicity for Bulkeley's program, and as an accomplished sailor and natural leader JFK made a very positive impression in his interview for the school.

Given the pounding that PT crews endured as they sped through the sea, Jack's pursuit of the assignment hinted at a self-destructive impulse. His mother noted a change in Jack's whole attitude to the war. "He is quite ready to die for the U.S.A. in order to keep the Japanese and the Germans from becoming the dominant people on their respective continents," she wrote, before going on to report his flippant observation that his dying "for the grand old flag" would probably not harm Joe Junior's political career either (Dallek 2003: 88). However jocular the tone of these ruminations on the risks he had embraced, they also reveal the conflicted emotions he was experiencing. Recalling the tales of knightly valor he had read as a child and the stories of martyrdom so common to his faith, Jack Kennedy may well have felt that heroic death at the hands of the enemy would put him forever ahead of his older brother, making even the latter's subsequent successes in some ways dependent on him.

With two sons in hazardous branches of the armed forces, Joe Kennedy was understandably agitated for their safety, and his influence may have ensured that, instead of being assigned to a war zone, Jack was retained as an instructor in Rhode Island. Anxious to prove himself, Jack in turn went to see his grand-father, whose political connections included David Walsh, chair of the Senate Naval Affairs Committee. Walsh was able to secure the eager warrior's transfer, first to Florida in January and then to the Solomon Islands in the South Pacific in March 1943. It proved a sobering, life-changing, and near-fatal experience. As his transport ship neared Guadalcanal it came under aerial attack, and when an effort was made to rescue a downed Japanese pilot, Kennedy was awed to watch the man's suicidal decision to open fire on the US vessel with his revolver. "It brought home very strongly," he wrote

Billings, "how long it's going to take to finish the war" (Dallek 2003: 91).

Having pulled strings to get to the front, Jack now shared his comrades' eagerness to return home as soon as possible; or so he told his parents, adding that they should urge his brother Joe not to rush to join him. He also shared the rank-and-file's derision for the navy's officer class, reporting sarcastically on the apparent surprise expressed by an admiral on learning that in the machine shop, they had, well, a lot of machinery. He also complained about the "old Captains and Commanders" brought out of retirement to manage supply stations who seemed clueless about how to move ships and cargo. Overall, he lamented the Navy's "superhuman ability ... to screw up everything they touch" (Dallek 2003: 93–94).

Jack arrived in a lull in the fighting following Guadalcanal's capture, but by June he was part of efforts to intercept Japanese convoys. His vessel *PT 109* was one of fifteen torpedo boats sent to the Blackett Strait in the Solomon Islands archipelago on the night of August 1. The ensuing clash had all the elements of a fiasco. Due to erratic communications and commands the attack was uncoordinated, and thirty-two torpedoes were fired without causing any damage to the Japanese ships. A moonless night meant that it was hard to tell friend from foe, sea from shore. However, propellers could create a phosphorescent trail in the sea, and fearing that this might give away his position, novice commander Kennedy throttled back his engines, making his normally high-speed vessel slow to respond when a Japanese destroyer loomed out of the darkness. Fifteen seconds later, a catastrophic collision followed. *PT 109* thus became the only vessel of its type to be rammed during the entire war. The destroyer sliced the boat in half, killing two crewmen and leaving the remaining eleven adrift in a sea of burning oil and dizzying gasoline fumes.

Later in his political career, when a young man asked JFK how he became a war hero, he replied: "Easy. I sunk my boat." Had the story ended there, it would have taken an extraordinary amount of "spin" to make Kennedy's war record a springboard for his political career, and even, during his presidency, the subject of a Hollywood film. But it did not end there, and it was Kennedy's actions in the days that followed that hinted at the cool-headed president he would become. Clinging for nine hours to the front half of *PT 109*, the terrified crewmen looked to JFK for leadership, and he gave it. He organized them into two groups to swim to the nearest land using a plank as floatation aid. His engineer Pat McMahon was seriously burned; Jack took the strap of his colleague's life-jacket between his teeth and towed him for five hours. Despite his own exhaustion, Kennedy then set out again to try to signal for help. Meantime, his commanders had concluded that no one could have survived the collision and moved away. It was noon the next day by the time Jack Kennedy returned to his crew, who had begun to fear that he had drowned.

After allowing a fellow crewman to make a further attempt to contact a ship in the strait the next night, Kennedy concluded by day three that the tiny island could not remain their refuge, not least because of a lack of fresh water. With his encouragement, the men moved camp to a larger, neighboring island, where a rainstorm and coconut milk alleviated their thirst. On the fifth night following the shipwreck, Kennedy and another crewman, Barney Ross, swam to another atoll, closer to the main strait, where they stumbled upon a canoe, a drum of fresh water, and some provisions which they took back to their comrades. During their absence, their colleagues had been spotted by two islanders who worked as scouts for the allied forces. Using his sheath knife, Kennedy carved a crude message on a coconut shell for the islanders to take for help:

> Native knows posit
> He can pilot 11 alive need
> Small boat
> Kennedy

The islanders reported to an English-speaking scout on an adjacent island and he in turn radioed to initiate the rescue. Supplies were brought immediately and then, almost a week after their patrol-boat sank, all survivors were ferried back to their base for medical attention (O'Brien 2005: 151).

The most visible injury to Jack Kennedy was lacerations to his feet from coral, but his physical ordeal certainly contributed to his back problems thereafter. It could also, however, be used to camouflage other illnesses, by attributing fevers and other sickness to malaria contracted while on military service rather than to his impaired adrenal function. Reporters for the Associated and United Press covering the campaign immediately seized upon the *PT 109* incident as good copy for the home front. Interviews with his crew and with other base officials were full of praise for Jack's courage in saving his crew. Back home, the *Boston Globe* ran the headline "Kennedy's Son is Hero in the Pacific," and spoke of the incident as "one of the great stories of heroism in this war." Other papers echoed the praise. The episode was a morale-boosting tale of a millionaire's son doing his bit for America while bonding with men from a far different background (Dallek 2003: 97–98).

Jack's rescue came as a shock to most of his family, since his father had never revealed that his son was missing in action. Rose Kennedy heard about it on the radio and came rushing into her husband's study. "I just turned on a news broadcast," she cried. "They say Jack's been saved. Saved from what?" (O'Brien 2005: 161). When Mrs. Pat McMahon learned of Kennedy's role in saving her husband she wrote him a letter of thanks, which Jack was moved to share with his erstwhile girlfriend Inga. "I suppose to you it was just part of your job," she wrote, "but Mr. McMahon was part of my life and if he had died I don't think I would have wanted to go on living." Somberly, Kennedy himself reflected on the "many McMahons that don't come through" (Leamer 2001: 192).

Joe Junior learned of Jack's missing-in-action status from a friend's letter, but only a few hours later he saw headlines about the rescue. To his father's bewilderment he did not immediately phone home to learn the details. Instead the eldest son wrote a bitingly sardonic letter, offering his parents "a few words of his own activities." While Jack had been nursed through yet more illnesses in 1941, Joe had volunteered for service and become a pilot escorting merchant vessels along the American eastern seaboard and in the Caribbean. More recently he had joined a new squadron of B-24 bomber pilots being prepared for deployment in Europe. At the end of a rigorous training schedule, in September 1943, he was granted leave to go home for his father's birthday. At a celebratory dinner, with Joe Junior seated near his father in a white naval uniform, a family friend proposed a toast: "To Ambassador Joe Kennedy, father of our hero, Lieutenant John F. Kennedy of the United States Navy." Later that evening, another house guest overheard Joe Junior angrily saying to himself in his room: "By God, I'll show them." Unaware of this episode, Rose Kennedy nevertheless sensed how much the news of Jack's exploits in the Pacific stung her eldest child. In her autobiography, she notes that it was probably the first time that Jack had won such a clear advantage over his older brother, and concedes that this "must have rankled Joe Jr." (Leamer 2001: 196–99).

Not long after, Joe's bomber squadron arrived in England and he was able to visit his sister Kathleen who was working in a London Red Cross center. She had stayed when the rest of the family returned to America, largely because of her relationship with William "Billy" Cavendish, Marquess of Hartington and heir to the duchy of Devonshire, including its palatial family home, Chatsworth. In May 1944, Kathleen and Billy married in a civil ceremony in Chelsea; the historic religious divide between Catholicism and Protestantism precluded a religious service in the church of either family. Joe Junior was the only Kennedy family member present and took his father's role in giving away the bride. In doing so, he joked that he risked his political future by losing Irish Catholic votes back home. The scandal that the wedding represented was enough to send Rose Kennedy into hospital, on the verge of a breakdown. Already a Boston paper had alluded to the fact that Kathleen's aristocratic fiancé was from "a family prominent in the defense and spread of Protestantism throughout the British realm" (O'Brien 2005: 178). This signaled to its Boston-Irish readers that the Kennedys' daughter was marrying into a family who not only were not Catholic, but implicated in the hated Protestant settlement of Ireland. "Kick," as she was known, was Jack's favorite sister, and under normal circumstances he would have made sure to attend the ceremony, but he was struggling anew with his back and had reluctantly agreed to surgery. With Kick's marriage, Joe's deployment to war-torn Britain, and Jack's surgery revealing disk degeneration in the spine, 1944 was shaping up to be a difficult year for the Kennedys.

While Joe Junior's squadron flew missions against German submarines in the Bay of Biscay, letters from home kept him up to date with the continuing media celebration of his brother's exploits. John Hersey's article in the *New Yorker* was reprinted in the bestselling *Reader's Digest* magazine. Joe Junior had already flown over thirty combat missions, which was sufficient for him to apply to return home. Instead, he insisted on remaining through the June D-Day landings, providing vital air cover for the invasion fleet. On August 10, after reading Hersey's article, he wrote to Jack praising his "intestinal fortitude," an inside joke since he knew all about Jack's recurrent colitis. At the same time as he congratulated Jack on his medal, Joe scoffed: "Where the hell were you when the destroyer hove into sight, and exactly what were your moves, and where the hell was your radar?" Jack's boat had not been equipped with radar but the point-scoring was obvious, especially since Joe concluded by saying that it "looks like I shall return home with the European campaign medal if I'm lucky" (Dallek 2003: 106).

Although Jack's commander had recommended him for a Silver Star for his bravery after the crash, he actually received the less prestigious Navy and Marine Corps Medal. This still put him in the lead in Joe's estimation, though. Aiming to draw level, two days after his letter to Jack, Joe volunteered for an acutely dangerous mission against the principal German V-1 rocket base. He was to lead one of two crews flying bombers packed with explosives over the Belgian coastal site. They were to activate a remote-control guidance device, and bail out at a low altitude. "If I don't come back," Joe told a friend, moments before taking off at 6 p.m. on August 12, "tell my dad that I love him very much." Twenty minutes after take-off, two huge explosions totally destroyed both planes well within British airspace; no human remains were ever found (Dallek 2003: 106).

It had been a quiet summer Sunday in Hyannis Port for the Kennedys. Joe Senior was napping and Rose was reading the newspaper when two priests unexpectedly came to the door. They needed to speak to Ambassador Kennedy urgently. They broke the news that Joe Junior was missing, presumed dead. The family struggled to come to terms with their loss. To friends, Joe Kennedy confided that unless he could find something new to absorb him, he would go mad: "All my plans for my own future were all tied up with young Joe and that has gone to smash" (Dallek 2003: 107). In later life, whenever he tried to speak of Joe's death, he would become choked with tears. Biographer Doris Kearns Goodwin notes that the grief-stricken Rose Kennedy, true to her faith, came to accept that even if she could not comprehend it, God had a reason for taking her firstborn son. Goodwin also believes that the death left Jack exposed and vulnerable, without the previously protective shield of knowing that Joe Junior bore the main burden of family expectation. He now "felt an 'unnamed responsibility' both to his parents and to his brothers and sisters" (Kearns Goodwin 1987: 699). It was Jack who went to meet his sister Kathleen at Boston's Logan Airport and held her as she sobbed. While family members agreed that it would be nice if someone wrote a book about Joe, Eunice Kennedy recalled that it was Jack who made it happen, gathering tributes and reminiscences over the next nine months from friends, classmates, former teachers, fellow flyers, a girlfriend and even Joe's valet. He "wrote the book," she said wistfully, "while the rest of us were still playing games" (O'Brien 2005: 176).

Five hundred copies of *As We Remember Joe* were printed privately and distributed. In his introduction, which he described to Lem Billings as "the best writing I ever did," Jack Kennedy averred: "If the Kennedy children amount to anything now or ever amount to anything, it will be due more to Joe's behavior and his constant example than to any other factor." Joe Junior, rather than his father, had set the standard that they all had to strive to match or better. Struggling once more to regain his health, Jack felt Joe Junior was now unassailable. "I'm shadow-boxing in a match the shadow is always going to win," he told Lem. Yet well before the grief at Joe's death had abated, the war claimed another. In mid-September Kathleen's English husband William Cavendish was killed by a German sniper. They had been married less than five months. As the war pressed on, both she and Jack learned of other friends lost. "Luckily I am a Kennedy," the resilient Kick wrote to Lem, " … and I know we've all got the ability to not be got down. There are lots of years ahead and lots of happiness left in the world though sometimes nowadays that's hard to believe" (Dallek 2003: 108).

2   Kennedy and the Democrats

Journalist JFK

Thanks to his father's influence, John F. Kennedy was able to spend most of the spring and early summer of 1945 testing his capabilities as a journalist for Hearst newspapers. In frail health, and with no clear decision made as to his future career, he covered the San Francisco conference that saw the formation of the United Nations. Between April 28 and May 28, he filed seventeen 300-word columns, ostensibly from the point of view of an American serviceman rather than the privileged son of a man who had alienated loyal New Dealers by his plotting against FDR. Much of the time Jack struck a cautionary note, warning that the powers of the UN were likely to be constrained because of the deep disagreements among its members. The Soviets in particular, he noted, were not about to entrust their security to anything other than the Red Army. Such misgivings were fairly widespread, except among liberal Democrats who had participated in Popular Front politics, and the Kennedy family was well removed from these circles.

Privately, Jack told an old naval buddy that he felt that people were not ready for a global government to enforce the peace. "We must face the truth that the people have not been horrified by war to a sufficient extent to force them to go to any extent rather than have another war ... ," he wrote. "War will exist until that distant day when the conscientious objector enjoys the same reputation and prestige that the warrior does today" (Schlesinger 1965: 87–88). This marked a reversal of the stance he had taken in his book *Why England Slept*. There, he had implied that the antiwar sentiment that the horrors of trench warfare instilled in many British people made it impossible for their government to rearm and thus required the appeasement policy of the late 1930s. The change of heart may have come from his war experience and the loss of his brother Joe. In addition, when he wrote of people not being sufficiently horrified, popular knowledge of the full atrocity of the war, in terms of the atomic bombs and the Nazi "final solution," lay in the future. At the same time, his comments reflect a persistent theme in his thinking, that the people only act wisely if their leaders make them aware of the full extent of the crisis to be faced. Kennedy thus believed in democracy, but was sanguine about its flaws. Like presidents before him, he hoped that his country would find in peace the moral equivalent of war as a stimulus for patriotic solidarity and sacrifice.

Given his father's position as a former ambassador to Great Britain, it was understandable that Jack's next journalistic assignment should be to cover the upcoming British election, as well as the next summit of the victorious powers at Potsdam. Although Kennedy himself was an admirer of Winston Churchill, he was clear-headed enough to sense the mood for change in Britain when he returned there in June 1945. On June 23 he predicted a socialist victory, although in later reports he suggested that Churchill might win narrowly. Despite this misjudgment in the final phase of the contest, he had tried to warn his American readers that it was "only a question of time before Labor gets an opportunity to form a government." In July, Churchill was comprehensively defeated.

In his private diary, Kennedy made it clear that he felt the British people had made the wrong choice. The failings of socialism lay in its inefficiency and its illiberal tendencies, he believed. "When one sees the iron hand with which the Trade Unions are governed, the whips cracked, the obligatory fee of the Trade Union Political representatives in Parliament," he noted, "you wonder about the liberalism of the Left. They must be most careful." At the same time, he recorded his dismay with the record of Franklin Roosevelt, who had died of a brain hemorrhage on April 12, 1945. In Kennedy's opinion he had left American capitalism weakened, not so much by the laws he secured as "through the emphasis on rights rather than responsibilities."

The Democratic Party after FDR

JFK's misgivings about FDR's legacy reflected his family's unease with the New Deal and the evolving liberalism within the Democratic Party. Both of the main parties were broad coalitions, defined more by pragmatic opposition to their rival than by ideological purity. For instance, the Kennedys' allegiance to the Democratic Party stemmed primarily from Republican hostility to the influence of immigrant groups like the Irish within the nation's politics, a position well represented by the prominent role of patrician Massachusetts senator, Henry Cabot Lodge, Sr. in the campaign between the 1890s and 1920s to restrict and regulate immigration. In the same period, the Boston-Irish allegiance to the Democratic Party had been strengthened by the long-running campaign for temperance reform, which branded the saloon a pernicious influence in American life and culminated in the Prohibition experiment. The Republican Party was the usual home for Temperance and other moral reformers who inveighed against immigrant corruption in the political system, pushing families like the Kennedys into the Democratic fold.

The Democratic Party itself, however, could not be regarded as a party mainly of liberals, despite the fact that the New Deal response to the Great Depression did give urban liberalism a greater role within the Democratic coalition than ever before. For generations before the 1930s, the foundations of the Democratic Party had been in the South, the region that championed local rather than national authority within the American republic. In the aftermath of the Civil War and Reconstruction, the South had become so solidly Democratic that the real contest for political power there occurred in the battle to win the party's nomination, rather than the general election that followed. At the heart of this development was the systematic disenfranchisement of African American freedmen, who had been the prime supporters of the Republicans, the party of Lincoln. As a result, because it was anathema to the white Southern political establishment, the question of civil rights was a major fissure in the Democratic Party of the 1940s.

By 1945, foreign policy differences between Republicans and Democrats could also explain party allegiance. The venerable

Republican Senator Lodge of Massachusetts had also been one of the principal opponents of the ratification of the Treaty of Versailles in 1918, the peace treaty that Democratic President Woodrow Wilson had negotiated as part of his efforts to make World War I "a war to end all wars." The repudiation of the treaty and the League of Nations that it had sought to found had been a powerful sign that isolationism remained strong. The Republican Party thereafter criticized the Democrats' internationalism as likely to drag the United States into war. As a result, Franklin Roosevelt had spent much of the 1930s placating neutralist feeling in the country, even as the militarism of the fascist dictators in Europe and the Japanese empire in Asia grew ever more threatening.

Kennedy's comment about the power of the trade unions in the Britain of 1945 was made against the backdrop of similar concerns among business leaders about the emergence of a powerful labor movement in the United States during the 1930s. Traditionally, organized labor had been weak and mainly confined to skilled workers who belonged to the American Federation of Labor (AFL), but during the mid- and late 1930s a new group, the Congress of Industrial Organizations (CIO), had led successful unionizing efforts in the nation's docks, mines, shipyards, and mass-production industries. FDR's administration had supported this effort to secure collective bargaining rights through the Wagner Act, which created the National Labor Relations Board. In return, the unions had developed political action committees which backed liberal Democratic candidates in major cities and across the Midwestern industrial heartland. But the role of the unions in American life remained controversial, especially since some of the most determined activists in the CIO's organizing drives were Communists who supported leftward-leaning candidates during what was known as the Popular Front period. The presence of Communists in some unions confirmed and amplified the fears of business leaders that the New Deal was a form of "creeping socialism" that would undermine the free market economy, which in their view was the foundation of American liberty.

The importance, by 1945, of both the South and organized labor in the Democratic Party exemplified the tensions that made the New Deal coalition less secure at the war's end than its four consecutive presidential victories might suggest. Arguably the most successful figure in American political history, Franklin Roosevelt had, from 1938, increasingly struggled against conservative opponents in Congress, and his death had catapulted a far less adept figure, Harry Truman, into the Oval Office. FDR had chosen the former senator from Missouri as his running mate in 1944 largely to avoid alienating rival wings of his party. He feared losing Southern support if he chose Henry Wallace, the Iowa-based progressive who had ruffled Southern feathers with his support for African American civil rights. At the same time, FDR could not fully placate the South by choosing his South Carolinian war cabinet colleague James Byrnes, a defender of segregation. Coming from a border state and with a reputation for party loyalty, Truman seemed the ideal compromise candidate, but with FDR's death he suddenly faced enormous challenges, and he had relatively little information on the policies that FDR had intended to pursue. Truman had not been briefed about the atomic bomb, for instance, yet it fell to him to be the only president to order the use of nuclear weapons, a step which gave international relations a new level of risk, and a legacy that would define John F. Kennedy's presidency.

From what we know of Joe Junior's politics, had he lived the Kennedy name would have been associated with the kind of isolationist, anti-labor position that his father espoused. With Joe's death, the pursuit of political prominence devolved to Jack, although in 1945 there was a brief period of hesitation on his part. Part of this reluctance stemmed from his continuing health concerns. Thanks to his father's contacts, he was able to attend the Potsdam conference in Germany, but on his return to London he fell seriously ill with a fever. Another source of his misgivings, however, was the understandable anxiety that in pursuing a political career he might be unable to be his own man. He told one reporter, "It was like being drafted. My father wanted his eldest son in politics. 'Wanted' isn't the right word. He *demanded* it. You know my father." As Robert Dallek concludes, for a man who prided himself on making up his own mind, "taking on his elder brother's identity was not Jack's idea of coming into his own" (Dallek 2003: 118–19).

Congressman JFK

By 1946, the Kennedys were in practice more residents of New York than of Massachusetts, although the family had several seasonal homes. But the Kennedys would have struggled to establish themselves among loyal New Deal Democrats in New York politics at this stage, and so they turned again to the Boston politics, where the Fitzgerald name as much as the Kennedy one had resonance. In April 1945 Joe Kennedy announced that he was making a half-million-dollar investment in his home state and accepted an offer to chair a commission on Massachusetts' economic future. In July he was conspicuously present at the launch of the USS *Joseph P. Kennedy*, named in honor of his fallen son. A much more emphatic move to prepare the ground for Jack's entry into politics was Joe's private offer to Congressman Jim Curley of the Eleventh Congressional District to cover debts arising from a recent fraud conviction, and to finance Curley's bid to become mayor of Boston. This would create a vacancy in the Eleventh for Jack, but only if he could win the primary against rivals with far more immediate connections to the District (Blair and Blair 1974: 398–99).

To do so, Jack would need to campaign, an exhausting process, particularly for a gaunt young man with acute back problems and other illnesses. He would also have to overcome the strong resentment of local activists, who felt that he had no real ties to the area. The *East Boston Leader* captured their feelings with a satirical ad that announced: "Congress seat for sale—No experience necessary—Applicant must live in New York or Florida—Only millionaires need apply" (Dallek 2003: 126). Long days of electioneering would begin with Jack's standing outside factory or dockyard gates shaking hands, proceed with hours of neighborhood canvassing, and end with a round of house parties organized by his sisters Eunice and Pat as a means to attract volunteers.

Jack's campaign slogan necessarily made a virtue of his youth, proclaiming "The New Generation Offers a Leader." It would be an emphasis that stayed with the Kennedy campaign team right the way through to the 1960 presidential race. Equally important was his war record. Joe Kennedy paid for 100,000 copies of John Hersey's "Survival," the *Reader's Digest* version of the *PT 109* story, to be distributed in the district. The unprecedented war-chest that Joe brought to the congressional race also paid for radio, newspaper and billboard advertising, and direct mail. Particularly successful was the elaborate invitation-only tea party hosted by the Kennedys at the Hotel Commander in Cambridge. Coming just three days before the primary, the event attracted 1500 guests, causing a traffic jam in Harvard Square that guaranteed the newspapers covered it. Overall, the race showed that Kennedy would campaign more as a representative of his illustrious family than as a loyal party man. On June 18 he won the primary comfortably, getting almost twice as many votes as his nearest rival in a crowded field.

The Eleventh District was a safe Democratic seat, which was just as well, since in 1946 the tide, statewide and nationally, was running with the Republicans. The soaring cost of living and the scarcity of goods in the shops and of housing to buy or rent fed a popular resentment that prompted the loss of both houses of Congress for the first time since 1930. In Massachusetts, the Democrats lost the US Senate race and the governorship. While Kennedy reminded voters that it had been the New Deal that had responded to the nation's needs, voters had sharper memories of the recent wave of strikes and a growing fear of Communist expansion in the postwar world. In his speeches during the campaign's final days, Kennedy warned of a "moral and physical" crisis due to the Soviets' "program of world aggression" (Dallek 2003: 132). Here, too, the rhetorical theme of international challenges that required extra patriotic effort in response would persist through Jack's later campaigns. Bucking the trend, he beat his Republican opponent by 69,093 votes to 26,007.

Kennedy's service in the House was undistinguished. His father's money ensured that both his congressional office in Washington and his office in his home district were expertly staffed, so that constituents looking for assistance were well served. His health remained poor and at this point in his life a sense of his own mortality seemed to reinforce his already strong sybaritic tendencies. Some weekends he would spend in New York with a divorcée, Florence Pritchett, fashion editor for the *New York Journal-American*. Others he would spend in Palm Beach with the equally sociable Florida congressman George Smathers. Jack's friend Ralph Horton recalled that, amidst a succession of pretty girls, it was sometimes difficult to keep up with precisely who Jack was dating.

The boudoir seemed to give Jack more satisfaction than the congressional chamber, but he established himself as a moderate Democrat. He was a freshman representative in the minority party and so could play only a meager role in Democratic efforts to salvage New Deal welfare programs from Republican efforts to dismantle them. He backed unsuccessful efforts to build low-cost public housing, as he had promised his constituents, and he voted against the Taft-Hartley Act, which undercut the rising power of organized labor, notably by outlawing the closed shop. He explained, however, that his opposition to Taft-Hartley was not because of uncritical support for labor but because he feared that it would inflame labor relations in a way that would benefit the Left, a prospect he dreaded.

As a member of the House Committee on Education and Labor, Kennedy insisted that Communist influence and labor malpractices had set the scene for successful Republican attacks. He himself pursued a Communist union organizer from Milwaukee named Harold Christoffel, alleging that the strike he had led in 1941 had been dictated by the US party's Soviet paymasters during the Nazi–Soviet pact era. Christoffel was eventually imprisoned for perjury, allowing the Kennedy camp later to boast that their man had "nailed" a Red subversive even earlier than his fellow class of '46 congressman, Richard Nixon. Nixon leapt to national notoriety through his role in the prosecution of prominent New Dealer Alger Hiss in 1947.

Jack's congressional experiences also taught him the cost of developing a political profile that was independent and not easily pigeonholed. Given his committee assignment, it was inevitable that he would have to take a stand on federal aid for education, and thereby risk amplifying the perception that he was very much a Catholic politician who heeded the needs of his Church. His call for aid to be allocated to the child rather than to the school was an obvious subterfuge designed to sidestep the charge that aid to parochial schools breached the constitutional line separating Church and state. His committee colleagues defeated his proposal, but the question of Kennedy's support for Church-backed policies would return.

If Jack's stance on this issue helps to explain his easy 1948 re-election victory in a heavily Catholic district, then his refusal to sign a petition urging clemency for Boston's Mayor James Curley, whose fraudulent wartime activities had eventually caught up with him, was a riskier maneuver. It placed him at odds with well-established Democratic members such as Representative John McCormack, and could have been seen by Curley's devout Boston following as treachery, given that he had stepped into Curley's congressional seat. President Truman's commutation of Curley's sentence may have reduced the urge for vengeance, but the threat of it may have played a small role in persuading Jack to delay his bid for a statewide office. More telling in this regard, though, were personal concerns. His Addison's disease was now so manifest in his susceptibility to infection and high fevers that when returning from England in September 1947 he was given the last rites aboard the liner the *Queen Mary*. Nine months of fitful recovery later, he was devastated to learn of the death of his favorite sister Kathleen in a plane crash in France in May 1948. Associates remarked on his grief and depression. He told columnist Joseph Alsop that he did not expect to live beyond the age of forty-five, and was just determined to make the most of it. His old friend Lem Billings later said that Jack had told him that thoughts of his sister used to distract him in Congressional hearings and prevent him sleeping at night. Private polls also told Kennedy that the incumbent Republican Robert Bradford was the favorite for the governorship, whereas his reelection to the House was assured.

Kennedy's interest in statewide office, however, was widely recognized, and like his contemporaries representatives Nixon and Smathers—who both moved up to the Senate in 1950 via Red-baiting campaigns—his intentions were clearly signalled by his position on the deepening tensions with the Soviet Union. The wartime alliance had only temporarily suppressed American mistrust of Communism, and by the time the second bomb was dropped on Japan in August 1945, the tension between the allies was widely recognized. During the remainder of the decade Americans interpreted world events largely within the framework of containing the Communist threat. When in 1946 Winston Churchill spoke of an iron curtain descending across Europe, his American audience accepted his analysis, and, despite the misgivings of Republican isolationists such as Senator Robert Taft of Ohio, a consensus emerged in Congress that enabled President Truman to win support for the Marshall Plan to aid European recovery, for the unprecedented engagement of the United States as a guarantor of European security via the North Atlantic Treaty Organization (NATO), and ultimately for continuing mobilization in what became known as the Cold War. John F. Kennedy supported these moves; in fact, he worried that the Truman administration was not resolute enough.

JFK moves to the Senate

By the time Jack Kennedy was plotting in earnest his move to statewide office, in 1949, this concern had deepened, with the fall of the Nationalist government in China. Led loudly by Henry Luce's publications, the press clamored that America had lost China to the Communists. Kennedy joined the chorus, declaring that what "our young men had saved [in World War II], our diplomats and our president have frittered away" (Dallek 2003: 160). When the initial phases of the Korean War went badly for American forces in 1950, he took the administration to task for its lack of preparedness. In November, he told a Harvard audience that he held the foreign policy leadership of Secretary of State Dean Acheson in little regard, and openly declared his delight that his contemporary Richard Nixon had beaten liberal Democrat Helen Douglas in the 1950 California Senate race. His family's fondness for the outspoken Red-baiting Republican senator from Wisconsin, Joseph McCarthy, added further weight to the view that Jack Kennedy was neither a loyal party man nor a member of its liberal wing.

A new kind of candidate

At the dawn of the 1950s the American political parties stood at a point of transition. Increasing suburbanization, migration westward and southward, and the transformation from a heavily industrial to a service economy meant that the grassroots structures of the two parties no longer corresponded with changing realities. Democratic Party chieftains continued to hold sway at the Party's national convention but their ability to deliver voters for presidential, statewide, even on occasion local office was faltering. Kennedy would need to court these men to win nominations but could potentially create his own campaign apparatus to deliver the vote in elections, especially as television increasingly provided a new way to reach the electorate.

The voters Kennedy courted might still be Catholic (40 percent of the Democratic Party was believed to be of this faith) and belong to labor unions, but after their move to the suburbs many of them had adopted Cold War centrist positions rather than Leftist ones. In the South, there were even signs that voters would consider a Republican presidential contender with either the martial appeal of an Eisenhower or the raw right-wing conservatism of a Barry Goldwater. While people spoke of a liberal consensus, partly because Eisenhower's "Modern Republicanism" seemed to accept the central elements of the New Deal such as Social Security and a limited but legitimate role for organized labor, there was an equally strong sense of the limits of reform, limits which made measures such as federal aid for education or public housing ambitious goals rather than political inevitabilities. Far more assured was the fact that any candidate who wanted to appeal to the nation, Democrat or Republican, would have to do so from a strongly anti-Communist position.

Family wealth ensured that Jack Kennedy could travel widely in pursuit of a better understanding of world affairs. In early 1951 he spent five weeks in Europe. On his return he presented a balanced report concluding that there was no immediate likelihood that the USSR would launch an attack in Europe while the US and its allies were engaged in Korea, but urging a military build-up as a deterrent—one that required NATO allies to match each American division with six of their own to ensure that costs were properly shared. In the fall of 1951 Kennedy took an even more unusual trip for an American congressman, to Israel, Iran, Pakistan, India, Singapore, Thailand, French Indochina (including Vietnam), Korea, and Japan, in order to learn first hand whether US policies were effective in containing Communist influence. His conclusions were bleak. "It is tragic to report," he told a radio audience, "that we have not only made no new friends, but we have lost old ones." He recognized that there was a clear danger that the US would be seen as the imperial successor to the old colonial powers, and thus an enemy to the nationalist aspirations evident in all these countries (Dallek 2003: 165–67).

Kennedy staffers Kenneth O'Donnell and David Powers have reported that it was while Jack was campaigning for the Democratic ticket in 1948 that he decided he would go for statewide office in 1952. The election of Democrat Paul Dever as governor of Massachusetts in 1948, and his reelection in 1950, defined Kennedy's options. If Dever decided to run for the US Senate in 1952, then the party would back him, but if Dever preferred to seek a third term, the Senate nomination would be open. To prepare for this challenge, Kennedy accepted hundreds of speaking engagements across the state, an exhausting schedule for someone suffering from increasingly acute back pain. Dave Powers remembered how JFK would grit his teeth and enter a hall "looking as fit and healthy as the light-heavyweight champion of the world" (O'Donnell and Powers 1972: 79). But once back at his hotel, he would need crutches to get upstairs and would soak in a hot bath for an hour before trying to sleep.

The incumbent senator seeking re-election in 1952 was three-time winner Henry Cabot Lodge, a member of the famous Boston Brahmin family, whose national profile had been boosted by his prominent role in persuading Dwight Eisenhower to seek the Republican nomination. Despite Truman's unexpected victory in 1948, the Republican Party had enjoyed a further resurgence in the early 1950s, in large measure due to the deepening Red Scare associated with Senator Joseph McCarthy's accusations of Communist subversion. With his promise to go to Korea and end the stalemated war, Eisenhower was favored to defeat any candidate the Democrats offered. There were those in the Party who therefore saw Lodge as very strongly placed to secure re-election. This appears to have been the view of the Lodge camp itself, which was slow to organize in 1952, and made the fatal mistake of underestimating Kennedy. The grueling visits to towns across the state had enabled Kennedy to put together a campaign team of enthusiastic volunteers under the hard-driving and driven leadership of his younger brother Bobby.

Jack's father, Joe Kennedy, was also a vital element in the campaign, albeit largely behind the scenes. His money paid for billboard, newspaper, radio, and television advertising. It covered the cost of Jack's campaign tours, of local offices, mailings and phone calls, and of the celebrated Kennedy "teas" that attracted over 70,000 women across the state. Just two weeks before Election Day, the *Boston Post* publicly endorsed Jack Kennedy in his race against Lodge, a move estimated to be worth at least 40,000 votes in a close contest. Later it was reported that the cash-strapped *Post* owner had received a loan of $500,000 on generous terms from Joe Kennedy; such was the ambassador's keenness to ensure victory.

In November, Kennedy won against the Republican tide that saw Dever lose the governorship and Massachusetts voters choose Eisenhower ahead of Adlai Stevenson by a margin of over 200,000. Kennedy finished ahead by only 70,737, a figure so close to the attendance at the Kennedy tea parties that journalists joked that Lodge had been drowned in tea. On election night, Jack's friend Torby Macdonald shrewdly predicted his victory because he represented "the best of the new generation. Not generation in age, but minorities, really. The newer arrived people." The statistics bore this out, with increased turnout especially in ethnic districts and a swing away from Lodge among both Catholic and Jewish voters. As Dallek concludes: "In voting for Jack, the minorities were not simply putting one of their own in the high reaches of government—they had been doing that for a number of years—but were saying that he and they had arrived at the center of American life and no longer felt self-conscious about their status as citizens of the Great Republic" (Dallek 2003: 176).

Another explanation for Kennedy's victory over Lodge was rumored to be the latter's role in securing the Republican nomination for Eisenhower ahead of the stalwart isolationist Robert Taft of Ohio. Unlike his famous isolationist forebear, Lodge was committed to international institutions like the UN and treaty obligations such as NATO. Taft supporters in Massachusetts, some claimed, took their vengeance. However limited their influence on the outcome, the disgruntled isolationists were symptomatic of the way the Republican Party was changing alongside the Democrats. Keen to unite the party, Eisenhower had reached out to its Right wing by choosing Richard Nixon as his running mate. The young Californian brought balance to the ticket. Ike was the choice of the Eastern establishment at a time when Senator McCarthy and others were casting doubt on the loyalty of Ivy Leaguers. Nixon gave the ticket not only youth and a West Coast base but also an appeal to those Republicans who had rallied to the increasing charges of treason in high places that flowed from the Hiss and Rosenberg spy trials. When JFK returned to Washington to take his seat in the Senate, he joined his contemporary Nixon who, as vice president, was Senate chair. As if to underline how close the Kennedys were to Nixon on the anti-Communist issue at this time, in early 1953 Robert Kennedy went to work on Joe McCarthy's investigative staff.

The Kennedy family's close association with McCarthy was destined to cause JFK problems, right up to the 1960 election. But in 1953 his main challenges were staffing his office, consolidating his home base, establishing his credentials as a foreign policy analyst, and, if the right girl could be found, getting married. His two key hires, who stayed with him into the White House, were Evelyn Lincoln, an experienced Capitol Hill secretary, and Theodore Sorensen, a twenty-four-year-old attorney from a progressive Republican background in Nebraska. Unusually for the Kennedy staff, Sorensen was a Unitarian and a conspicuous liberal—far more so than his new boss. He proved an exceptionally hardworking staffer, analytically shrewd and with a rare speechwriting gift that would excite envy among Kennedy's contemporaries.

Kennedy and anti-Communism

One of Sorensen's first tasks was to craft three speeches embodying Kennedy's forty proposals for New England economic renewal. The program fulfilled a campaign pledge, and 30,000 copies of the collected speeches were circulated back home to assure voters that they had made the right choice. Kennedy proved equally swift in establishing himself as an opinionated commentator on world affairs. Popular fear of Communism meant that it was easier to attack the Eisenhower administration from a hawkish than from a dovish position. The proposed "New Look" defense policy, which cut back on conventional forces and relied on "massive retaliation" with nuclear weapons, imperiled the nation, Kennedy declared. Senator Stuart Symington of Missouri would similarly speak of a "bomber gap." It was a charge, later couched in terms of a "missile gap," that Kennedy would make again in the 1960 campaign (Dallek 2003: 184–85).

Being an aggressive advocate of defense spending remained politically expedient for any ambitious politician throughout the fifties. Although Eisenhower kept his promise and ended the Korean conflict, criticism of the administration for failing to contain the Communist threat continued, with Kennedy among the critics. At the beginning of his presidency Eisenhower was able to reach an accommodation with Senator Taft, leader of the Republican Right, shortly before the latter's death from cancer in July 1953, but he still struggled to satisfy his right-wing critics, and this partly explains why he allowed the McCarthy hearings to continue. Eisenhower personally loathed the Wisconsin senator, especially after he accused one of the president's mentors, General George Marshall, of being part of "a conspiracy so immense and an infamy so black as to dwarf any previous such venture in the history of man" (McCarthy 1951). Fearing that a public response would play into the demagogue's hands, Eisenhower pursued a quiet policy of noncooperation with McCarthy's committee, and waited for him to destroy himself. Between April and June 1954 the blatantly arbitrary nature of McCarthy's charges was exposed in televised Senate hearings investigating Communist influence in the armed forces. In early December 1954 the Senate voted to censure McCarthy.

The only Senate Democrat not recorded as voting to censure McCarthy was JFK. This fact would be used regularly by liberals to explain their mistrust of Kennedy. In reality, cordial relations between Jack and McCarthy had largely ended by 1954 because of Jack's blocking of two appointments McCarthy had sought for his friends Owen Brewster and Robert Lee. However, like Eisenhower, Kennedy was wary of McCarthy's popularity with the public. Ex-governor Paul Dever summed up McCarthy's appeal to Catholic Massachusetts voters by declaring that the Wisconsin senator "could beat Archbishop Cushing in a two man election fight in South Boston" (Dallek 2003: 190). Add to this the fact that Bobby Kennedy had worked for McCarthy until July 1953 and Joe Kennedy's pro-McCarthy sentiment, and it is easy to understand why Kennedy attempted to use his medical unavailability in December 1954 as a means of avoiding an explicit vote against McCarthy.

Marriage to Jacqueline Bouvier

While settling into his Senate role, Kennedy had also been advancing his courtship of a beautiful and bright Catholic socialite, Jacqueline Bouvier. Despite the womanizing that preceded and continued after the marriage, friends agree that Jack found there was something special about Jackie. "He saw her as a kindred spirit," Lem Billings said, while Chuck Spalding declared "You could see it in his eyes; he'd follow her around the room watching to see what she'd do next. Jackie *interested* him, which was not true of many women." Spalding even speculated that Jackie was unwittingly attracted to the philandering Kennedy because he reminded her subconsciously of her own errant father, "Black Jack" Bouvier (Dallek 2003: 193–94). Whatever the basis of their attraction, the couple married on September 12, 1953. The event was lavishly covered by the press and thereafter the stylish Jackie added to the already considerable Kennedy mystique. Twelve years his junior, she also enhanced Kennedy's aura of youthfulness. Together they became the image of the husband and wife campaign team.

Courting the liberals through intellectualism

At the same time, Kennedy continued to develop other elements of his appeal. During the 1950s, the nomination of Adlai Stevenson for the presidency in 1952 and 1956 demonstrated the hold that liberals, particularly those associated with the group Americans for Democratic Action, held over the party's convention. Stevenson was the darling of the party's so-called "eggheads," intellectuals who were drawn to his wit and composure, even though his successive defeats suggested his limitations in terms of popular appeal. To liberals, a candidate who could declare that, if the Republicans stopped telling lies about his party he might stop telling the truth about them, was their voice. Where Eisenhower was homely and Joe McCarthy was crude, Stevenson was cerebral, and if Kennedy was to become president he would need to be seen as equally intellectual.

Kennedy's rivals for the 1960 nomination had begun to emerge. If the party returned to the down-to-earth, almost folksy appeal of Harry Truman, then Kennedy would have little chance against a trio of Southern senators. Lyndon Johnson, the youngest ever majority leader in the Senate, was building a formidable reputation as a legislative tactician, and would be expected to deliver the important Electoral College votes of his home state of Texas. But in the early 1950s he was seen as more of a regional than a national figure. Equally folksy, but from a border state, Senator Estes Kefauver of Tennessee would show in 1956 that a Southern candidate could attract Northern voters in the emerging primary contests. Like Johnson, he was careful to avoid being portrayed as a hardline segregationist, although he was far less popular with his fellow senators than the Texan. Tall and good-looking, Senator Stuart Symington of Missouri was a third contender. He was making a name for himself as a critic of Eisenhower's defense policy, although his limitations as a speaker had led some to declare that he was the ideal candidate right up to the moment he opened his mouth.

Beyond Kennedy's Southern rivals, there was Hubert Humphrey of Minnesota, a favorite of liberals since his successful floor fight for a strong civil rights plank at the 1948 convention, and a leading defender of organized labor. Humphrey's strong commitment to racial justice was likely to antagonize Southerners, however, and he also had a reputation for losing some supporters by his tendency to speak at length on any subject that came his way. Finally, Kennedy had to be wary of Stevenson himself, since despite declarations that he would not seek a third nomination it was widely reported that he would be willing to be drafted by the convention, as he had been in 1952.

Two events greatly enhanced Kennedy's chances in relation to his future rivals: the publication of his Pulitzer Prize-winning historical study, *Profiles in Courage*, and his performance at the 1956 national convention in Chicago, where he came close to securing the vice presidential nomination. The first appealed to liberal intellectuals, although probably not enough to stifle their mistrust, while the second made Kennedy into a truly national figure for the first time, due to TV exposure, and also cemented his belief that he could win the nomination, and the presidency itself.

Continuing health problems

However, before either of these events, Kennedy had to take radical steps to try to deal with his severe back problems. He had already resigned himself to a daily regime of cortisone to control his Addison's disease, but the deteriorating state of his back and the subsequent pain and limited mobility seemed to require surgical intervention. By the spring of 1954, X-rays showed that his fifth lumbar vertebra had essentially disintegrated, probably due to osteoporosis, a side effect of prolonged steroid use. He had to use crutches to get around the Senate, and was relieved that his office neighbor, Richard Nixon, as Senate chair, was compassionate enough to allow regular pairing of votes so that his absence did not give the Republicans an unfair advantage. The medical prognosis was not good. Without surgery, it was predicted that he would lose the ability to walk, but due to the low state of his immune system any elaborate surgery carried a heavy risk of infection. There was a 50 percent chance that the surgery would be successful, but there was also a 50 percent chance that Kennedy would die from postoperative infection.

The surgery to insert a metal plate to stabilize Kennedy's spine took place on October 21. In the aftermath a severe infection put him into a coma, and he received the last rites. Rose Kennedy recalled how her husband Joe's "entire body shook with anger and sorrow" at the prospect of losing another of his precious children (Kearns Goodwin 1987: 775). But Kennedy recovered, and by December, having missed the censure vote on McCarthy, he was able to recuperate at the family's Palm Beach home. The suppurating state of the wound in his lower back visibly signaled that the plate had itself become infected. In February, further surgery was needed, with the shattered spinal cartilage being replaced by a bone graft. Another period of recuperation in Florida followed, and he did not return to Washington until May 1954. Among the Senate colleagues who greeted him most warmly was Vice President Richard Nixon.

Profiles in Courage

During his lengthy period of illness and convalescence, Kennedy got the idea of writing a book on the subject of political courage.

Initially drawn to the example of famed Massachusetts figure John Quincy Adams, in what became *Profiles in Courage* Kennedy also told the stories of seven other senators who risked their political careers by making principled stands that ran contrary to the preferences of their parties, states, or home regions.

The closest example in Kennedy's own career had been his support for the construction of the St. Lawrence Seaway to facilitate cargo shipments to the Great Lakes region, which was opposed by New England interests who feared the potential damage to the port of Boston. His more recent evasiveness over the McCarthy issue had seemed a good deal less courageous, and given his father's important investments in Chicago the Seaway proposal might be seen as an instance where family interests loomed larger than local ones, even though Kennedy couched his support in terms of a victory for the national interest.

With fulsome support from his father, the book climbed rapidly in the *New York Times* bestseller list. Despite rumors that it was more the work of Theodore Sorensen and other advisors than of Kennedy, *Profiles* gave the senator an intellectual standing that none of his rivals, save perhaps Stevenson, could muster. When columnist Drew Pearson stated on television that the book was "ghostwritten," Kennedy successfully secured a retraction from both Pearson and the network (Dallek 2003: 199).

Ahead of the 1956 election, Kennedy and his advisors also decided that they needed to establish their dominance over the Massachusetts Democratic Party, in order to control the national convention delegation. In practice this meant overturning the influence of longstanding Congressman John McCormack, who operated through his in-state ally William Burke, the State Committee chairman. Carefully cultivating various grudges that local rivals held against Burke, the Kennedy team quietly built up an alternate group of delegates. They eventually ousted Burke by a vote of 47 to 31, in a three-hour committee meeting that teetered on the brink of fisticuffs. This local victory, in the mudslinging world of internal party politics, also gave Kennedy some credibility with the hard-nosed political bosses in states such as Illinois, New York, Ohio, and Pennsylvania, all of whom would have a role at the national convention.

Vice presidential contest, 1956

While health problems to a large extent dominated Kennedy's life in 1953–54, by 1956 the health problems of others had changed the political landscape in his favor. In the summer of 1955, Lyndon Johnson, whose mastery of the Senate had made him a contender for the presidency, suffered a severe heart attack that put him out of contention. Soon after, in September, President Eisenhower's own heart attack focused attention on the vice presidency, with liberal Republicans and Democrats anguished by the thought that Richard Nixon, the persecutor of Alger Hiss, was only a weak heartbeat away from the presidency. In planning for the 1956 campaign, Democrats faced the reality that, while voters had proven ready to give the party control of Congress, they were so charmed by Eisenhower that he would be difficult to defeat. Perhaps they would change their mind if Democrats played up the likelihood that Ike would not survive a second term, and that consequently a vote for Ike was actually a vote for Nixon. This made the choice of vice president a more headline-grabbing story than usual in the 1956 campaign.

Kennedy already recognized that, in his dream of becoming president, he faced the obstacle of anti-Catholicism. In February 1956, *Look* journalist Fletcher Knebel listed Jack among his potential running mates for Adlai Stevenson and reported that, contrary to the orthodox view of Catholicism as a negative feature because of the strong rejection of Al Smith's candidacy in 1928, it would boost Stevenson's chances. The indefatigable Sorensen prepared a statistical study that showed that if Catholics in key states who had voted for Eisenhower in 1952 were inspired to vote Democratic in 1956 by the presence of a Catholic candidate, they would provide the margin of victory. This was seen as particularly important because Stevenson was believed to have lost supporters after his divorce. However, Stevenson himself was widely rumored to prefer a Southerner, or at least a Border state running mate. Perhaps partly to appease JFK's deep-pocketed father, Stevenson asked Jack to narrate a film about the Democratic Party that was to open the convention. This would make use of Jack's glamorous image to appeal to delegates, but, more than Stevenson intended, it also served as a highly positive platform for JFK's introduction to the party nationwide.

At the August convention, Stevenson seemed to reward Jack further by asking him to give the nomination address. However flattering this appeared, it was also a clear sign that Kennedy was not going to be Stevenson's vice presidential choice. Ironically, by the time Stevenson announced that he would underline the democratic character of the Democratic Party by allowing the convention to choose the vice president, his actions had given Kennedy a party profile that made his bid to win over delegates possible, if still a long shot.

According to Kennedy aides Kenny O'Donnell and Dave Powers, Stevenson had miscalculated, believing that he could use JFK to strengthen his standing with "big city Democratic bosses, many of them Irish Catholics" without jeopardizing the "previously arranged Stevenson–Estes Kefauver ticket." The nominee then discovered that he might be forced to have Kennedy on the ticket. O'Donnell and Powers, who shared a general Kennedy disdain for Stevenson, conclude that it reminded them "of the story about the Irish girl who worked so hard at converting her Jewish boyfriend to Catholicism that he became a priest" (O'Donnell and Powers 1972: 117–18). More seriously, they explain the surge for Kennedy among both Northern and Southern delegations as proof of the power of television and of the short-term calculations of the delegates: they wanted a vice presidential choice who would help their own local election chances, and the glamorous Kennedy came over so well on TV that they reckoned he might just make a difference.

Although the Kennedy team believed that the vice presidential slot had effectively already been given to Kefauver, they may have been misled by their dislike for Stevenson. The latter resented Kefauver's primary campaigning, and may well have wanted to make Kefauver prove his appeal. At one stage in a series of tallies that provided the main talking point of the convention, Kennedy came within forty votes of victory. He ran surprisingly well among some of the Deep South delegations, who saw Kefauver as too liberal on civil rights, but he could not secure wholehearted support from Northern liberals, given the very public lack of support for his selection from the "grande dame" of the liberal wing, Eleanor Roosevelt.

Ironically, leading Catholic political figures like David Lawrence of Pennsylvania and Mike DiSalle of Ohio also balked because they feared that the Party would blame Catholics if the ticket went down to defeat in November against the hugely popular Eisenhower. In addition, Jack's rival Kefauver was very much the preferred candidate among farm state delegates, who remembered Kennedy's recent failure to support efforts to raise crop subsidies. When it became clear that Kefauver had the majority he needed, Kennedy graciously addressed the convention, asking it to make Kefauver's selection unanimous.

Although it was a defeat of sorts, the Chicago convention was in key respects a triumph for Kennedy, and an experience that made him believe that he could win in 1960. First and foremost, he had been in the national spotlight three times in the course of the televised convention, and each time his charismatic appeal had been evident. Second, he had learned a lot from the extemporized campaign to win over delegates for his candidacy. If he could come so close to victory with little preparation, he mused, imagine how well he could do with four years of campaigning behind him. The experience revealed the weakness of seemingly formidable rivals like Johnson, who believed that they could win the nomination simply by using their congressional influence at the convention itself. It also showed that if Kennedy could maintain his moderation on the civil rights question he would get support from Southern state delegations, whose members would not only oppose liberals like Hubert Humphrey but turn on those they saw as renegades in their ranks, like Kefauver, and maybe even Johnson himself.

At the same time, the convention confirmed that Jack had a problem with the party's liberal wing, rooted in memories of his father's conduct while an ambassador and deepened by Jack's failure to vote against Joe McCarthy. And there were the Catholic bosses who felt threatened by the prospect of a Catholic presidential bid: if it succeeded it would somehow belittle what they had achieved at the state level, and if it failed it would reinforce the barriers against them. In this respect, faltering party discipline worked in Kennedy's favor, as bosses like Lawrence and DiSalle would struggle to control their own state delegations if they stood out against a candidate who had demonstrated his ability to turn out the vote by his performances in the nonbinding primary contests.

In 1956 Jack Kennedy ultimately benefited from not being on a losing team. In the November election Stevenson won only six Southern states plus Missouri; he could not even carry his home state of Illinois. Jack campaigned loyally for Stevenson–Kefauver, and his brother Bobby, at Stevenson's request, was part of the nominee's campaign train. Jack's efforts could not change the outcome, even in Massachusetts, but speaking in twenty-four states sustained his growing national reputation. Bobby was scathing about the ineptitude of the Stevenson operation, declaring that it offered a case study of what *not* to do in a presidential campaign. Four years later, Bobby would have the chance to show how things should be done. By that stage, Bobby had acquired a reputation as the most ruthless of the Kennedy brothers, becoming in many ways his older brother's protector and enforcer. Even while they remarked on the difference between the urbane and cool Jack, and the devout and intense Bobby, observers noted that the two seemed to communicate telepathically. It was to be the strongest bond Jack Kennedy ever enjoyed. Bobby's loyalty would carry him to the White House and would be a vital asset while he was president.

In key respects, then, the 1956 convention marked the start of Kennedy's 1960 campaign. Certainly he set his sights on the presidency at this point. Even his landslide 1958 Senate reelection victory was significant only insofar as it confirmed his vote-getting potential. By the same token, his actual performance in the Senate was primarily calculated to strengthen a presidential bid. In this respect, he benefited from a clash of rivals. Since Senate Majority Leader Lyndon Johnson regarded Kefauver as his main rival for the nomination in 1960, he denied him a place on the influential Foreign Relations Committee, allowing Kennedy to take it instead. This may have been Johnson's way of setting up Kennedy to be his vice presidential pick. In 1955, seeking to boost his son's vice presidential chances, Joe Kennedy had offered to underwrite a presidential bid by Johnson, only to have the Texan brusquely (and in Bobby Kennedy's view, unforgivably) decline. Nevertheless, the overture may have created the impression in Johnson's mind that he could get the young Massachusetts senator as his vice president. Hence Johnson indulged Kennedy's well-known willingness to comment on foreign policy via a conspicuous

Committee assignment because this would ultimately benefit a generously financed Johnson–Kennedy ticket.

As his fortieth birthday approached, in May 1957, Kennedy could celebrate his recently announced Pulitzer Prize for history, a boost to his intellectual credentials among liberals, but also lament that his youth made most people see him as a vice presidential rather than presidential candidate. Despite his heart attack, Johnson was a vigorous figure who would be fifty-two in 1960, and so well placed to contest the election against the likely Republican nominee, the by-then forty-seven-year-old vice president Richard Nixon, a man some saw as having been middle aged almost from birth. If Kennedy helped Johnson win the White House, this might begin the process of overturning the Al Smith legend that no Catholic could be elected president. But Kennedy was not prepared to wait his turn, perhaps because his ill health (a closely guarded secret in key respects) argued against delay. The challenge was to unite the disparate Party behind him, despite its racial and ideological cleavages.

Candidate Kennedy and the South

In the mid-1950s the race question gained prominence, partly because of the reaction of the white South to the US Supreme Court's 1954 *Brown* decision outlawing segregated schools, but also because President Eisenhower was tepid at best in his support for the Court. For Southern leaders like Lyndon Johnson, opposition to the ruling, known as "Massive Resistance," was alarming. Johnson, like his rival Kefauver, was one of the few Southern congressional figures who refused to sign the Southern Manifesto pledging defiance to school desegregation. But seeing racial moderates losing office across the South, Johnson realized that he could neither join the segregationist clamor nor stand out against it without running serious political risks.

The media coverage of the Montgomery bus boycott in 1956 not only brought a young and eloquent black Baptist preacher, Martin Luther King, to national prominence, it evoked sympathy in Northern states whose delegates would be unwilling to support the Texan, unless he separated himself from the South in a way that risked support in Dixie itself. The Supreme Court's use of the *Brown* precedent to outlaw bus segregation in Montgomery in December 1956 confirmed that progress on desegregation was likely to be an important political issue in the 1960 presidential race, especially since the Communist bloc readily seized upon racial incidents in their propaganda efforts in the developing world. While segregationists charged that advocates of reform were really Communists intent on fomenting disorder in America, reformers countered that the mistreatment of African Americans was damaging the nation in the ongoing Cold War. For both Johnson and Kennedy, therefore, simultaneously placating liberals and segregationists became a recurrent challenge.

As Senate majority leader, Johnson tried to bolster his presidential hopes by securing passage of the 1957 Civil Rights Act, the first such measure since 1875. Earlier efforts had typically died in congressional committees, which were dominated by Southern chairmen by virtue of their seniority. The 1957 bill was likely to go before the Judiciary Committee, whose Senate chair James Eastland of Mississippi was a rabid segregationist. When liberals attempted to avoid this by invoking procedural rule XIV, Jack Kennedy opposed the move to endear himself to Southern colleagues, since he knew that there were enough votes to progress the bill via a discharge petition. Days later, aware that the part of the bill which would give the attorney general broad powers to intervene in the South was unlikely to pass, Kennedy felt able to speak and vote in its favor to appease Northern liberal critics.

At the same time, Johnson, aware that liberals had no confidence that Southern white juries would convict a registrar who frustrated African American voter registration efforts, agreed to an amendment that affirmed the right of all Americans to serve on juries but provided that civil contempt cases should be heard before a judge sitting alone rather than before a jury. This led Kennedy to back the amendment for its promise of interracial juries, but to join Southerners in opposing the denial of jury trials for civil contempt defendants. His stance gained sympathy from Southerners and mistrust from African Americans in equal measure.

Candidate Kennedy: the unions and the media

Kennedy used his place on the Foreign Relations Committee to deliver a critique of administration foreign policy. Speaking against the possibility of US support for the French in their war against Algerian freedom fighters in 1957, he repeated his warning, made in 1954 in the context of US support for the French in Indochina, against siding with imperialist powers against legitimate nationalist aspirations. Only by placing itself on the side of freedom, he declared, could the US be assured of success in its Cold War fight for the allegiance of what he called "the uncommitted millions in Asia and Africa." He underlined his views in an article in *Foreign Affairs*, stating that "the forces of nationalism are rewriting the geopolitical map" and adding that the administration must step back from the "apocalyptic solutions" of atomic warfare and adopt a "new realism," which he failed to define (Dallek 2003: 222–23). Judging by his support for economic aid programs, this new realism consisted of balancing military preparedness with energetic diplomacy.

While Kennedy was not at the forefront of those who took the Eisenhower administration to task following the Soviets' successful launch of a space satellite, Sputnik, in October 1957, he could not resist warning of the "grave peril" produced by the administration's readiness to put "fiscal security ahead of national security" (Dallek 2003: 224). From August 1958 onwards, he warned of an approaching period of danger in which Soviet missile capabilities would outstrip America's. This alleged "missile gap," within a broader criticism of a tired, even complacent administration, would be a vital element in his 1960 campaign. In office he might temper rearmament with an Alliance for Progress in Latin America and eventually disarmament talks, but first he intended to follow the maxim "arm, to parley."

Perhaps equally revealing of the president he would become, Senator Kennedy was an indifferent legislator. Despite five years in the Senate, by 1958 he had not attached his name to a major piece of legislation. To the consternation of some colleagues and the dismay of his father, Kennedy's main effort to legislate came in the sphere of labor relations. Given the readiness of Republicans to exploit such initiatives in order to rein in further what they saw as the damaging influence of trade unions, Bobby Kennedy's work for the Senate committee on racketeering and Jack's willingness to join the probe into organized labor ran the risk of alienating labor chieftains, whose political action committees remained a vital force within the Democratic Party. In March 1958, Jack introduced a measure to limit the use of union funds for improper purposes and to require independent auditing. The bill built upon investigations that had exposed the nefarious activities of Teamsters' leaders Dave Beck and Jimmy Hoffa, sinister gangster-like figures whose on-screen appearances made the Kennedy brothers look like public crusaders. Caught between business critics who saw it as too weak and labor opponents who judged it draconian, the bill was shelved, although the more restrictive Landrum-Griffin Act of 1959 dealt with many of the same issues. Bobby had by that stage switched his attention to the pursuit of Mafia bosses, although he dealt with both crusades in his 1960 account, *The Enemy Within.*

The Kennedy-led probe into organized labor had prompted the head of the AFL-CIO, George Meany, to lament loudly "God save us from our friends." In general, however, it seemed to do Jack's public standing no harm. The Republicans were unable to find a serious candidate to run against him in 1958 and he coasted to a record-breaking reelection victory, with 73.6 percent of the vote. By this stage, Kennedy had become a media phenomenon, the symbol of the new breed of celebrity politician, and a mainstay of popular magazines due to the plethora of human interest stories devoted to him and his extraordinary family. Kennedy attributed his frequent appearance in *Life* and other magazines to his "beautiful wife," who in November 1957 had given him a daughter, Caroline. His more boastful father was more insistent that the record sales of magazines that placed his son's picture on the cover and the record attendances at the many fundraising dinners Jack attended across the country were down to only one thing: his son's universal appeal. Nevertheless, the conspicuous presence of his rich father, as well as the obvious adulation of much of the popular press, antagonized many envious political colleagues. Kennedy remained more popular with the public than he was inside the Senate, or within his Party. Among liberals, deep mistrust persisted, and among those African American leaders who had monitored his performance there were deeper doubts than there were in segregationist circles. In the murky underworld where organized crime and union racketeering met, there was no doubt, just a potentially lethal hatred. In 1960, he would have to best both Democratic rivals and an equally formidable campaigner in Richard Nixon, and he would have to disprove the popular belief that no Catholic could be elected president.

3   The 1960 campaign

A good time to run

The four-year presidential election gap ensures that, every twenty years since 1800, Americans have chosen a president to lead them firmly into a new decade. On six consecutive occasions from 1840 to 1980 the president elected in this "zero" year died in office. Among them were the assassinated presidents Abraham Lincoln, James Garfield, William McKinley, and, of course, John F. Kennedy. Only Ronald Reagan's recovery from the gunshot wound he suffered in 1981 ended this fateful cycle. If the pattern was known to the politicians of 1960, however, it was a weak deterrent. On the Republican side, Vice President Richard Nixon was the clear front-runner, and he soon became the putative party nominee when his liberal rival, Governor Nelson Rockefeller of New York, declined to run. Rockefeller did, however, continue to cause problems for Nixon, as he strove to appease both Rockefeller liberals and right-wing Republicans, increasingly identified with Arizona Senator Barry Goldwater.

On the Democratic side, the field was much more crowded. In the primaries Kennedy jostled for the nomination with liberal stalwart Hubert Humphrey, both men striving to prove their vote-getting potential. Since most primary contests in this period were nonbinding in their allocation of convention delegates, the nomination was not secure until the convention itself, and other contenders—Senate Majority Leader Lyndon Johnson of Texas, Senator Stuart Symington of Missouri, and twice-nominated liberal standard-bearer Governor Adlai Stevenson of Illinois—positioned themselves for a move when the party gathered in Los Angeles. Stevenson in particular denied any wish for a third nomination, yet still hoped to be drafted by his convention supporters.

The auguries for Democrats in 1960 were promising. First and foremost, the hugely popular Eisenhower was prevented from running for a third term by the Twenty-second Amendment, ratified in 1951. Ironically, it had been championed by the Republicans after the four consecutive terms of Franklin Roosevelt. But in 1960 it promised to benefit their opponents, since no Republican could match Ike's appeal. Four years earlier, in spite of Eisenhower's landslide victory, the Democrats had gained ground in Congress—two further seats in the House for a majority of 33, and one Senate seat for a majority of two in the upper chamber. The midterm elections saw further Democratic gains. Richard Nixon recalled election night in 1958 as one of the most depressing he had ever known. The statistics, he wrote later, "still make me wince" (Nixon 1978: 220). The Democratic majority swelled to 130 in the House and to 28 in the Senate. Admission of Hawaii and Alaska as full states of the union in 1959 confirmed Democratic dominance. Hawaii had one Republican and one Democrat in the Senate, but its sole congressman was a Democrat. Both of Alaska's senators and its solitary representative in the House were Democrats.

A series of setbacks for the Republican administration, on both foreign and domestic fronts, strengthened the positive tide for the Democrats. The 1956 Suez Crisis sowed discord among the NATO powers and gave the Soviets scope for influence in Nasser's Egypt. It also made the Soviet suppression of the Hungarian revolt easier, and the inability of the US to respond gave the lie to Secretary of State J. Foster Dulles' lofty words about "rolling back" the Iron Curtain. The successful launch of a Russian communications satellite, Sputnik, in 1957 shook Americans' confidence in their technological superiority bolstering the plausibility of those like Kennedy and Symington, who suggested that there was a "missile gap" developing in the Soviets' favor. The overthrow of the pro-American Batista regime in Cuba and the growing impression that Fidel Castro's regime was Communist-oriented deepened the sense that the Cold War was turning in the Reds' favor.

Eisenhower's use of troops to enforce desegregation at Little Rock's Central High School balked the flow of sympathy for the president among white Southerners, and his administration's reluctance to stimulate the economy, despite a sharp recession beginning in 1957, added further impetus to those who claimed that the Republicans had run out of ideas. The shooting down of a U-2 spy plane in 1960 and the subsequent acrimonious and inconclusive summit between Eisenhower and Khrushchev, alongside faltering economic indicators, meant that the Republicans could not run effectively on a "peace and prosperity" platform. The contrast between the ageing and often ill Eisenhower and the glamorous young senator from Massachusetts (whose own health problems were a carefully guarded secret) seemed to underscore the latter's appeal as the standard-bearer for those who wanted change. Ike's personal standing in the polls remained high, but his party seemed to inherit the blame for his mistakes. Pundits sensed that the electorate, unable to have Ike, might seek a change.

The primaries

At the same time, youth was a key Kennedy weakness. He seemed a young man in a hurry, pushed into the limelight by his father's money and his glamorous wife and family rather than by proven leadership. Nixon was close in age to Kennedy but did not look it, and he had enjoyed the publicity of being vice president, showing courage when his entourage was attacked on a tour of Latin America in 1958, and an ability to debate the Soviet premier in the televised "kitchen debate" at the opening of the American National Exhibition in Moscow in 1959. In the 1960 campaign, Nixon would claim that the times were too dangerous to entrust the presidency to so inexperienced a candidate as JFK, a point also made by his Democratic rivals.

The strategy of the Kennedy camp was to secure the Democratic nomination by winning primary victories, in order to prove to party bosses that JFK was the candidate who would best benefit all Democratic Party candidates in November. At the same time, using their formidable financial resources they would organize individual states, identifying people who were likely to be delegates, negotiating with party bosses, and striving to get them to commit to Kennedy ahead of the convention. The only other candidate who chose to enter the primary contests was Hubert Humphrey, a well-known liberal from Minnesota who had shot to prominence by persuading the 1948 convention to place a liberal civil rights plank in the party platform, to the anger of Deep South delegates who had marched out of the convention in disgust.

Humphrey hoped to prove that his liberalism would boost turnout among African Americans and trade unionists in the Midwest and Northeast, and that this ability to contest the battleground states would offset his unpopularity in the South. He was more popular with organized labor than Kennedy and, coming from Minnesota, he had worked in the Senate to support farm subsidies in a way that JFK had not. Humphrey's optimism, however, blinded him to the insuperable obstacles he faced. He had a limited home base compared to his rivals. Minnesota had only 11 Electoral College votes in the presidential contest, whereas Massachusetts had 16, Missouri 13, Texas 24 and Illinois 27. Compared to Kennedy he had hardly any money to finance a national campaign, and he was loathed by Southern segregationists, who controlled the Electoral College votes of the South.

Humphrey chose to launch his campaign in Minnesota's neighboring state of Wisconsin in April, making its primary the first contested one of the season. He believed that he could carry the western third of the state because its population mirrored Minnesota's and watched TV and listened to radio coming out of Minneapolis–St. Paul, giving him "name recognition." He also hoped to get union support in industrial cities like Milwaukee and Racine, and to carry the liberal student vote in the state capital Madison, which had voted strongly for Stevenson in 1956. Kennedy, on the other hand, hoped to use the Wisconsin contest to eliminate Humphrey quickly. If Humphrey could not win in neighboring Wisconsin, he should quit immediately because he would have little chance nationally. The Kennedy message was that Humphrey could not hope to win a national contest, whereas Kennedy could. This swayed some unions and thus shrank Humphrey's resources further.

Kennedy had in every way a much richer and bigger campaign than Humphrey's. Just the size of the extended Kennedy family meant that every Wisconsin community of 300 people or more was visited by a member of the Kennedy clan. While Humphrey bounced along chilly rural roads in an old bus with no heating, Kennedy traveled by private plane. Chagrined, Humphrey declared "I feel like an independent merchant competing against a chain store" (Sorensen 1965: 135). Humphrey was also angered by what he felt was conspicuous media favoritism, but ultimately it was the press that kept his campaign alive. In the end, it was widely reported in the newspapers that Kennedy's large margin of victory in Milwaukee and around Green Bay suggested that thousands of Catholic Republicans had crossed over to vote for him in these districts, whereas his failure to carry four congressional districts in the west of the state could be explained by the predominantly Lutheran religious affiliation of the residents.

Despite winning 56 percent of the overall vote and carrying six of ten congressional districts, Kennedy was portrayed as a candidate who polarized voters along religious lines. In a CBS broadcast with legendary anchorman Walter Cronkite, pollster Elmo Roper called religion the single most important issue in the election. The *New York Times* published an editorial, "Result: Negative," which stressed that the margin of victory for Kennedy was below expectations and that his dependence on the Catholic bloc was a weakness. *Time* magazine echoed this negative assessment (Kallina 2010: 59). Ever since the presidential campaign of Alfred E. Smith in 1928, the standard wisdom was that a Catholic could not win the White House. By failing to win over the Lutheran rural vote, Kennedy had raised the specter that his Catholicism would doom the Democratic ticket. To disprove this, he would have to win the next primary, in West Virginia.

If Humphrey had withdrawn after his defeat in Wisconsin, an unopposed Kennedy victory in West Virginia would have had little significance. Thus complaints from the Kennedy camp that Humphrey was a misguided "spoiler" candidate were themselves misjudged. Anger fueled Humphrey's decision to continue. His campaign had been the victim of dirty tricks in Wisconsin, in particular the mysterious appearance of anti-Catholic leaflets in predominantly Catholic neighborhoods. It later emerged that a Kennedy volunteer had mailed the offensive items, although it was never clear whether he did so on his own initiative, to drive up the Catholic voter turnout. Humphrey rashly declared that impoverished West Virginia, barely 5 percent Catholic, with the miners' union as a strong political lobby, was "made for my politics and not Jack Kennedy's" (Donaldson 2007: 53).

In reality, West Virginian politics was made for the Kennedys. Despite the media furor, the state was never likely to vote on religious grounds. Newspaper commentators failed to report that Catholic Al Smith had carried West Virginia in the 1928 primary, and even more significantly they ignored the fact that, unlike surrounding states, West Virginia had a large proportion of residents (59 percent) of no religion at all. The premise of West Virginia politics was not God but Mammon. The state's acute poverty underpinned the practice of candidates paying officials in the individual counties to get on the ballot or slate of candidates. Theodore White, whose account of Kennedy's campaign is generally glowing to the point of adulation, is candid about the sordid state of West Virginian politics, which was all about money—"hot money, under-the-table money, open money" (White 1961: 99). Along with the accusations of electoral fraud in Illinois and Texas in November, the West Virginia primary result lends the greatest substance to the accusations of those who charge that Joseph Kennedy, possibly in collusion with organized crime, bought his son's 1960 election victory.

The slating practice was a thin mask for vote-buying. The standard rate was $2 per vote, which, to be fair, had to cover the cost of driving voters to the polls and manning the polling stations. With hardly any money of his own, Humphrey spent barely $30,000, $2,000 of it on TV air time. Kennedy spent $34,000 on TV and at least $200,000 on the primary contest overall. It may easily have been ten times that amount. At the same time, the Kennedys actively worked to deter outside financial contributions and labor support for Humphrey. One Humphrey supporter from New York, Bill Benton, explained that they had told him that any further donations to Humphrey would be seen as an act of war, and retribution would follow. Similarly, national union leaders told subordinates that a victory for Humphrey would simply open the way for the nomination of Symington or Johnson, Southerners with anti-union track records. As a result, little labor help materialized for Humphrey. The injustice clearly incensed him, and in late April, having spent even the money set aside for his daughter's wedding to buy one last TV spot, he declared peevishly, "I can't afford to run through this state with a little black bag and a check book" (Kallina 2010: 65).

In the wake of the Wisconsin result, the religious issue was preeminent and Kennedy addressed it shrewdly, linking his defense to his wartime heroism in a state that venerated military service. "Nobody asked me if I was a Catholic when I joined the United States Navy," Kennedy grew used to responding, adding pointedly "Nobody asked my brother if he was a Catholic or a Protestant before he climbed into an American bomber to fly his last mission" (Kallina 2010: 64). The line taken by Kennedy in West Virginia implied that anyone who rejected Kennedy was a potential bigot, a position that outflanked opponents and still allowed him to benefit from any Catholic solidarity that his candidacy enjoyed. Humphrey's choice of the song "Give Me That Old-Time Religion" was hardly a subtle signal, but it did not deliver at the polls in the way that hard cash did.

Underlining the ruthlessness with which the Kennedy campaign set out to destroy Humphrey, they recruited Franklin Delano Roosevelt, Jr. to tour a state whose residents still revered FDR Senior for the relief he had given them during the hungry thirties. The devotion to the late president was so profound that one journalist claimed that, for many, it was almost a case of "God's son coming down and saying it was alright to vote for a Catholic" (Kallina 2010: 67). Late in the campaign, Roosevelt Junior, ignoring the reality that Humphrey had not dodged the draft but had been deemed medically unfit due to a double hernia that still required him to wear a truss, remarked casually that although Humphrey was a good Democrat, "I don't know where he was in World War II." In a state with a high percentage of veterans, there was similarly little subtlety in the practice of introducing Kennedy on TV as "the only veteran in the West Virginia primary."

At the same time as his campaign played dirty, Kennedy demonstrated his skills as a debater. On May 5, in a televised debate, he illustrated his grasp of local people's problems by showing the meager basket of surplus food that was currently allocated to poor families. No American family should face such misery, he declared, and promised to increase food allowances if elected. Even Humphrey had to concede that this was "dramatic and effective" (Donaldson 2007: 56–57).

Wary of how their early projections of results had led the press to portray the Wisconsin victory as disappointing, Bobby Kennedy and his team were deliberately pessimistic in their reports of any polling lead. On the weekend before the May 10 poll, senior staffer Theodore Sorensen told Michigan politicians, "We don't know what's going to happen," while campaign press secretary Pierre Salinger felt that the margin of Kennedy's lead was no more than 3 percent (Kallina 2010: 66). Election Day was wet and drizzly, and JFK decided that he would prefer to await the result at home in Washington. Together with journalist Ben Bradlee and his wife, Jack and Jackie went to the movies. Arriving too late to be admitted to the hit movie *Suddenly Last Summer*, they walked to another theater to see what Bradlee recalled as a "nasty" soft porn flick called *Private Property*. Returning home at 11:30 that evening, Jack found a message: call Bobby at once. "As he put the phone down," Theodore White reported, "he burst out with a very un-Senatorial war whoop" (O'Brien 2005: 455). He had won comfortably, 236,510 to 152,187, comprehensively proving that he could win a state with few Catholic voters. The next day Humphrey ended his candidacy, but not before Bobby Kennedy had worsened relations between the rivals by visiting the Humphrey head-quarters and crassly kissing an ashen-faced and obviously seething Mrs. Humphrey on the cheek in an ill-judged gesture of reconciliation.

The West Virginia result was amplified by Kennedy's victory the same day in Nebraska. Further victories followed: Maryland on May 17 and Oregon on May 20. Kennedy had won all ten primary contests he had entered and the Democratic Party bosses took notice. The doubts they had harbored in abundance when Kennedy had announced his candidacy at the start of the year had largely abated. Even before West Virginia proved that his vote-getting potential was not confined to Catholics, the Kennedy campaign had spent a lot of time flattering, negotiating with, and if need be threatening political bosses and so-called favorite sons in seven key states. New York was in some respects the most complex, due its factionalism. Carmine De Sapio, head of the fabled Tammany Hall machine, could no longer deliver the city due to the power of his rivals: state party chairman Michael Prenderghast and borough bosses Charles Buckley (the Bronx) and Joseph Sharkey (Brooklyn); upstate bosses Daniel O'Connell in Albany and Peter Crotty in Buffalo had to be courted too.

A further obstacle was the hostile presence of the former first lady, Eleanor Roosevelt, whose dislike of JFK grew out of her abiding hatred of his father. Kennedy made several largely unsuccessful efforts to neutralize her influence. As early as 1958, she had talked disparagingly on a TV show of how Joe Kennedy was spending "oodles of money" all over the country to get his son elected president, prompting Jack to call for her to back up her claims. Lacking proof, Eleanor backed down in public in early 1959, although the correspondence between the two revealed unresolved animosity. Mrs. Roosevelt would work to stop Kennedy and to spur Stevenson on, until the nomination was Kennedy's. Her even deeper revulsion at the prospect of a Nixon presidency would then ensure unity.

Amassing a winning total

An early target for the Kennedy camp was the 64-strong delegation from Ohio, and this meant negotiations with Governor Michael DiSalle. He was rumored to be considering backing Stuart Symington, but was vulnerable due to his sagging popularity. Many governors were facing disaffected electorates due to the tax hikes required to fund facilities, especially schools for the baby boom generation. Private polling carried out for Kennedy by Lou Harris revealed that he could defeat DiSalle if he entered the Ohio primary, which was timed to coincide with the Wisconsin race. Having marshaled support from DiSalle's in-state rivals, the Kennedy camp sent Bobby to deliver their message in no uncertain terms. The manner in which the hard-nosed Bobby spelt out to DiSalle what would happen if he failed to pledge publicly to deliver his delegation to Kennedy was graphically recalled by one witness, Connecticut politico John Bailey. "Bobby was all over DiSalle," he said, "like a fly on shit." The pledge was made soon after Kennedy announced his candidacy in January. Disappointed liberal senator Wayne Morse greeted the pledge with the declaration that Ohio no longer had a favorite son, but "a favorite stooge"

(Kallina 2010: 53–55). Other bosses realized that they might not be able to fob off the Kennedys, once the Catholic question had been answered.

After West Virginia, the campaign worked hard to secure commitments from delegates in New York and Michigan, and Mayor Daley of Chicago quietly promised to bring in the Illinois delegation. The large delegations from California, Pennsylvania, and New Jersey held out. All three had Democratic governors. New Jersey governor Robert Meyner wanted the publicity of being his state's candidate on the first ballot, and would then switch in the second round to give Kennedy the nomination. Despite the West Virginia result, governor and fellow Catholic David Lawrence continued to fret that anti-Catholic sentiment, galvanized by a Kennedy presidential bid, might undermine his own bid for reelection in Pennsylvania. He also had pro-Stevenson leanings, despite the fact that by June there were strong rumors that the former Illinois governor could not count on the backing of even his home state, given Mayor Daley's influence.

Governor Pat Brown of California remained a problem for Kennedy. The two men did not have a good personal relationship, especially after Brown began their very first meeting by bluntly asking Kennedy if he had Addison's disease. Nominally, they came to a deal whereby Kennedy agreed not to run in the California primary in return for Brown's promise that if JFK won the primaries he entered he could count on Brown's support at the Los Angeles convention. Unfortunately the governor's ability to deliver his delegation, weak when the deal was struck, diminished further as the convention neared and local Democrats fought to be delegates at a convention in their home state. California Democratic clubs were dominated by liberal activists who mistrusted Kennedy and remained sentimentally attached to Adlai Stevenson. Eleanor Roosevelt actively cultivated their mistrust at the convention itself, and Brown so resented the constant pressure from Bobby Kennedy for him to commit that he angrily referred to Bobby as a "punk kid." He let it be known that he was only with JFK for the first ballot. The Kennedy camp sensed that, if they faltered on that ballot, their chance might have gone (Kallina 2010: 70–71).

While small in numbers, the delegations from the Great Plains (North and South Dakota, Nebraska, Kansas, and Oklahoma) and

Mountain states (Idaho, Montana, Utah, Wyoming, Colorado, Nevada, Arizona) were important. They should have bolstered Lyndon Johnson's bid for the nomination, enabling him to add their votes to his guaranteed Southern ones (nearly 30 percent of the convention total). Had the 128 delegates from the Mountain West been in the Johnson camp, a Kennedy victory on the first ballot would have been almost impossible. The shared economic interests of agriculture and extractive industries, especially oil, made this a logical alliance, and Johnson's Senate record as a backer of federally constructed dam projects should have strengthened it even further. But Johnson dithered over his candidacy and foolishly believed that his Senate colleagues could deliver their state delegations. By the time he tried to organize in these states he discovered the Kennedys were already entrenched. Over the Memorial Day weekend of 1960, Johnson's top campaign aide, James Rowe (who had pleaded with him to start preparatory work for the 1960 race as early as 1958), phoned him from Montana and advised him to wipe the state off his itinerary since it was Kennedy's. Entrusted with the task of delivering the Mountain states for his older brother, Edward Kennedy had earned begrudging respect in Montana by staying on a bucking bronco for five seconds, but even he conceded that if Johnson had campaigned early he could have "locked up" the region "without any difficulty at all" (Caro 2012: 91).

The Kennedy campaign still feared a "Draft Stevenson" movement. Jack Kennedy had broken his journey back from his Oregon primary victory by stopping off at Adlai Stevenson's home in Illinois. Months earlier, via Connecticut Governor Abraham Ribicoff, he had tried unsuccessfully to get Stevenson's endorsement by offering him the post of secretary of state in a Kennedy administration. Now he spoke to the two-time nominee directly, with the connivance of Arthur Schlesinger, Jr., the Harvard historian who had become Kennedy's conduit to the liberal lobby group, Americans for Democratic Action. After the meeting, Stevenson wrote Schlesinger explaining that he wanted to be consistent in his refusal to take sides ahead of the convention, saying only that he would not join any "Stop Kennedy" movements. Kennedy's own impression was that Stevenson was either hoping for a deadlocked convention that would draft him as the nominee, or covertly maneuvering for the same outcome in order to secure the nomination for Lyndon Johnson.

Stevenson's associates recalled an unharmonious meeting that had seen Kennedy explode at Stevenson's prevarication with the words "We are going to have to shit all over you." Stevenson was certainly apt to tell friends how ill-mannered Kennedy was, and how little he appreciated the start which Stevenson had given him by his decision to leave open the choice of vice president at the 1956 convention. But such blunt speaking doesn't sound like Jack—it's more Bobby's style. Privately JFK dismissed Stevenson as a "goddam weeper" and a "switcher," by which he meant a bisexual, although Adlai's popularity with women puzzled Kennedy. He even asked Stevenson's friend Clayton Fritchey to explain why women were said to go mad for Adlai. Fritchey felt it was because they sensed that Stevenson truly liked them. "He likes to talk to them, to be around them. Do you like them?" Fritchey added. "I wouldn't go that far," Jack replied (Dallek 2003: 254).

As the convention neared, with Kennedy's position as frontrunner obvious to all, his opponents went on the attack in ways that revealed the intensity of the competition. Former President Harry Truman complained at a nationally televised press conference that the convention was being "rigged" for Kennedy. A Symington supporter, Truman felt the Massachusetts senator lacked "maturity and experience," and had risen to prominence through Joe Kennedy's money and connections rather than as a result of achievement. When reporters asked whether his disapproval had an anti-Catholic component, Truman quipped, "I'm not against the Pope. I'm against the Pop" (Rorabaugh 2009: 70–71).

Enemies leapt on any Kennedy mistake. When Kennedy suggested that Eisenhower might have apologized to the Soviets for the U-2 spy plane incident, Johnson pointedly accused him of playing into Soviet hands by fomenting division instead of supporting his president. "I'm not prepared to apologize to Mr. Khrushchev," he told cheering crowds. Governor Brown of California declared that the dangerous world situation required a mature, calm, worldly wise leader like Adlai Stevenson. A full-page Johnson ad that ran in eighteen cities declared, "We cannot afford to gamble with inexperience, immaturity." More abrasively, LBJ reminded people of Daddy Kennedy's wartime defeatism. To Bobby Kennedy's enduring fury, Johnson smeared Joe Kennedy as an appeaser and a Nazi sympathizer with the words, "I wasn't any Chamberlain umbrella man. I never thought Hitler was right." Worse yet for the Kennedys, Johnson's allies raised the health issue. India Edwards, a prominent leader in the Democratic Party's women's division, declared to a press conference that JFK had Addison's disease and would not be alive today "if not for cortisone." This drew an immediate, and frankly mendacious, denial from the Kennedy camp. Kennedy's physicians issued false statements that he did not have the disease, which in classic cases was characterized by a lethargy that his already lengthy campaigning clearly belied. Bobby Kennedy described these "despicable tactics" as "a sure sign of the desperation of the opposition" (Caro 2012: 94–97).

The convention

Democratic national chairman Paul Butler had deliberately placed the convention in Los Angeles to associate the party with better economic conditions and Hollywood glamor. The LA backdrop would play well on the newly dominant medium of television, with the convention's events moved forward each day to ensure that West Coast time did not mean missing East Coast primetime audiences. The convention's emphasis on television—visible in the 10-by-16-foot "big screen" behind the podium and speakers' use of teleprompters for the first time—benefitted Kennedy. In the weekend before the July 11 opening, the mingling of movie stars with twenty members of the extended Kennedy family provided photo opportunities that boosted the front-runner's profile, but more importantly the large delegations caucused to agree their choice for president. On Sunday, the Illinois delegation largely followed Mayor Daley's recommendation, assigning JFK 59.5 votes (each delegate had 0.5 of a vote), Symington 6.5, and Stevenson 2, with the remaining two delegates uncommitted on the first ballot. When the convention opened on Monday, New York announced 102 votes for Kennedy, and the Pennsylvania delegation, rebelling against Governor Lawrence, came out overwhelmingly for Kennedy, with 64 votes. JFK had moved rapidly towards the required total of 761, and the press began to say a Kennedy victory was inevitable.

Over the same weekend, the Party's platform committee met to hammer out the policy positions on which its candidates would ostensibly run. At its head was a liberal, former Connecticut governor Chester Bowles, who was known to be a strong advocate of civil rights reform as well as a Kennedy supporter. In 1956 the Democratic platform had contained a weak civil rights plank, in a vain effort to appease the white South. Bowles was determined not to make this mistake, and instead included a strong demand for federal action to strengthen racial equality in voting, education, housing and employment. The platform even endorsed the lunch counter sit-in protest movement which had swept the segregated South in the spring and summer of 1960. Bowles calculated that the platform would be denounced by the Southern delegations in public, but that it might increase the African American vote in key Northern battleground states like Illinois, Pennsylvania, and Ohio. He also knew well that it would not be an easy platform for a Southern politician like Johnson to champion at the convention, and that it would give the pragmatic Kennedy less room to court Southerners. The platform also endorsed the policy demands of the major trade unions of the AFL-CIO.

At the same time, reporters learned that the AFL-CIO top brass had sent word to labor members who were convention delegates that they must give no support to Lyndon Johnson's bid for the presidency, since he was "an arch foe of labor." Inside the convention, an NAACP-organized rally was marked by cheers for Hubert Humphrey but boos and catcalls whenever Johnson was even mentioned. Seeking a chance to boost his candidacy, Johnson responded to a Kennedy campaign wire asking whether JFK could address the Texan delegation—which Johnson received as head of the delegation—by publicly urging a televised event where both the Massachusetts and Texan delegations would hear the two candidates debate the issues. Not being the leader of the Massachusetts delegation nor wanting to give LBJ a larger platform, Kennedy replied that he would be happy to appear alone before the Texan delegation. Despite the intrinsic bias against him, he left the delegation amused by his wit and impressed by his calm demeanor. Johnson boasted at the event that he had answered all 45 roll calls during the round-the-clock sessions debating the 1957 Civil Rights Bill, whereas "certain other senators" had been there barely ten times. Kennedy smiled at this reference and commended the majority leader on his extraordinary record, but added, to grins from his audience, that since LBJ did not mention any names, Kennedy would assume that Johnson must have been talking about someone other than him. Even members of LBJ's inner circle felt the event had gone in Kennedy's favor. (Caro 2012: 98, 103–5).

Nevertheless, Kennedy could not afford to be complacent. On July 13, the same day that Kennedy entered the Texan den, the main convention hall witnessed lavish demonstrations in favor of Stevenson. His arrival on the floor was greeted by a seemingly spontaneous outburst of adulation from the galleries, as thousands of his backers from California Democratic Clubs paraded down into the main hall, conspicuously applauded by his main supporter, Eleanor Roosevelt. Stevenson himself was persuaded to take the stage, but he failed to announce his candidacy and thus capitalize on the occasion. The clamor for Stevenson did allow Hubert Humphrey to enjoy a small act of revenge. Pressed by Bobby Kennedy to endorse Jack and bring the Minnesota delegation with him, he told Bobby to go to hell, and the next morning announced for Stevenson. It was small consolation, since by Wednesday, July 13, the Kennedy camp calculated that they had the votes to win on the first ballot, and so it proved, despite a powerful, emotional speech nominating Stevenson from Humphrey's Senate colleague from Minnesota, Eugene McCarthy. Urging delegates not to abandon their former standard-bearer Stevenson, McCarthy provided the rhetorical high spot of the week and signaled his own immunity to Kennedy's charm. A devout Catholic, McCarthy was outraged by JFK's playboy antics and considered him a bad representative of his church. But McCarthy's speech, while theatrical, made little difference. Once Wyoming cast its 15 votes in Kennedy's favor he had exceeded the required majority of 761 by 4 votes; his final tally was 806.

Kennedy's first-round victory at the convention was secured by primary victories, successful negotiations with party bosses, the securing of Western state delegates, and a high overall level of organization during what had essentially been a four-year campaign.

Along the way, Kennedy had become the prototype for the tele-vised candidate: young, glamorous, and able to feed the media's appetite for stories both personal and political. His beautiful wife, extended family, and wealthy lifestyle played as large a part as his policy speeches in securing "free media" exposure. Joe Kennedy's money was the foundation for winning the nomination. When Jack told the press club that he had received a telegram from his father after the West Virginia primary that told him to buy only the votes necessary to win, because Pop was not prepared to fund a landslide, the joke had the ring of truth. But winning the nomi-nation was not the same as winning the presidency, and a key element in the presidential campaign had to be selected: a vice presidential running mate. If Joe's money was the essential factor in the nomination race, Lyndon Johnson's hold on the South was fundamental to victory in one of the tightest presidential contests in American history.

Choosing a winning ticket

Winning the election was rooted in the peculiar mathematics of the US Electoral College, which assigned each state votes on the basis of its number of congressmen plus two senators. Most Americans in 1960 told pollsters that they were Democrats, despite the fact that they had elected a Republican president in two consecutive contests, and by an increasing margin. The Democratic Party's strength was rooted in the Southern states of the former Confederacy and in the urban industrial heartlands of the East and Midwest, where it was associated with a multiethnic vote that had once been largely made up of Catholics, including the Irish, and eastern Europeans, including many Jewish-Americans. By 1960, the multiethnic vote came increasingly from Hispanic and African American voters. With the help of organized labor in getting out the minority vote, Kennedy expected to surge in the large industrial cities, and various studies suggested that he would also benefit from a middle-class Catholic vote in the suburbs of the Northeast and Midwest.

His problems began in the South, where his Catholicism and the party's strong liberal civil rights platform would alienate the largely white electorate. He was also likely to lose the farm belt of the Midwest and Far West, since he had opposed farm subsidies during his Senate career, and here too there would be pockets of devout Protestants alarmed at the prospect of a Catholic in the Oval Office. The simple fact was that JFK had to get the majority of electoral votes from the largest states because he was weak in the lightly populated, rural ones. Ideally he needed to carry California, Illinois, Ohio, Michigan, New York, Pennsylvania, and Texas. But it was more likely that Nixon would take the first three, producing a split in Electoral College votes of 121 to 84 in JFK's favor. This made Texas crucial—a loss there and Nixon would lead in the large state league, 108 to 97. This could be a telling advantage, especially since Kennedy could not count on solid support from the Southern states, several of which had seen segregationists campaigning to select a slate of uncommitted electors who would bargain with both Nixon and Kennedy when the Electoral College met in December. In a close election, they might even be able to throw the contest into the House of Representatives.

Almost as soon as he won the nomination, therefore, Kennedy had to make his vice presidential pick, and although some consideration was given to Missouri Senator Stuart Symington, he quickly realized that the logical candidate was Lyndon Johnson of Texas, who had come second in the ballot for the presidential nomination, with 409 votes. But Kennedy was hesitant. Johnson was certainly anathema to Jack's brother Bobby, and potentially also to the union bosses and African American voters who might help JFK win in the industrial states. Johnson was also the most powerful Senate majority leader that Congress had seen in the twentieth century—why would he take the offer? His Texan predecessor, James Nance Garner, had famously described his role as vice president to Franklin Delano Roosevelt as "not worth a pitcher of piss." Kennedy risked the embarrassment of having his offer turned down. Given his conduct during the nomination fight, Johnson might exploit any offer made to weaken JFK; he and his Texan colleague House Speaker Sam Rayburn had gone so far as to visit Eisenhower to ask the Republican president to assist efforts to deny Kennedy the nomination. Thus making an offer to Johnson was a gamble. Kennedy was known for his political calculation, however, and the math pointed to Johnson as the choice who could make the difference.

At around eight o'clock on Thursday, July 14, Kennedy phoned Lyndon Johnson's suite and, when Lady Bird Johnson answered, he asked to speak to her husband. "Can I come down to speak with you?" Kennedy asked, and they agreed to meet at ten. The Johnson suite (7333) was two floors below Kennedy's headquarters (Suite 9333), although most nights Jack had slipped away to an apartment his father had rented to allow him to escape media scrutiny. A mass of reporters had taken up post by the elevators on the ninth floor, waiting to see who would be summoned by the nominee for what they assumed would be a series of vice presidential interviews. A few journalists had even positioned themselves outside the doors of likely choices, but Johnson was not on their list. The press definitely did not see Kennedy sneak down the dimly lit back stairs, to arrive at Suite 7333 at about ten fifteen. Johnson gave in person the congratulations he had sent Kennedy by telegram immediately after his victory, but Kennedy was keen to do business: was Johnson available for the vice presidency? LBJ confirmed that he was, but added that there were obstacles. He would only take the job if his mentor Sam Rayburn could be persuaded that it was the right thing to do, and Kennedy should know that on his own side he would have to placate certain labor and liberal leaders who were anti-Johnson. Kennedy promised to call back before noon. Returning to his suite, he told a shocked Kenny O'Donnell that it looked as if Johnson would take the job.

Accounts of the rest of the day's events are contradictory, and largely revolve around Bobby Kennedy's efforts to rescind the offer. Bobby had a considerable capacity for hatred, which Johnson amply triggered. Feelings were also inflamed within the Johnson camp. Senator Robert Kerr of Oklahoma was so livid that Johnson would consider joining the Kennedy ticket that he threatened to kill Johnson and Lady Bird, and actually struck longtime Johnson aide Bobby Baker, so hard that he saw stars. In subsequent oral histories, Bobby Kennedy insisted that his brother had intended nothing more than a courtesy call with a *pro forma* offer that he fully expected Johnson to reject, and was astonished that Johnson instead seized his chance. If the offer was not a serious one, though, why did Jack double check the potential benefits of having Texas's Electoral College votes before he visited Johnson, and why did he happily tell leading Northern bosses and share in their delight at Johnson's willingness to serve? Moreover, why did he go and get Sam Rayburn's acceptance of the ticket, as Johnson had requested? If he wanted to rescind the offer, it would have been easy to cite Rayburn as the stumbling block. At the same time, Bobby Kennedy's attempts to persuade Johnson to withdraw are undeniable. They may have reflected a genuine concern that union hostility to Johnson might trigger a raucous convention fight that would tarnish the ticket from the outset, but the main reason was Bobby's loathing of the Texan. Only a phone call to JFK himself at around 3.30 confirmed the Kennedy–Johnson ticket. Asked about his brother's conduct, Jack blithely told LBJ that "Bobby's been out of touch" (Schlesinger 1965: 56).

To answer the question why Johnson surrendered his position as the most powerful figure in Congress in favor of a role that amounted to understudy, one first has to appreciate how much he yearned to be president, and then realize that the historical record suggested that the only route to power open to Johnson was the vice presidency. If he declined to serve, he would remain a Southern senator, with the same prejudices working against him after Kennedy completed what might be two terms. Worse still, without Johnson's support, Kennedy might well lose to Nixon, extending Republican control over the White House, and in defeat the party's liberals would be happy to target Johnson as its cause. This would potentially scupper a future presidential bid and make his increasingly difficult relationship with liberals in the Senate even more difficult, had he continued as majority leader. Serving on a losing ticket did not carry this risk and might even promote a Johnson candidacy as a way of reviving party fortunes.

Defending his choice of Johnson to his unhappy aides, JFK at one point declared that, as the youngest candidate for the presidency, his vice presidential pick was largely irrelevant. "You've traveled with me enough to know that I'm not going to die in office," he said with a smile. At the same time, the core appeal of the vice presidency for ambitious figures is that it lies just a heartbeat away from the presidency, and several voices in the Johnson camp, not least the candidate, had talked about Kennedy's health troubles in ways that suggested they knew he was far more physically fragile than his image suggested. Given what ultimately happened to Kennedy in Johnson's home state of Texas in November 1963, any suggestion that LBJ took the vice presidency in anticipation of stepping into a dead man's shoes sparks conspiracy theories. He was certainly aware that a man who had struggled to cope with the Senate due to health problems might falter under the burdens of the presidency, but perhaps the most compelling reasons for his decision were the many negative outcomes he could predict if he turned the office down. It was better to be damned for what he did than for what he failed to do.

Political realities swayed the labor leaders and bosses who had reacted negatively to the choice of Johnson. They saw that he made the Democratic ticket more competitive, and they loathed Nixon. On Thursday night, convention chairman Leroy Collins of Florida declared that Johnson had been nominated as vice president by acclamation, and the next morning the two nominees met with African American delegates to reassure them that the ticket was fully behind the civil rights measures promised in the platform. Johnson promised them more progress in the next four years than in the previous hundred (1961 marked the start of the centennial of the Civil War). The finale of the convention, Kennedy's acceptance speech, was held in the LA Coliseum, a football stadium that easily accommodated the 80,000 spectators, but proved a poor venue for the 35 million television viewers. It was too large to be lavishly decorated. Its capacity of 110,000 meant that it was not filled, and Kennedy's position at its center produced acoustic problems beyond the amplification available. Harsh lights blanched the candidate and rendered the background a blur of sinister shadows. They also attracted insects, which visibly darted around Kennedy and even entered his mouth as he tried unsuccessfully to project his voice. Under an open night sky it was a far from stellar performance to launch what Kennedy termed his "New Frontier." The polls showed a modest bounce in approval for Kennedy, but the speech certainly failed to impress the "middle-of-the-road" voters that Kennedy needed to reclaim from Eisenhower. Eager to reassure them, the campaign rhetoric would thereafter stress the energy Kennedy would bring to the defense of America in the Cold War.

The presidential campaign

Since the Red Scare of the late 1940s, foreign policy issues had tended to favor the Republicans, and they were certainly seen as Richard Nixon's forte. His problems on the eve of the Republican convention paralleled Kennedy's, with the challenge of maintaining unity in the face of tensions between the Goldwater conservatives, who deplored the "creeping socialism" of the Eisenhower years, and the Rockefeller liberals, who wanted to boost the economy through federal spending and to act vigorously on civil rights. Nixon was a moderate liberal on civil rights and this may explain why he ignored calls to pursue a Southern strategy that would appeal to white Southerners angered by what they saw as outside interference in racial matters. In what became known as the "Treaty of Fifth Avenue," Nixon negotiated an agreement with Nelson Rockefeller to place a civil rights plank in the platform that mirrored the liberal Democratic one, in order to compete for Northern African American votes. It also called for increased defense spending in a way that implicitly criticized Eisenhower's policy, significantly souring relations with the president, who had spent much of his two terms trying to rein in defense costs. Despite their anger, the conservatives' standard bearer Barry Goldwater declined to challenge Nixon for the nomination, urging the convention's delegates to work hard to elect the Californian, while at the same time working harder to "take this party back" from the liberal establishment. The 1964 convention which would see the GOP nominate Goldwater on a conservative platform was the eventual outcome of the failure of Nixon's attempt to win a third term for "middle-of-the-road" Republicanism (Rorabaugh 2009: 107–14).

Nixon's bid for Northern liberal and minority voters, rather than Southern white voters, was reflected also in his choice of vice president, former Massachusetts Senator Henry Cabot Lodge. Due largely to his familiarity to voters as ambassador to the United Nations, where he had been seen denouncing Soviet misdeeds, Lodge was supposed to strengthen Nixon in the Northeast states, especially with respect to the black vote in New York, but in the campaign he proved a liability. A lethargic campaigner whom Kennedy had defeated in his first Senate race, Lodge came across as arrogant and out of touch, and was far from a team player. The contrast between the negative impact of Lodge on the Republican ticket and the hugely positive effect of Johnson on the Democratic side was a key element in Kennedy's narrow victory. Lodge could neither deliver his home state nor prevent the loss of New York, a key Electoral College state. Johnson held Texas and campaigned effectively across the South, enabling Kennedy to concentrate his efforts elsewhere.

While the strategic mistakes Nixon made at the July convention would ultimately haunt him, the immediate perception was that the event was a triumph. Even Kennedy aide Theodore Sorensen conceded that Nixon's acceptance speech was "brilliant." It skillfully presented him as an experienced statesman who knew the practicalities of being president, and who could combine a resolute defense of American interests with a sophisticated understanding of global affairs. After the convention, polls showed him ahead of Kennedy. Nixon believed that he would win because of his experience, but only after a drawn-out campaign that would necessitate him keeping resources in reserve for the closing weeks. He made that final sprint needlessly taxing by promising in his acceptance address that he would campaign in all fifty states before Election Day.

Pointlessly adding to the already energy-sapping toll of traveling was just one example of the tactical errors that Nixon made. It compounded his dismal press relations: the press pack had to endure the same exhausting campaign schedule as the candidate. And, in stark contrast to Kennedy's cultivation of the media, the Nixon team did little to make their life easier. Even the most basic courtesy, such as ensuring that reporters were given transcripts of Nixon's speeches, was not in place. Unable to see the press as an ally, Nixon made them into an enemy. Admittedly they were predisposed to be so, even though most newspaper publishers were Republicans. As far Nixon was concerned, reporters took delight in demeaning him. On August 24, an ill-tempered President Eisenhower was leaving his weekly press conference when a reporter asked him to give a specific example of a decision Nixon had shaped as his vice president. Believing the session had ended and testily wanting to tell the reporter to leave his question till the following week, Eisenhower snapped "Give me a week and

I might think of one" (Rorabaugh 2009: 122). The remark seemed to say that he would be hard pressed to name a single contribution Nixon had made in the last seven and a half years, and that was how an eager press presented it.

Ike's gaffe was not Nixon's only piece of bad luck. During an August campaign trip to North Carolina, he banged his knee sharply on a car door and the resulting wound became infected. Within days the badly swollen joint required him to be hospitalized, blowing a hole in what was already an overbooked schedule. By the time he returned to the campaign trail on September 12, he had demanded his team schedule visits to 37 states in 21 days to make up for lost time, ignoring the need for recuperation. By mixing in rescheduled locations Nixon made his itinerary less efficient than Kennedy's, which concentrated on specific regions before each long haul flight. Predictably, Nixon caught a severe cold, with a high fever, night sweats, and daytime chills.

The Catholic question

But if Nixon made mistakes, the Kennedy team also played smart. During Nixon's hospitalization they had acquired a telling report from a polling research firm on the impact of anti-Catholicism. The report argued that Kennedy had already lost those voters who would be alienated by his Catholicism, and that, ironically, public discussion of the issue was now likely to win votes for Kennedy. He would get votes from outraged Catholics, minority groups, and those disposed to "resent overt prejudice." At the same time, the Nixon camp had been gingerly seeking to profit from Protestant groups animated by the threat they perceived in a Catholic president. Devout Texan Baptist and insurance millionaire Carr Collins, for instance, purchased airtime on two Dallas radio stations in order to lambast Kennedy. The Nixon camp hoped to capitalize on Protestant fears, but clandestinely, lest the backlash to prejudice prove larger than the appeal to the prejudiced. On September 8, however, a story broke about a meeting of Protestant clergy that explicitly attacked the Kennedy candidacy on religious grounds. The presence among the clergy of renowned pastor Norman Vincent Peale, bestselling author of *The Power of Positive Thinking*, drew headlines. The group was essentially demanding a "Protestants only" rule for the presidency, and this provided Kennedy with an ideal opportunity to address the issue in a way that would rally support. To magnify the occasion, he agreed to address a televised meeting of the Greater Houston Ministerial Association on September 12. The Kennedy team set up the event and placed the preachers they believed to be the meanest looking in the front rows. No viewer could doubt who the bad guys were.

In his opening remarks Kennedy noted and heartily agreed with the Constitution's requirement of a strict separation of Church and state. "I am not the Catholic candidate for president," he said pointedly. "I am the Democratic Party's candidate for president who happens to be Catholic." After his eloquent statement, he gracefully and effectively dealt with a series of antagonistic questions from his unfriendly studio audience, in a way that won over his much larger TV audience. He emerged as a champion of religious freedom. Insulted Catholics felt powerfully inclined to support him and members of other minority groups, notably Jewish Americans, also felt intense sympathy. These would be important electoral elements in Kennedy's victories in Northern states. Even in Texas, Kennedy's Houston performance won him begrudging admirers and boosted his support among the state's Catholic Latino population. His campaign was so pleased with the event that they circulated edited copies: a five-minute version to play in Protestant areas to put critics on the defensive, and a longer thirty-minute version, used most often in Catholic areas to rally the troops. In the battleground states of New York, Illinois, Pennsylvania, and Ohio the program aired many times.

The TV debates

In 1960 the television networks were reeling from the aftermath of the quiz show scandals that had revealed rigged contests, and from a torrent of criticism that they were the worst aspect of mass culture, playing to the lowest common denominator. Fearing a political backlash, their top executives wanted to present a more civic, sophisticated image. Coverage of politics was limited, however, by the strict "equal time" rule. A station that interviewed

Kennedy would then have to give the same amount of airtime not just to Nixon but to all other candidates (in 1960 there 12 additional minor candidates). The rule thus barred a debate confined to just the major party candidates. However, during a special summer session, called by Johnson and Rayburn at a time when they had hoped it might boost the Texan's presidential hopes, Congress voted to suspend the equal time rule, and the networks offered the two candidates the chance to debate.

Eisenhower strongly advised Nixon to decline, believing it could only help his opponent, but other GOP leaders felt that no free media opportunity should be ignored. Nixon also knew that if he declined the press response would be hostile. Polls showed that a majority of Americans wanted a televised debate. And, after watching Kennedy's lackluster acceptance speech, Nixon felt confident that he could beat him in debate. The two major TV events of his political career—the 1952 Checkers speech defending himself against corruption charges and the 1959 "kitchen debate" with Khrushchev—had gone firmly in his favor. Nixon had excelled in debate point-scoring since high school, and he believed that this would give him an edge. He failed to realize that these televised debates would be more about image than substance.

Nixon also made a series of tactical errors in relation to the debates. He agreed to four, beginning on September 26, and believed that the audience would grow. He was unperturbed by the decision to make the first debate about domestic policy, since he felt that this would mean that the second on foreign policy (his strength) would have the larger audience. In practice, the novelty of a televised debate ensured that the first had the largest audience. Nixon also insisted that there should be no audience in the studio, but in practice the empty studio benefited the cool style of Kennedy. Without an audience, the network producers insisted that they needed to be able to show reaction shots to liven up their coverage, and this would work greatly to Nixon's disadvantage. Similarly, neither side were interested in vice presidential debates, yet Lodge had far greater television experience than Johnson, and a poor performance by the latter before a national audience might have helped Nixon.

There were further serious errors at the first debate. On September 26, Nixon was in no shape to appear on television. He was still running a high temperature, and his recent weight loss caused his shirt collar to gape and accentuated his deep-set eyes and heavy jowls. His revised travel schedule had exhausted him, and on arrival he banged his damaged knee. Kennedy, on the other hand, had taken a break in Florida and focused with his staff on preparing for the debate. Ironically, the medical regimen that Kennedy was following for his adrenal deficiency had the side effect of facilitating tanning. His deep-rooted illness made him look a model of health, whereas Nixon's temporary bout of sickness appeared to signal profound anxiety and unease, as he sweated under the overhead lights. He needed expert make-up, yet accepted only a light dusting with powder, which streaked to produce a ghoulish effect. During the debate the cameras caught Nixon mopping his brow, licking sweat off his upper lip, and nodding in agreement with Kennedy's words. Kennedy, meanwhile, looked cool and unflustered, and took notes. Seeing Nixon on a monitor in the Chicago studio, Mayor Daley blurted out, "My God, they've embalmed him before he even died." When the program ended, Nixon's press secretary received so many enquiries about his boss that he issued a blanket press statement: "Mr. Nixon is in excellent health and looks good in person" (Rorabaugh 2009: 154).

There was a marked difference of opinion between TV viewers and radio listeners. Viewers rated Kennedy more highly but listeners had the contest closer, and even a slight majority judging it a win for Nixon. But the impact of the debate has been exaggerated. In reality even those who saw Kennedy as winning the debate did not change their minds about who they would vote for. Arguably the debate's most tangible effect was to raise public awareness and so boost turnout. Those viewers who watched all four debates felt the candidates were evenly matched, which was confirmed by the election itself. Instead of seeing the first debate as the hallmark of a slick TV campaign that guaranteed a Kennedy triumph, it is more accurate to see it as a temporary gain made significant by other steps that his campaign took in the closing weeks. The high turnout, for example, was also a product of a significant voter registration drive. By early October, Democrats had signed up 8.5 million new voters in key states such as New York, Illinois, Pennsylvania, and California; all except the last of these states went for Kennedy in November.

A *focused campaign*

The chief message from Kennedy in 1960 was "It is time to get this country moving again," a dynamic theme that capitalized on the contrast between the ageing president and the youthful candidate. Nixon stood on the message "Experience Counts," but the Republican platform had largely staked out a position of moderate change, hoping to split the Democrats if they tried to be more radical and to attract conservative-oriented independent voters.

At rallies, Kennedy astutely selected proposals that could appeal to key constituencies. He spoke about the need for health insurance for the elderly, which addressed a key concern among older voters, and he urged federal aid to school districts struggling to cope with the demands of the baby boom and a mobile population. On civil rights, he endorsed the liberal platform and used the issue to illustrate the Eisenhower presidency's inertia. He declared that there were areas of discrimination that the president could address directly by executive order, citing the example of federally funded housing. In this area, he said, discrimination could be eliminated by "a stroke of the pen" (Dallek 2003: 292). The overarching concern for voters remained foreign policy, where Kennedy tried to capitalize on the sense that the Soviets had caught up with the US in the Cold War contest. Yet here the Republicans had a stronger record than the Democrats, since memories of the stalemate in Korea were still fresh.

Vice presidential contributions to victory

By mid-October, Kennedy had a four-point lead in the polls. His campaign recognized, however, that this lead could disappear quickly in key states. Lyndon Johnson campaigned hard in the South to prevent Nixon replicating or extending Eisenhower's gains among conservative whites. Aboard a train that traveled from Washington, DC to New Orleans, LBJ entertained 1,247 local party leaders, reminding them of the deals that could be done if the party ticket regained the White House with Southern help—deals that would tackle poverty, rural development, education, and healthcare. But if Kennedy won with little Southern help, the rewards would go elsewhere. Polling in the South saw a

10 percent surge in Kennedy's rating in October. For the rest of the campaign Johnson focused on the vital task of keeping Texas Democratic. Days before the election, he and his wife Lady Bird were walking through the lobby of the Adolphus Hotel in Dallas when they were confronted by Republican protesters led by Congressman Bruce Alger. Seeing the TV crews and alert to the publicity possibilities, Johnson moved towards rather than away from the placard-waving crowd, enabling the cameras to capture the crudely chanting hecklers' mistreatment of his calm and stately wife, upon whom this "mink-coat mob" spat fulsomely. This spectacle, the antithesis of Southern hospitality, angered many Southerners, notably Georgia Senator Richard Russell, a conservative who revered Lady Bird. He spent two days campaigning in conservative east Texas, calling the faithful back to the party (Rorabaugh 2009: 134–37).

While Johnson helped Kennedy in the South, Nixon's running mate Henry Cabot Lodge blundered in the North. At a campaign stop in Spanish Harlem, Lodge pledged that Nixon would name an African American in his cabinet. Nixon had in no way authorized Lodge to make such a promise, which had little effect on the Hispanic crowd to which it was addressed. Relayed in the media, it allowed the Democrats to take the high ground by insisting that their cabinet would be based solely on merit, and forced Nixon to backtrack on his running mate's words. By the time Lodge conceded that he could not make such a pledge, the Republicans had managed three self-inflicted wounds: they had nurtured mistrust among African Americans by giving empty promises, they had done the same among white Southerners by openly courting the black vote, and they had alienated independents by their crass politicking, which strengthened the attachment of the epithet "tricky" to "Dickey" Nixon (Rorabaugh 2009: 165–66).

Civil rights and King's release

Just a week later, Martin Luther King, Jr. was arrested among a group of sit-in demonstrators at an Atlanta department store restaurant. While city mayor William Hartsfield was able to secure the swift release of most of the protesters, King was held due to a previously imposed DeKalb County parole order for driving without a Georgia state permit. Segregationist judge Oscar Mitchell eagerly sentenced King to four months' hard labor for breach of parole, and he was spirited away in the middle of the night to distant Reidsville state penitentiary. Fearing a lynching, King's heavily pregnant wife Coretta phoned Harris Wofford, a Kennedy aide who had supported the civil rights cause in the past. Wofford had another civil rights sympathizer, Sargent Shriver, JFK's brother-in-law, talk the candidate into calling Mrs. King, which he did on October 26. The next day, Bobby Kennedy pressed Judge Mitchell to order the civil rights leader's release, and by the evening King was back with his wife.

During the week King had been in jail, Nixon had stayed silent, despite pleas from African American supporters such as Jackie Robinson that he should take a public stand. On the Sunday before the election, the Kennedy campaign distributed leaflets outside black churches carrying the title "'No Comment' Nixon Versus a Candidate with a Heart, Senator Kennedy." After the election proved so close, this incident was held to have made the difference, with Eisenhower blaming Nixon's loss on a "couple of phone calls." Ironically, while the episode is supposed to have shown Kennedy's commitment to civil rights, it actually demonstrated his continued closeness to Southern white politicians, such as Georgia Governor Vandiver, and his willingness to do backroom deals with them.

The closing gap

As polling day neared, JFK was wary, more so than most of his staff. Nixon had always planned a crescendo of effort in the last week. One quarter of his TV budget was spent in the last week, saturating the airwaves in an unprecedented blitz. Another key resource used at this stage was President Eisenhower. Since no Republican since 1876 had won the White House without carrying New York, the president joined Nixon and Lodge for a full day's campaigning there on November 2. Given Eisenhower's widespread popularity, postelection analysts pondered why he was not used more extensively, notably in swing states like Illinois or Texas. At least part of the answer was that Nixon was pressed by

Mrs. Eisenhower and the president's doctor to limit Ike's campaigning on health grounds. During an ostensibly nonpolitical presidential visit to Michigan in mid-October, Eisenhower had become so enraged by a United Auto Workers leaflet equating Republican anti-Catholicism with the Ku Klux Klan that his blood pressure spiked and his heartbeat became rapid and irregular. Extensive campaigning, Nixon was warned, might trigger another heart attack or stroke.

This certainly worked in Kennedy's favor. Talking to a friend, Jack commented that he could feel the votes draining away with every word Eisenhower uttered. Had Ike been well enough to campaign in more places, even a few days earlier, Nixon might have emerged the victor on November 8. A Nixon telethon on election eve was judged by many to be his best TV appearance of the campaign, with the Republican candidate at ease, talking lucidly to average Americans about their problems. Anxious Democrats urged a Kennedy response, but the supposedly lavishly funded campaign had no money left.

JFK had to hope that his call for change and renewed effort in foreign policy would win favor. Gallup had reported in July that most Americans saw US–Soviet relations as the number one issue. Khrushchev had reacted to the U-2 spy plane incident by aborting his summit with Eisenhower and by boasting about the power of Soviet missile technology. The threat seemed to have grown, and yet the administration seemed untroubled. The 1959 Cuban Revolution had taken a leftward tilt, giving Communism an unprecedented foothold in the Americas, just ninety miles off the Florida coast. In October, despite a CIA briefing informing him of the secret training of an invasion force in Guatemala, Kennedy complained about the Eisenhower administration's failure to support anti-Castro rebels. This placed Nixon in the position of deploring his rival's saber-rattling in order to preserve secrecy, or at least its vestiges. In reality Nixon still hoped that the force would land in Cuba before Election Day, enabling him to benefit from their success, or at least from a "rally around the flag" effect that would impel patriotic Americans to back the administration. Liberals were alarmed by Kennedy's comments, which seemed to signal his preference for intervention. It might also mean that, were an invasion to occur before the election, JFK could claim that it was a brazen attempt to blunt his criticism of Eisenhower's inaction. Fortunately, November 8 arrived peacefully.

Election night 1960

Kennedy and Nixon voted early in their respective home states on opposite sides of the continent, then waited for the polls to close and the results to emerge. Connecticut's result came first. Kennedy had carried the state by 306,000 votes due to a high turnout in the industrial cities, especially among African American voters, and a strong Jewish and Catholic vote in the suburbs—all signs that he would also do well in New York, New Jersey, and Pennsylvania. TV networks began talking rashly of a Kennedy victory. Jack himself remained wary, recognizing that the count would swing Nixon's way once more rural Midwestern and Western states reported. He also retained his fabled sense of humor, telling Sorensen that he had just taken a call from Lyndon Johnson who had said, "I hear *you're* losing Ohio, but *we're* doing fine in Pennsylvania." A lead of nearly 2 million votes for Kennedy at midnight halved in the next hour, as Western state tallies came in. At 3.20 a.m. Eastern Time, Nixon mournfully told television reporters, "If the present trend continues, Senator Kennedy will be the next president," but he did not formally concede. This annoyed some in the Kennedy camp but Jack observed that in Nixon's position he wouldn't have conceded either. With that, he went to bed, and awoke to find that the Secret Service had been deployed around his home, a sign that he was now president-elect.

While the popular vote does not decide presidential elections, it is seen as giving the victory greater authority and legitimacy. For Kennedy, the margin was razor thin. He had won 49.72 percent of the popular vote, compared to Nixon's 49.6 percent, a difference that averaged out at one half-vote per election precinct across the country. This was reflected in close contests in several states. Amidst cries of corruption, Kennedy carried Texas by 46,233 votes and Illinois by only 8,858 votes. He also carried several other states by narrow margins: Missouri by 9,980, Delaware by 3,217, Nevada by 2,493, New Mexico by 2,294, and Hawaii by just 115. Conversely, Nixon carried California only after the absentee postal ballots had been counted, giving him a final majority of

35,623, while he carried Arkansas by 1,144 and Montana by 6,950 votes. If Nixon had won Illinois and Texas, however, he would have been president, and so they have been the focus of investigations. Texas law made no provision for a challenge in presidential contests, but extant records show that in several counties more votes were cast that there were registered voters. In addition, in counties without mechanical voting voters were required to strike out the names of all the candidates they did not support, leaving just their choice. In 1960 the Texas presidential ballot had four names on it, so voters had to cross out three names; otherwise their vote should have been disallowed. In precincts that favored Nixon, local officials voided 40 percent of the ballots, whereas in Starr County on the Mexican border, where voters went overwhelmingly for Kennedy, officials discounted just 1.5 percent.

Illinois was equally suspect, although it should be noted that what happened there was in keeping with normal practice both before and after the 1960 election. Eight years later, a Chicago precinct captain explained the approach to ballot counting: "We don't know how many we got until we find out how many we need." While critics have insisted that organized crime bought votes at the behest of Joe Kennedy to ensure his son's victory, this lurid thesis ignores the norms of Cook County machine politics. Mayor Daley had instructed his precinct captains to ensure a fixed margin of victory in their ward or risk losing their posts, and often their city job. In 1960, Chicago recorded an impressive 89.3 percent turnout, despite the fact that a number of Republicans discovered when they tried to vote that they had somehow fallen off the registration rolls. This turnout was more artificial than real. As in Texas, there were several wards where the number of votes cast was larger than the number of persons registered, and among those participating were several deceased residents. Republicans were able to secure a partial recount in Illinois, and a commission investigated but found too little evidence of wrongdoing to invalidate the result. Local GOP members also knew that there had been irregularities in the southern Illinois counties they controlled. It was not so much that one side stole the election, rather one side was more successful in a dubious battle.

Nixon always said that he had rejected calls that he should challenge the election result because he did not want the nation to face a period of chronic uncertainty at a time of international peril. Given the cynicism that often greets any claim that Nixon was capable of a noble act, it is fair to add that he also knew that such a legal process was unlikely to be successful. Even if the Illinois result had been overturned, he would still have needed Texas to be victorious. For whatever reason, at noon Eastern Time on November 9, Nixon formally conceded the election to Kennedy.

Others were less readily reconciled. On December 15 a retired New Hampshire postal worker, Richard Paul Pavlick, was arrested by the Secret Service while waiting to kill the president-elect at his family's home in West Palm Beach, Florida. Asked why he wanted to kill JFK, Pavlick said it was because he hated the idea that money had bought the presidency. Four days earlier when the family had headed to church, he had been ready to crash his car, filled with dynamite, into the Kennedy motorcade, but had stopped when he saw Jackie and the children. He was placed in a psychiatric institution until 1966. The scruples of a deranged man spared Kennedy from becoming the first president killed before he was inaugurated.

Kennedy was his party's nominee in no small measure because of his father's money, his brother's energetic campaign management, his rivals' mistakes, and his own media-friendly style. He became America's president because he nullified the question of religion and capitalized on his opponent's errors, notably in relation to the first televised debate and the King imprisonment. Despite a gulf in style, the policy differences between the two candidates were relatively minor, with Americans largely endorsing stability at home and resolute defense abroad. The slim margin of victory urged caution. Kennedy now had to govern in a way that lived up to his promise and yet kept his party and the nation united. It would be a challenge.

4 "Let us begin"

Triumph, fiascoes, and crises

The transition: Choosing a team

As Jack Kennedy struggled to form his administration, he complained that during his lengthy campaign for the White House he had concentrated on meeting people who could help him win, and met too few who could help him govern. He knew people in politics, journalism, the unions, and the New England universities, especially Harvard, but his immediate circle lacked the bankers, high-ranking military officers, diplomats, and industrialists whose executive talents he now sought. To identify suitable candidates for top jobs he turned to sage veterans of the Truman years—legal counsel Clark Clifford, ex-Secretary of State Dean Acheson, and especially Robert Lovett, a Wall Street investment banker who had worked in the Defense Department. JFK's brother-in-law Sargent Shriver also helped with the recruitment challenge.

Adding to the pressures on the new president, Jackie gave birth to a son, John Junior, on November 25, 1960 by Caesarean section. As with Caroline's birth, Kennedy was not there, but hurried back by plane. Like his own father, Jack was a doting if sometimes absent figure, and during his presidency he would often invoke the image of children, and of the future they might experience, to underline the importance of what he was striving to achieve. He wanted their world to be a richer, safer place, and predictably saw American power as the key to progress.

The 1953 presidential transition from Truman to Eisenhower had been deemed so poor that the Brookings Institution, a leading Washington think tank, had organized a project to improve the process, and Clifford acted as JFK's link to this study. At the same time, Kennedy read *Presidential Power* and conferred with its author Richard Neustadt about how to run the White House. He also read a series of reports on policies and organization written by specially formed task forces, all in an attempt to hit the ground running.

Kennedy was determined to break with Eisenhower's committee-heavy style of governing. This had given the appearance of an excessive delegation of authority, notably to Ike's Chief of Staff Sherman Adams and to his first secretary of state, John Foster Dulles. Kennedy decided that he would not have a Chief of Staff, and he was determined to oversee foreign policy closely, being effectively his own secretary of state. In marked contrast to Eisenhower, he was to display a reluctance to engage his Cabinet in broad policy discussions. Having taught himself to speed read, Kennedy would begin his day by devouring the morning newspapers and then fire off memos and phone calls to aides and officials asking for information and action.

Given his narrow margin of victory, Kennedy felt that he needed to reassure the center right, especially in Congress but also more broadly in the electorate, and so he began by announcing that he would be retaining J. Edgar Hoover as Director of the Federal Bureau of Investigation (FBI) and Allen Dulles as Director of the Central Intelligence Agency (CIA). Hoover had made the FBI a personal fiefdom and Kennedy was well aware that FBI surveillance meant that Hoover had ample material that could embarrass the Kennedys. Dulles was similarly a near-legendary figure at the CIA. The Company, as it was known, had enjoyed considerable latitude in terms of executive oversight during the Eisenhower years, partly because Dulles' relationship with his brother, Secretary of State John Foster Dulles, gave the semblance of close supervision.

In 1960, the CIA's standing was high, and Kennedy had reason to believe that men like Allen Dulles and his deputy Richard Bissell would give him sound advice. Dulles and Bissell had given the president-elect a briefing on November 18, explaining the CIA's plan to topple Fidel Castro by landing a contingent of trained Cuban freedom fighters who would either ignite a general uprising or establish themselves as guerilla fighters in the Escambray

Mountains. An assassination plot against Castro was timed to coincide with the landing. Since Kennedy had criticized the Eisenhower administration for doing too little to liberate Cuba, he could hardly fail to back the CIA's plans. However, he did stress to the Agency that there would be no direct US military involvement. Fatefully, the CIA did not believe this, instead assuming that Kennedy would bail out a failing operation.

Kennedy had won the election on the basis that he would not only prosecute the Cold War more vigorously, he would tackle the faltering economy as well. Consequently, the Defense and Treasury Cabinet posts were vital. In both cases, he appointed business figures who were Republicans. Kennedy had wanted Lovett to be treasury secretary, but citing failing health Lovett recommended C. Douglas Dillon. Extremely well connected in the financial world and experienced in international diplomacy, Dillon sent a powerful signal of reassurance to the financial markets. In 1953, Eisenhower had tried to instill greater efficiency in defense procurement by bringing in as Defense Secretary Charles Wilson, the head of the giant auto-maker General Motors, who had told a congressional hearing that what was good for America was good for GM, and vice versa. Kennedy, in like manner, appointed Robert McNamara, one of the so-called "whizz kids," whose systems analysis approach had helped to turn around the fortunes of GM's rival, the Ford Motor Company. What impressed Kennedy most about the steely, intellectual McNamara was his "toughness," displayed in his insistence that he must be left to run his own department and choose his own subordinates, and would not be expected to participate in the capital's social whirl. Through his appointments Kennedy thus reassured moderate conservatives (Dallek 2003: 310–13).

After securing the nomination, JFK had asked Adlai Stevenson to prepare a report on foreign policy problems, even though Stevenson's disingenuous behavior during the nomination contest had left Kennedy determined not to offer him any post at all, let alone secretary of state. Kennedy was not a generous winner. After a post-election meeting with Nixon, he told close aide Ken O'Donnell, "It was just as well for all of us that he didn't quite make it." Similarly, while Eisenhower was reported to have revised his opinion of Kennedy upwards after their December 6 meeting,

Kennedy told his brother Bobby dismissively that Ike was poorly informed on many subjects that he should have known intimately (Dallek 2003: 301, 303; see Plate 1).

The Kennedy competitive streak was apt to harden judgments and, after courting him at various points in the campaign, Jack judged Stevenson to be sly and not tough enough. Only fear of a liberal outcry induced him to offer the two-time presidential nominee the UN ambassadorship. Other liberals gained similarly second-tier roles: Chester Bowles as an under secretary of state, Arthur Schlesinger, Jr. as a White House aide, and Walter Heller as head of the Council of Economic Advisors. JFK worried that otherwise he would be perceived as a captive to liberals, a group that was more influential inside the Democratic Party than it was in the nation at large.

JFK had wanted to make the powerful chairman of the Senate Foreign Relations Committee William Fulbright his secretary of state, but the Arkansas senator realized that his defense of segregation was likely to stir antagonism at home and abroad, and said that he preferred to stay in the Senate. A process of elimination brought the post to Dean Rusk, a liberal Georgian who had worked with Acheson and Lovett during the Truman years. Lovett had recommended Acheson, an abrasive and outspoken figure, but Kennedy insisted that he wanted to control foreign policy. Lovett then said that if what Kennedy really wanted was an *under* secretary, Rusk would be perfect.

Whereas McNamara's strength had won JFK's admiration, Rusk appealed because of his diffidence—the ideal secretary of state for a president who wanted to steer his own course. Far more influential in policy matters was McGeorge Bundy as National Security Advisor, the first in a line of advisors, culminating in Henry Kissinger, who tended to eclipse the State Department. Bundy abolished the National Security Council committee structure established by Eisenhower. He relied largely on his own staff and formulated policy with the president and small *ad hoc* teams. As a result, Kennedy met the full NSC only monthly, for briefings or to endorse already agreed security decisions. While this gave Kennedy the personal control he desired, it also weakened the presidency as an institution, giving it fewer structures for the management and review of policies. The dangers of this shift became more apparent under Lyndon Johnson, notably in relation to Vietnam, but it was JFK who initiated the trend.

The Cabinet appointment that sparked most comment was JFK's selection of his brother Robert Kennedy as attorney general. It drew predictable complaints of nepotism, especially since Bobby had no previous legal career to justify his elevation. JFK told several people that his father had insisted, but given the two brothers' closeness their supposed mutual reluctance was probably feigned for the press's benefit.

For Jack's part, Bobby's place at the head of the Justice Department put him in charge of managing the administration's civil rights policy, which JFK perceived as a damage limitation exercise. Southern resistance to African American demands for equality was a source of international embarrassment and added greatly to the difficulty of handling Congress, where seniority ensured that Southerners dominated the committees and thus the progress of all legislation. In the wake of the 1960 lunch counter sit-ins, the growing civil rights movement was planning protests that would garner headlines and increase the pressure for reform. Bobby's job at Justice was to protect the president from the squeeze of these conflicting forces. Technically, he would also be in charge of the FBI, and thus able to watch over Hoover's maneuvering. At the same time, the Senate anti-racketeering investigations had fueled in Bobby a crusading desire to expose and prosecute corrupt union officials like Jimmy Hoffa and their criminal associates. Only time would tell if Bobby's multiple tasks would enable him to protect his brother or add to his perils.

While JFK was reluctant to engage in Cabinet-style government, he liked working with the people he knew best. He had a small, devoted White House staff, most of them loyalists from earlier campaigns. Ken O'Donnell was his appointments secretary. A terse, abrasive man, he guarded the Oval Office entrance on one side, protecting the president from timewasters. Kennedy had retained Evelyn Lincoln as his personal secretary, and Jack's friends and favored aides knew that it was easier to get to see him via her office. Dave Powers, like O'Donnell, was one of the so-called "Irish Mafia." Deeply loyal to Jack, he helped keep the new president amused, a task that included ensuring a steady, almost daily supply of women for Jack's pleasure. While many senior figures turned a blind eye to Kennedy's womanizing, others, such as press secretary Pierre Salinger, simply accepted it. Shortly after the election victory, a tipsy Salinger boasted to reporters that if the outgoing administration had been known for its love of golf, Kennedy's would be noted for its "fucking" (Giglio 2006: 33).

Despite service in both House and Senate, Kennedy had limited ties he could use with Congress. A longstanding associate, Larry O'Brien, was given responsibility for lobbying for the president's program. In his memoirs, he speaks of trying to build "an invisible bridge down Pennsylvania Avenue" from the White House to the Capitol (quoted in Giglio 2006: 38). Previously, over forty individual congressional relations offices had bargained with lawmakers on behalf of their department or agency, regardless of the president's priorities. Now they were all to coordinate their efforts with O'Brien. He and his staff warned legislators of impending measures and made a pitch on how each bill might go over in their home district or state. O'Brien was authorized to accommodate amendments that boosted support and to distribute patronage, although officially this was supposed to be overseen by the Democratic National Committee chairman, John Bailey.

Word soon got around that a call from O'Brien's office was likely to be good news, whereas Bailey's calls were commiserations. O'Brien worked hard but it was an uphill struggle. Congressional leaders did not feel any need to kowtow to Kennedy. Many had been elected with larger majorities than he had, several remembered him as an indifferent legislator during his time on Capitol Hill, and conservatives, both Republican and Southern Democrat, felt that opposition to his proposals was likely to win them more support back home than would cooperation.

Potentially Lyndon Johnson, the one-time master of the Senate, could have been a help to Kennedy in congressional relations. However, when Johnson wrote to Kennedy requesting a much more direct role in policy formulation, his bid for power was strongly rejected, even if the rejection took the form of JFK's failure to acknowledge LBJ's presumptuous memorandum. Shortly thereafter LBJ made a bid to retain some of his former influence in the Senate, and was rejected by his erstwhile colleagues on the grounds that his continued participation in the Democratic caucus would infringe the constitutional separation of powers. Johnson spent much of his vice presidency sulking, pining for appreciation and yet remaining largely silent in meetings, since he did not believe that a vice president should be seen to challenge the president in open discussion. By 1963 he was regarded by many journalists as "yesterday's man." "Whatever happened to Lyndon Johnson?" was the common question. Among the White House staff, despite JFK's clear instruction that Johnson be shown respect, LBJ was often an object of derision because of his crass, rustic ways. By 1963 there was even speculation that he might be replaced on the ticket for 1964.

The inaugural address

A far more central figure than Johnson in Kennedy's deliberations was Theodore Sorensen. Sometimes referred to as JFK's "intellectual blood bank," the Nebraskan was far more than just a speechwriter, but in the winter of 1960–61, the crafting of Kennedy's inaugural address was obviously central to his role. Reinforcing the sense of change, JFK asked Sorensen to create an address that would give his presidency a brand identity, just as FDR's "We have nothing to fear, but fear itself" speech had set a confident tone for his approach to the Great Depression. With a keen sense of history, Kennedy urged Sorensen to look to Jefferson's first inaugural, and Lincoln's second, as well as the latter's famed Gettysburg Address. Churchill's wartime speeches were another source of inspiration.

Like Lincoln's speeches, the inaugural should marry cadence with brevity; an admonition that fitted the new television era well. Sorensen has also recalled that, while the speech drew on Kennedy's experience as a member of a new generation (described in the address as "born in this century, tempered by war, [and] disciplined by a harsh and bitter peace"), the president required him to avoid the use of the first person pronoun as far as possible. Following Jefferson's call to heal divisions, the speech deliberately focused on foreign rather than domestic policy, since the latter was more clearly divisive. Advisors insisted that the civil rights issue needed acknowledgement in the final draft, and it came obliquely and fleetingly, with a reference to the new generation's commitment to the defense of human rights "at home and around the world" (Sorensen 2008: 221).

The day before the inauguration, heavy snow fell in Washington, and it took teams of workmen to ensure that the areas around the Capitol were clear and passable. January 20 dawned clear but cold, with most dignitaries glad to be bundled up in overcoats and hats over formal dress, to guard against the chill. At Kennedy's request, the businessman's Homburg hat, favored by Eisenhower, was supplanted by the courtlier top hat, although the press noted that Kennedy wore his as little as possible. While others shivered, JFK stood bareheaded and without an overcoat during the hours of ceremony, taking only a surreptitious sip of soup or coffee to offset the chill (Dallek 2003: 322).

Kennedy had agreed to invite the distinguished poet Robert Frost to speak at the ceremony, although he jested that he risked being upstaged by a finer wordsmith. Frost wrote a special poem for the occasion, but in the event, bright sunlight and a gusty wind prevented the eighty-six-year-old from reading it. Had he done so, his audience might not have enjoyed his mock epic on the place of poetry in a new "Augustan age," with its allusions to the independence struggles of the time:

> We see how seriously the races swarm
> In their attempts at sovereignty and form.
> They are our wards we think to some extent
> For the time being and with their consent,
> To teach them how Democracy is meant.

Instead, Frost recited from memory his poem "The Gift Outright," which seems at first a simple sonnet in celebration of America's Manifest Destiny, except that its parenthetical line "(The deed of gift was many deeds of war)" offers a far more somber reading, noting the costs of claiming both land and liberty.

Kennedy had fretted like a poet, not just over every one of his 1,355 words, but over his performance. He kept a reading copy of the speech with him and took every spare moment to consign the address to memory, reading it aloud in his bathtub and at the breakfast table. It was his first address to the nation as president and it ultimately won lasting praise for its call to fellow Americans to "ask not what your country can do for you—ask what you can do for your country." But Kennedy was also mindful that in rallying the nation he was simultaneously addressing the world. Here, too, the rhetoric was soaring but the precise policy implications were unclear. In his second paragraph, he reminded listeners that he was well aware of his responsibilities in a nuclear age. Unlike his forebears, he noted, he lived in a world that contained "the power to abolish all forms of human poverty and all forms of human life." Nevertheless, after linking Cold War America to its revolutionary foundations, he went on to make a seemingly open-ended commitment to the defense of freedom. "Let every nation know, whether it wishes us well or ill," he proclaimed, "that we shall pay any price, bear any burden, meet any hardship, support any friend, oppose any foe to assure the survival and success of liberty."

Urging unity upon established allies, the speech focused more on the emergent nations, where Kennedy knew the Cold War was most competitive. To those "struggling to break the bonds of mass misery," he pledged that America would "help them help themselves." It would do so not simply to combat Communism but "because it is right" and because "a free society that cannot help the many who are poor ... cannot save the few who are rich." Kennedy spoke especially to the peoples of Latin America, offering them "a new alliance for progress," but at same time, and obviously implying Cuba, he reasserted the traditional Monroe Doctrine that forbade any other power from interfering in the affairs of the Western hemisphere.

Kennedy wanted to leave the door open for talks with the Soviet Union, even as he spoke forcefully about his devotion to freedom's defense. Within his own party there were hawks like Acheson, who saw the USSR as still committed to Stalin's goal of world domination, and doves like Stevenson and Bowles, who believed that Premier Khrushchev's denunciation of Stalin offered a new era of reform, as the Soviet leader tried to improve his people's living standards by reining in the military budget. The inaugural melded both sets of voices, containing enough to please the hard-liners while leaving the diplomatic path still open. He would not negotiate out of fear, Kennedy had pledged, but he would not fear to negotiate.

The speech was a triumph, drawing praise from Republicans and the wider press. The *New Yorker* magazine hoped that the address would "revive a taste for good oratory." Khrushchev permitted both *Pravda* and *Izvestia* to publish Kennedy's text in full. Polls showed that the candidate who had commanded less than half the electorate's support in November was now approved by almost three-quarters of Americans. Sorensen had penned a masterpiece, and Kennedy, who had once struggled to deliver his public addresses, had performed like a virtuoso.

After standing for hours watching the floats and marching bands, the first lady retreated to the White House for a rest while the new president continued on to a round of parties. Jackie joined him in the early evening but soon withdrew, leaving Jack to continue his tour of inaugural balls, which ended in the early hours of the next morning with a visit to journalist Joseph Alsop's party in Georgetown. "I fed him terrapin," Alsop recalled. Yet later that morning Kennedy was at his desk, eager to begin. Natural adrenalin and a more settled regime of physiotherapy, alongside his medication, appeared to have stabilized his health, which was rarely questioned now. His first action was to sign an executive order doubling the ration of surplus commodities distributed to families on welfare. He had not forgotten the poverty he saw during the West Virginia primary campaign (O'Brien 2005: 518–21).

Kennedy and Congress

Not every promise would be met so swiftly, with the stroke of a pen. To improve his legislative prospects, Kennedy joined House Speaker Sam Rayburn in a bid to expand membership of the Rules Committee from twelve to fifteen. Currently, Chairman Howard Smith of Virginia marshaled a bipartisan conservative coalition to bottle up civil rights, economic, educational, and health reform proposals. After an eleven-day struggle, the expansion was approved by just one vote, but since 101 of the 262 Democrats in the House were Southerners, reforms that now made it to the floor for debate still faced an uphill battle.

Rayburn's death in late 1961 made Kennedy's task even harder. There were two new Democratic leaders in Congress, and neither Senator Mike Mansfield nor Congressman James McCormack was as effective in shepherding the party as his predecessor had been.

Liberal hopes were set to be frustrated, as Kennedy's team concluded that they did not have the votes to legislate in several areas. Although the sluggish economy, with 7 percent unemployment, provided justification for a stimulus package, there was little chance that the Federal Reserve would cut interest rates or that the new Congress would pass a public works bill. Kennedy himself believed that seeking a tax cut would undercut his larger message of national sacrifice. The best he could do in the short term was to accelerate existing appropriations and use the gloomy economic situation to induce Congress to expand Social Security benefits, raise the minimum wage, and subsidize low- and middle-income housing construction. The cash injected would, it was hoped, spark recovery.

Immediate overseas crises: Laos, the Congo, and Cuba

In a farewell meeting with Eisenhower on the eve of the inauguration, Kennedy listened as the departing president ran through the list of geopolitical crises that required immediate attention. He stressed the dangerous situation in Laos, a Southeast Asian country where civil war was tilting in favor of Communist-backed forces. Eschewing the usual "domino" metaphor that described the dire consequences for the region if one part of it became Communist, Eisenhower referred to Laos as the "cork in the bottle," and seemed to imply that it should be kept neutral, even if that required US military intervention. There was also continuing instability in the Congo, where former Prime Minister Patrice Lumumba had been murdered in circumstances that prompted the Soviets to question the role of the UN peacekeeping force. At the same time, there was the growing and more immediately embarrassing problem of Castro's Cuba, which offered the Soviets an ally barely eight minutes by plane from the US mainland. Kennedy should give his full backing to CIA plans to eliminate this threat, Eisenhower recommended.

Kennedy's most prominent statements on foreign policy in the Senate had stressed the need to acknowledge the legitimate nationalist aspirations of peoples in the developing world, and his campaign biography had even alluded to Castro as being in the

Latin American tradition of Simon Bolivar, so Eisenhower felt that the young Democrat needed to be reminded of the need for containment. He also remained angry at Kennedy's charge that a "missile gap" had developed in the Soviets' favor during the General's years in power. Covert surveillance confirmed the complete opposite, and in Ike's view fully justified his efforts to rein in defense spending, out of fear that it would ultimately distort the US economy in a disastrous way. To amplify his point, Eisenhower had given a farewell address that identified what he called the "military–industrial complex," which threatened the future of the American republic. Thus Kennedy took office with his predecessor warning that he was likely to need to engage in military actions to contain Communism, but that he should not destabilize the nation's finances and economic structures by unrestrained defense spending.

JFK's initial stance on US–Soviet relations

In practice, Kennedy paid at least as much attention to Khrushchev's January 6 speech as he did to Eisenhower's January 17 farewell address. The Soviet leader's speech had been flagged by US Ambassador Llewellyn Thompson. Eager to retain his Moscow post in the new administration, Thompson declared that "the speech should be read in its entirety by everyone having to do with Soviet affairs," since it condensed "Khrushchev's point of view as Communist and propagandist." Accordingly, Kennedy distributed the speech to his top people, urging them to "read, mark, learn, and inwardly digest" Khrushchev's message (Kempe 2011: 76).

The president carried a copy with him and would read extracts to Cabinet members, dinner companions, and other colleagues, inviting their comments on its aggressive tone. Khrushchev had proclaimed "We will beat the United States with small wars of liberation. We will nibble them to exhaustion all over the globe, in South America, Africa, and Southeast Asia." Khrushchev also indicated that the Berlin situation (where the British, French, and Americans occupied the west of the city while the eastern, Soviet sector was the capital of East Germany) was no longer acceptable. What Thompson had failed to do was offer the correct context for the speech, which had been delivered to party officials as a distillation of the position agreed at the conference of Communist parties the previous November, a meeting where Khrushchev had tried to limit the visibility of the Sino–Soviet split and to counter Mao's claim that any desire for peaceful coexistence with the West was intrinsically counterrevolutionary. In this context, the speech was more archetypal party propaganda than evidence of a crucial shift in Soviet policy (Kempe 2011: 78–80).

The speech's reception offset the impact of gestures made by Khrushchev and intended to signal a new beginning in US–Soviet relations, following the aborted summit due to the U-2 spy plane incident. On January 25, Kennedy had been able to announce that two American airmen shot down over the Barentz Sea had been released by Moscow. Khrushchev had deliberately delayed their release, lest it benefit Nixon's candidacy, and therefore believed that he, as much as anyone, secured Kennedy's narrow victory. He also sent JFK a congratulatory telegram on his inauguration, relaxed other anti-American policies, and privately urged an early summit meeting. But these gestures towards détente did not alter the impression made by the January 6 speech, which seemed to confirm an aggressive strategy, evident in Soviet actions in Laos, the Congo, and Cuba. Equally importantly, they did not alter the political reality that Kennedy, without a strong electoral mandate, recognized that both his leverage with Congress and his standing with the people rested on cultivating a sense of solidarity in the face of a common threat. Domestically, fear was the new administration's ally.

When Kennedy delivered his first State of the Union address on January 30, he invoked Lincoln's Gettysburg Address by declaring that, in this "hour of national peril," Americans "shall have to test anew whether a nation organized and governed such as ours can endure." While much of the speech detailed economic difficulties, Kennedy also explained the perilous international situation in Laos, the Congo, and Cuba. Alluding to Khrushchev's address, he warned of the Soviet and Chinese Communist threat. "We must never be lulled," he declared, "into believing that either power has yielded its ambitions for world domination, ambitions which they forcefully restated only a short time ago." Announcing a comprehensive defense review to be completed by the end of February, Kennedy listed immediate steps to increase airlift capacity, to accelerate Polaris submarine deployment, to expand international aid, especially in connection with the Alliance for Progress and the newly created Peace Corps, and to back the United Nations in the wake of Soviet attacks on its role in the Congo. To underline how strongly his address responded to Khrushchev's "wars of liberation" speech, he concluded that the hopes of all mankind rested not just on the Congress, but "upon the peasant in Laos, the fisherman in Nigeria, [and] the exile from Cuba."

The Bay of Pigs operation

The exile from Cuba was very much on the president's mind in the weeks that followed, as the CIA-backed invasion force in Guatemala attracted unwelcome attention and its handlers warned that it had a limited "shelf-life." At the same time, General Lyman Lemnitzer worried that Soviet aid was enabling Castro to tighten his hold on the island "with disastrous consequences to the security of the Western Hemisphere." The CIA had escaped strict scrutiny in the past, and given the Kennedy administration's aversion to institutional structures there was even less chance of rigorous oversight. In essence, Kennedy asked the invasion's advocates to be its critics. When the Joint Chiefs of Staff (JCS) were asked to evaluate the CIA plans in late January, for instance, they did not complete their usual assessment because the operation's secret nature denied them precise data.

Kennedy's trust in CIA director Dulles and his deputy Bissell would prove misplaced, since neither man gave sufficient weight to the limited character of Castro's domestic opponents or to clarifying the operational plans for the force once ashore. Intelligence reports suggested no imminent domestic threat to Castro, and while the original Trinidad landing site might have permitted the force's effective dispersion into the mountains, the revised Bay of Pigs site had marshlands that eliminated that option. Such challenges to the proposed scheme were not brought to the president's attention and his inexperienced team asked too few questions.

The operation also threatened larger policy goals. Kennedy's broad policy towards Latin America, the Alliance for Progress, rested on his realization that the gap between the continent's poor and its established oligarchs provided fertile soil for Communist subversion. Better homes, better schools, better living standards, and land and tax reforms were needed to ensure that modernization gave the people a vested interest in liberal democracy. Kennedy was also well aware that past US interventions had instilled a profound mistrust of the Yankee. As Arthur Schlesinger warned in a prescient memo, if the Kennedy administration was to begin its term with an invasion of Cuba, this mistrust would be powerfully reaffirmed. "It would fix a malevolent image ... in the minds of millions" (Dallek 2003: 358).

Consequently, in all his meetings about the Bay of Pigs operation, Kennedy stressed that this had to be a Cuban exile operation, which is why he wanted a quiet landing with the first military assaults made from the mountains. When the initial plan for a landing at Trinidad was described to him, he rejected it as too "spectacular." At a February 11 meeting he sought "a plan where US assistance would be less obvious." Bissell responded quickly with a new scheme for a landing in the thinly populated swamp area of the Zapata Peninsula, but he failed to report that this ended any chance of the group forming a mountain guerilla base. Instead of querying the implications of this switch closely, the Kennedy team was impressed with Bissell's apparent gift for swift improvisation. On March 15, NSA Bundy applauded his "remarkable job of reframing the landing plan so as to make it unspectacular and quiet, and plausibly Cuban in its essentials" (Dallek 2003: 360). The new location was accepted too readily.

At the same time, the CIA was telling the administration that the Cuban force gathered under its guidance in Guatemala would have to leave soon, that it could only be held together inside the US for a limited period, and that if it were disbanded the political damage would be considerable. Given that Kennedy assumed that the most probable, worst-case scenario was that the landed force would have to adapt to guerilla warfare in the Escambray Mountains, going ahead seemed preferable than having hundreds of disaffected Cubans vociferously denouncing him for failing to back their efforts to topple Communism. After all, the JCS report had said that "the plan has a fair chance of ultimate success." Kennedy interpreted this as an endorsement rather than a cautionary assessment signaling no better than a 30 percent chance, and those odds assumed appropriate US military support, notably in the air.

Oblivious to this, Kennedy asked the CIA to make clear to the Cuban Brigade that "U.S. strike forces would not be allowed to participate in or support the invasion in any way" (US Department of State 1997: 177).

Believing that he had made his requirements clear, Kennedy responded to questions about the rumored invasion at an April 12 press conference by declaring: "This Government will do everything it can ... to make sure that there are no Americans involved in any actions inside Cuba" (Dallek 2003: 363). Still worried that the quiet landing would attract negative attention, he ordered Bissell to reduce the number of planes participating in a preliminary air strike from sixteen to eight, even though the planes would be flown by Cuban pilots taking off from a non-US location (Nicaragua). As a result, on Saturday, April 15, 1961, eight B-26 bombers hit three Cuban airfields but only eliminated a few of Castro's three dozen combat planes.

Still more fatefully for the expedition, on the morning of the invasion itself Kennedy canceled a dawn air strike, realizing at the last moment that the planes could not plausibly come from a landing strip that had been seized by the Brigade before it even came ashore. CIA planners said at the time that this order "would probably mean the failure of the mission." While the reality was that the scheme was ill conceived throughout, without effective air strikes the anti-Castro forces lost vital supplies when Cuban planes sank one of their vessels, and by noon on April 18 they were pinned down with little prospect of escape. Reviewing the unfolding disaster with the JCS and CIA in the early hours of April 19, Kennedy faced and firmly rejected repeated demands to commit US forces. He suspected that the operation's backers had just assumed he would try to save face and intervene at the last. "Well," he told Dave Powers, "they had me figured all wrong" (Dallek 2003: 363–65).

A subsequent review of the fiasco, in which 114 of the CIA's trainees were killed and 1,189 taken prisoner, rejected the idea that the canceled air strikes had caused the defeat. The CIA rather than JFK was to blame. The report concluded: "The Agency became so wrapped up in the military operation that it failed to appraise the chances of success realistically" (Dallek 2003: 366). Kennedy was not the main culprit but he took the blame anyway. In a press statement he accepted "sole responsibility" and quoted what he claimed to be "an old saying that victory has a hundred fathers and defeat is an orphan." By acknowledging his mistakes the president won support. A Gallup poll at the end of April indicated an 83 percent approval rating, which Kennedy joked about privately: "The worse I do, the more popular I get." The parallels between the wartime praise he won after the sinking of his patrol boat and the popularity he now enjoyed, after presiding over a comprehensive foreign policy failure that left Castro stronger and his own competency in doubt, did not escape him.

Instead of weakening Communism, Kennedy had cemented it in Cuba, boosted its appeal in Latin America, and raised Moscow's standing across the developing world. The fact that the operation had begun under the Eisenhower administration and had been overseen by Dulles, a Republican, helped to ensure that patriotism trumped partisanship. Both Dulles and Bissell would be replaced. On April 21, Kennedy set up a task force for Castro's overthrow by all means "short of outright war." Barely two weeks later, he told the National Security Council that, in essence, regime change was US policy; there could be no coexistence with Castro in the long term, since he threatened subversion in other Latin American republics. In the short term the only realistic option was a range of clandestine operations to destabilize Cuba (Dallek 2003: 366–72). Ominously, after tears and self-recriminations ("How could I have been so stupid?" was the refrain), the Kennedy brothers responded to the Bay of Pigs with plans for vengeance. Equally deep emotions were stirred in those in the CIA and anti-Castro Cuban community who felt that the outcome on the Zapata Peninsula could have different if the Kennedys had shown courage and commitment.

Repercussions of the Bay of Pigs failure

Convinced that the Bay of Pigs fiasco was due partly to press coverage that alerted Castro to the impending threat, the president used his April 20 address to the American Newspaper Publishers to urge self-censorship in reporting news that impacted on national security. Liberals like Chester Bowles who had leaked their misgivings about the Cuban mission were chastised, and would eventually be pushed out. While Kennedy apologists typically see the Bay of Pigs as ultimately beneficial—as helping in the development of Kennedy's skepticism towards the Joint Chiefs and CIA, as laying the foundation for his more astute management of the 1962 Cuban Missile Crisis, and as a counsel of restraint that dissuaded Kennedy from full-scale troop deployments to Southeast Asia—the debacle was a setback that amplified fears among European allies that the new administration was ill equipped for world leadership. He learned from his mistakes, is the claim, but this should not obscure how greatly he erred in the first place. As he supposedly told Dulles, in other countries a leader who had showed the same level of incompetence would have had to resign.

The public failure of this attempt to topple Castro further complicated prospects for a US–Soviet summit. Part of Kennedy's foreign policy critique had been that Eisenhower had not pursued talks with Khrushchev vigorously enough, but the international reaction to the Bay of Pigs debacle forced a reconsideration. What were the political risks of a meeting between a weakened president and an emboldened Khrushchev, determined to wring concessions over the vexed question of Berlin? Asked to finalize plans in early May, Kennedy hesitated.

The Vienna Summit: Initial plans

Coming into the meeting, the two sides faced pressures that headed them in opposite directions. Kennedy needed to reassure European allies and at the same time demonstrate toughness to his American constituents in the wake of the Cuban fiasco. Ideally, he wanted a quiet acceptance that Laos should remain a neutral zone, and progress on a nuclear test ban treaty. Khrushchev, meanwhile, needed to negate Chinese rumors that his quest for coexistence with the West amounted to a betrayal of the revolution, and to placate his East German ally Walter Ulbricht, who was demanding action to stem the heavy outflow of well-educated refugees from his country to the West via Berlin.

On arms control, the Soviet premier shared Kennedy's misgivings about the prospect of a Chinese H-bomb and recognized that ultimately his country's resources needed to go into raising living standards. He also knew, however, that freezing the existing situation gave the advantage to the US in missile technology and that Soviet prestige was vitally linked to its image as a technological innovator, as reflected in the current cosmonaut program that had made Yuri Gagarin the first man to orbit the Earth. Given the vested interests on all sides, arms talks would make only slow progress, and so in Khrushchev's opinion issues such as Berlin needed to be addressed as more immediate priorities.

From Kennedy's point of view, a meeting focused on resolving the anomalous position of Berlin, a divided city inside Communist-controlled East Germany, was a depressing prospect. Former Secretary of State Dean Acheson had recently reiterated that for the West the only acceptable solution to the Berlin problem was German reunification. Since this was a distant possibility, Kennedy had to resist Soviet efforts to undermine Western rights in Berlin, which in Acheson's view were the key to power status in Europe. As the 1948 airlift had demonstrated, protecting Berlin meant persuading Moscow that the US was willing to use all its forces to defend it. Accordingly, in early April Kennedy had asked the Pentagon to examine how it would break any fresh attempt to blockade Berlin.

While others doubted the wisdom of summitry, both Kennedy and Khrushchev shared a curiosity about each other that a brief encounter in Washington in 1959 had not assuaged. Kennedy wanted to find out what the volatile Khrushchev was really like and, equally importantly, he told Ken O'Donnell, "I have to show him we can be just as tough as he is" (Beschloss 1991: 77).

Civil rights protests and Southern resistance: Kennedy's dilemma

At the same time, Kennedy needed to improve his foreign policy performance since his domestic record was looking weak. His only legislative success was the Area Redevelopment Act that directed federal aid to projects in West Virginia and nine other states with acute areas of poverty. The other high-priority domestic goals—college scholarships, federal aid to elementary and secondary education, health insurance for the aged, and tax reform—all languished in committee. Pollster Lou Harris urged Kennedy to press for an education bill by September, the start of the school year, and then to focus on health care. Legislative victories would yield a political dividend in the 1962 midterm congressional elections, he argued. But Southern resistance blocked the way.

Wary of Kennedy's courtship of the white South, civil rights leaders complained that their expectations of the new president were not being met. To turn up the heat, the Congress of Racial Equality (CORE) launched its Freedom Rides, taking buses of integrated riders south to test compliance with court-ordered desegregation of terminal facilities. The organizers knew that this was likely to provoke vigilante aggression, and on May 15 one bus was firebombed and another attacked on arrival in Birmingham, Alabama. The riders were attacked again in Montgomery by a mob that also bludgeoned a Justice Department official who tried to intervene. Images of the violence circulated nationally and internationally, further tarnishing Kennedy's image in Europe ahead of his summit with Khrushchev.

Eager to safeguard his brother, Bobby Kennedy sent marshals to protect Martin Luther King in Montgomery and then negotiated an armed escort for the Freedom Riders, who were intent on continuing to Jackson, Mississippi. State authorities were prepared to provide what amounted to protective custody only on condition that they could arrest the demonstrators on arrival. Speedily convicted on minor charges, they were then sent to Parchman, Mississippi's notorious maximum security prison. For the young activists from CORE and the Student Nonviolent Coordinating Committee (SNCC), Kennedy's connivance in their imprisonment began a process of disillusionment with liberal officials.

"Going to the Moon"

Anxious to revive his flagging leadership, Kennedy delivered what he termed a "second State of the Union" address on May 25, to alert the nation to the "extraordinary challenges" currently being faced. To show the world that he was serious about the prospect of a nuclear confrontation and to rally the nation by underlining the gravity of the threat, he urged a $700 million increase in defense spending, with a tripling of expenditure on civil defense, including fallout shelters. To lever more money into the economy, and out of a Congress reluctant to fund public works and welfare projects, he announced that the nation should seek to land a man on the Moon before the decade's end. Experts advised Kennedy that this could enable the US to overtake the Soviet Union in space technology. Lagging behind the USSR, America had completed its first manned space flight on May 5. Committing to achieving a Moon landing was presented as an affirmation of faith in America, and few politicians dare do otherwise.

The Vienna Summit: Wooing Europe

Notwithstanding a warning from Bobby Kennedy, via Soviet agent Georgi Bolshakov, that JFK's harsh rhetoric did not signal an unwillingness to negotiate, Khrushchev read the May speech as confirmation that the young president was the uncertain puppet of his Pentagon and CIA masters. He told Presidium colleagues that he had determined to settle the Berlin question within the next 6 months. The USSR would sign its own peace treaty with East Germany (the DDR), thus abrogating the Potsdam agreement on Berlin. The DDR would then seal off the city, ending the exodus of refugees from its ailing economy. He calculated that the French and the British, fearful of war, would reinforce Kennedy's hesitancy, and thus there would be no effective Western response. In the longer term, this would end hopes of German reunification and sow dissension in the NATO ranks, as their mistrust of the US intensified.

Kennedy landed at Orly airport near Paris on May 31 as a diminished figure, compared to the day of his inauguration. The Bay of Pigs stained his foreign policy record, an ill-disciplined Congress blocked his domestic priorities, pictures of American citizens being beaten in the streets on racial grounds circulated internationally, and to top it all his back problems had returned. He was obliged to resort to crutches in private, and away from the White House—where he took up to five hot showers a day and soaked in the swimming pool most afternoons—pain relief came through a disturbingly large range of medications.

His personal physician Dr. Janet Travell and White House medical staff member Admiral George Burkley flew with him to Europe on Air Force One. Travell gave Kennedy injections of procaine for his back, along with corticosteroids for his Addison's disease. The latter left him very vulnerable to infection, especially urinary problems aggravated by his sexual promiscuity. Burkley's records show the penicillin and other antibiotics he prescribed, as well as pills to help Kennedy sleep. Neither doctor knew that Dr. Max Jacobson, known among celebrities as "Dr. Feelgood" followed Kennedy to Paris and thence to Vienna, in order to continue his own course of injections with the president. Asked about the undisclosed contents of these injections, Kennedy declared "I don't care if it's horse piss. It works." However, given the subsequent death of one of Jacobson's patients from amphetamine addiction, biographers have understandably expressed concern over JFK's unmonitored drug use (Dallek 2003: 397–99).

The Paris trip was a triumph in terms of the restoration of Kennedy's public image, not least because of growing fascination with the first lady. His private negotiations with de Gaulle required him to give the senior statesman respect, despite the difficulties that Gaullist unilateralism caused in NATO and US–Soviet relations. Asked about Khrushchev's increasingly threatening behavior over the Berlin question, de Gaulle was sanguine. "If he had wanted a war over Berlin," he observed, "he would have acted already." De Gaulle spoke more respectfully of Kennedy after the visit, but did not alter his policies to accommodate the American "Grand Strategy." For his part, Kennedy proceeded to Vienna with the senior statesman's advice that Khrushchev's belligerence was a bluff. Ambassador Thompson also reiterated his own counsel that the president should avoid any discussion of ideology with the Soviet premier, since this would play to the latter's strengths (Kempe 2011: 214).

The Vienna Summit: A setback

With his back pain deadened by drugs and a tightly laced corset, Kennedy greeted the Soviet premier at the US ambassador's residence in Vienna on June 3. After posing for photographs of the obligatory handshake, the two parties moved inside. The exchanges quickly fell into a pattern of relatively brief Kennedy statements and longer Khrushchev ones. The first real clash came when Khrushchev took offense at Kennedy's repeated use of the word "miscalculation," in the course of explaining why better bilateral relations were vital in the nuclear age. The term was an attempt to inhibit the USSR in its international dissemination of the ideas that would inspire revolution. "We will not make war by mistake," he said, adding that Kennedy should "bury the word in cold storage and never use it again." After lunch, the two leaders, accompanied only by their interpreters, took a stroll in the residence grounds. Watching from an upstairs window, Kennedy aide Ken O'Donnell saw Khrushchev circle JFK, shaking his finger and snapping "like a terrier." O'Donnell also noticed that Kennedy winced in pain as he leaned over to attend to what Khrushchev was saying (O'Donnell and Powers 1972: 296).

The afternoon session did not go well for Kennedy. Khrushchev insisted that the greatest risk to world peace came from the American tendency to see the wave of revolution sweeping the world as a product of Soviet subversion, rather than native grievance. "Castro is not a Communist," he said at one point, "but US policy can make him one." Kennedy responded by asking Khrushchev to consider how the USSR might respond to the arrival of a pro-Western regime in Poland, an analogy that ceded more to Soviet claims to influence in Eastern Europe than had any previous President. It hinted at JFK's readiness to accept the continent's division (Kempe 2011: 230–34).

Talks resumed the next morning at the Soviet embassy. Overnight the delegations had made progress on an agreement to back a neutral regime in Laos, but talks between the two principals seemed as ill-starred as ever. Contrary to private hints from agent Bolshakov to Bobby Kennedy that there would be flexibility on the nuclear test ban issue, Khrushchev reiterated his view that what was needed was a wider arms control agreement and that the USSR could tolerate no more than three inspection visits, with the agreement being monitored by a commission of three officials: US, Soviet, and nonaligned. Despite Kennedy's warning that without a test ban there would be nuclear weapons proliferation, Khrushchev gave no ground. Instead he turned to Berlin, where Soviet patience had been exhausted (Beschloss 1991: 211–15).

While he would prefer to reach an agreement with Kennedy, Khrushchev declared that he was determined to sign a peace treaty with the DDR and thus ratify the division of Germany that the Great Patriotic War had produced. Once that treaty was signed, the DDR would have the sovereign right to accept or deny existing occupation rights in Berlin. Kennedy strove to be firm: "We are in Berlin not by agreement with the East Germans," he said, "but by contractual rights." He elaborated that loss of these rights would destroy international confidence in US pledges, especially in Western Europe. "If we were to leave West Berlin, Europe would be abandoned as well," he declared, "So when we are talking about West Berlin, we are also talking about Western Europe." While Kennedy gave the appearance of rejecting Khrushchev's policy, his reference to West Berlin rather than Berlin in its entirety was a tacit acceptance of the division of Germany that Khrushchev wished to secure.

Emboldened, Khrushchev declared that the Soviet Union would sign a peace treaty with the DDR and that any violation of the DDR's sovereignty would be regarded by the Soviets as "an act of open aggression." When Kennedy asked if Western rights and access to West Berlin would remain after the treaty, Khrushchev said they would not. While Moscow could transfer its rights to the DDR, Kennedy replied, it could not surrender American rights. Khrushchev offered a face-saving solution—a six-month period for negotiations on German reunification, but the abrogation of the Potsdam agreement if no settlement was obtained. Throwing the term "miscalculation" back in Kennedy's face, he said that the US should not misjudge Soviet resolve. "If the US should start a war over Berlin, let it be so." He then presented Kennedy with a formal aide-memoire on the Berlin question, documenting his ultimatum that it must be resolved within six months (Kempe 2011: 242–49).

With the talks scheduled to finish at this point, a desperate Kennedy asked for one more meeting with Khrushchev with just interpreters present. "I can't leave here without giving it one more try," he confided to O'Donnell, implying that he still believed that he could make the Soviet leader appreciate that he would not be intimidated. Acknowledging the importance of Berlin at the outset of this last exchange, he asked Khrushchev not to "present him with a situation so deeply involving" US national interests; in short, not to box him into a potentially nuclear confrontation. Khrushchev reiterated that they could try the face-saving device of a time-limited negotiating period over Germany, but nothing would save the status quo, which humiliated the USSR. Perhaps the DDR would accede to a UN agreement on the status of Berlin as a free city that would allow both US and Soviet troops to remain, but that was for them to determine. Slamming his hand on the table for emphasis, he declared, "I want peace. But if you want war, that is your problem." His decision to sign a peace treaty with the DDR was "firm and irrevocable." It would happen in December, regardless. "If that is true," Kennedy responded, "it's going to be a cold winter." The chill was already present.

State Department official Charles Bohlen was already briefing reporters about friendly talks when Kennedy decided that journalists should know that the atmosphere had been "somber." Press Secretary Salinger stayed behind in Vienna to spread the word about Khrushchev's belligerence, while Kennedy himself gave *New York Times* columnist James Reston "a grim picture." Khrushchev had roughed him up because of the Bay of Pigs "mess" and this gave him "a terrible problem." He would have to prove that he had "guts" to make Khrushchev see sense. On the plane to London, Kennedy told O'Donnell that he kept thinking of all the children who might die because of "an argument about access rights on an *autobahn*. ... If I'm going to threaten Russia with a nuclear war, it will have to be for much bigger and more important reasons than that." He carped about West German expectations of American action, when with US troops to protect them they had become "the fastest-growing industrial power in the world." The next day, British Prime Minister Harold Macmillan spared the obviously weary president a further round of diplomatic negotiations with his Cabinet. Privately, he listened to Kennedy's complaints about Khrushchev the "barbarian," and they agreed to make contingency plans for the impending crisis (Beschloss 1991: 227).

In a television address on his return, Kennedy told the American people that they and the Soviets gave "wholly different meanings to the same words—war, peace, democracy, and popular will," even "right and wrong." Nevertheless, they owed mankind the fullest effort to avoid an armed clash (Dallek 2003: 416).

The Berlin crisis

The aide memoire summarizing Soviet demands was made public on June 10, and thereafter the absence of a US rejoinder prompted press speculation that Kennedy's leadership abilities were once more in doubt. Behind the scenes, Berlin had become his obsession. According to his friend, *Newsweek* editor Ben Bradlee, he talked of little else through the rest of June. At a June 29 NSC meeting he had Dean Acheson outline the options. Acheson was de facto head of the hardliners on Berlin, supported by the Joint Chiefs in his calls for a conspicuous military build-up to intimidate Moscow.

Advocates of a subtler diplomatic approach were disparagingly known as SLOBS ("softliners on Berlin"). Prominent among them were Ambassador Thompson, Harvard foreign policy consultant Henry Kissinger, Charles Bohlen at the State Department, and Kennedy aides Ted Sorensen and Arthur Schlesinger. McNamara and Bundy were also sympathetic to this less confrontational approach. Kennedy kept the pressure up on his advisors for carefully calibrated, practical options. He wanted a larger choice than "holocaust or humiliation" (Beschloss 1991: 246).

On July 19 Kennedy approved a plan to supply Berlin by air, if necessary, and move six divisions to Europe ahead of Khrushchev's December deadline. He rejected Acheson's call for a national emergency declaration, and his demand that reserves be called up no later than September. Both were seen as needlessly panicky and provocative. Addressing the nation on July 25, Kennedy called for further defense spending and a boost in army manpower to one million men. While willing to "remove any irritants," he would not surrender West Berlin's freedom. It was "the great testing place of Western courage and will." He ended by asking Americans for their prayers to help him bear the heavy and constant burdens of his office.

Throughout the speech, however, he referred explicitly to West Berlin, a stress on only one portion of the divided city that was reinforced by the July 30 comments of Senator William Fulbright on ABC television. Fulbright said that the Communists had the power to close the border and that he didn't understand why the East Germans had not done so. Fulbright corrected his statement on August 4, affirming the treaty rights of freedom of movement across Berlin, but Kennedy never spoke out against Fulbright's initial comments. Talking with Walt Rostow, he mused that Khrushchev would have to do something to stop the flow of refugees, maybe even build a wall, and that he would not be able to prevent it. NATO would unite to defend West Berlin but was unprepared to act to keep East Berlin open (Kempe 2011: 315–16).

The Wall

Early on the morning of August 13, East German security forces threw barriers across all access points from East to West Berlin. While this seemed to fulfill expectations in some circles, it did not immediately end the crisis. Kennedy told McNamara that he expected the latest events to increase pressure for military action. Nonetheless, on reflection he was in private prepared to admit that the outcome was a godsend. If Khrushchev had intended to seize West Berlin, there would have been no need for a wall. "It's not a very nice solution," he conceded, "but a wall is a hell of a lot better than a war." Accepting the wall, however, meant placating disturbed American allies, most of all West Germany, which was facing fresh elections in which Berlin Mayor Willy Brandt was challenging long-time incumbent Chancellor Konrad Adenauer.

Kennedy needed to reassure his NATO allies that US commitment to their security had not wavered. Vice President Johnson was dispatched to Berlin to greet a fresh detachment of US troops, who would come by road through the Eastern zone to reassert access rights. The hero of the 1948 Berlin Airlift, General Lucius Clay, was also sent to his old post as a symbol of reassurance. En route, Clay regaled Johnson with stories from 1948, all in support of his view that the only way to deal with the Soviets was to stand up to them. If he were president, he said, he would tear down the Wall. Observers compared the rapturous reception the two men received in Berlin on August 19 to that given allied troops during the liberation of Paris in 1944.

Meanwhile, Khrushchev announced renewed nuclear arms testing, a move that compelled Kennedy to resume underground tests despite his calls for a test ban agreement. His first, unreported response to the news was characteristically brusque: "Fucked again." When UN Ambassador Adlai Stevenson complained about his decision to resume testing on September 3, Kennedy retorted that he'd had no choice. They had spat in his eye three times—space, Cuba, the Wall had all made the Soviets look tough, he said. He could not keep backing down (Beschloss 1991: 307). Echoing Clay's view of the Russians, Khrushchev told Soviet scientist Andrei Sakharov that he needed the tests because Americans only understood the language of military strength. Just as importantly, the new tests would remind the Third World of Soviet power (Dallek 2003: 429).

Although Clay was a potent symbol for West Berliners, for Kennedy he was a risk since he was intent on probing Soviet resolve. When a nail-biting standoff involving tanks occurred on October 28, he used his brother Bobby's contacts with Georgi Bolshakov to get messages privately to Khrushchev (Kempe 2011: 479). Nonetheless, Kennedy managed the Berlin crisis well once it occurred, and recognized that its safe resolution required him to persist with diplomacy. He did so in the face of renewed pressure for retaliatory measures that had to assume the possibility of nuclear war. Briefed by the JCS on September 13, Kennedy learned that the vast nuclear superiority of the US ensured that, in the event of an imminent Soviet attack, he could strike first with 1,685 nuclear warheads. While American fatalities might be as high as 15 million due to strikes on densely populated urban areas, and Western Europe would certainly face a death toll in the tens of millions, he could be confident that the US attack would leave Soviet society devastated (Beschloss 1991: 309–10).

Dining with press secretary Salinger in New York on September 24, ahead of Kennedy's address to the United Nations, Soviet spokesman Mikhail Kharmalov delivered a message from Khrushchev: "The storm in Berlin is over." The next day, using one of Sorensen's epigrams, Kennedy told the world's representatives that "Mankind must put an end to war—or war will put an end to mankind." Challenging the USSR to a "peace race" rather than an arms race, he ended his speech by inviting the assembly to be part of the generation that could "save succeeding generations from the scourge of war. ... For together we shall save our planet—or together we shall perish in its flames."

Liberals had harbored doubts about Jack Kennedy. They had feared that he was too much his father's son. His early months in office had sent mixed signals; there had been dismay at the botched Cuban invasion and concern over the escalating Berlin crisis, countered by pride in the style and ambition of the witty young president. As 1961 drew to a close, fear over Joe's influence was to vanish. The senior Kennedy suffered a massive and devastating stroke that left him partially paralyzed and virtually speechless. To all questions, his response was "No, no, no." Small wonder that Christmas 1961 found the Kennedys in somber and reflective mood.

5 Brinkmanship

The Missile Crisis and other challenges

January 1962 completed Kennedy's first year as president. It had been challenging and instructive. In his speeches, he was apt to refer to the times as demanding greater sacrifices and more effort, yet the plethora of foreign and domestic problems that he confronted shocked him. After the comprehensive failure of the Bay of Pigs invasion, his wife Jackie reported that he cried in a way that she had only previously seen during the worst times of his back surgery. Learning that the Soviets had resumed nuclear testing, he could not contain his anger that Khrushchev had broken a promise. "That fucking liar," he railed to colleagues. Taunted by Dallas newspaper publisher E.M. Dealey at a White House lunch for not being the "man on horseback" the nation needed but instead coming across like a man "riding Caroline's [JFK's daughter] tricycle," Kennedy was clearly riled. Observing that it was easier to talk about wars than to fight them, he added the schoolyard-style boast "I'm just as tough as you are" (Dallek 2003: 366, 429, 433).

Like other presidents, Kennedy was learning that what confronted him almost every day were critical issues and desperately difficult problems. Minor, readily resolvable matters should not, and usually did not, get to his desk. Every day was different, but his basic routine was to read the press while still in bed, then attend his National Security briefing, before going to the Oval Office for the scheduled round of meetings and phone calls. He would take a break at some point in the afternoon, often swimming in the White House pool; sometimes he was joined by two lissome girls on the staff, nicknamed Fiddle and Faddle. He would see the children before they went to bed and attend formal dinners and receptions, and commonly work on papers late into the night.

Vietnam

Although 1961 had been dominated by Cuba and Berlin in terms of foreign policy, with both casting a shadow over US–Soviet relations, Kennedy had also had to deal with the Congolese civil war in Africa, instability in the Dominican Republic in the Caribbean, and a deepening conflict in Laos in Southeast Asia, which at one point threatened to require US troops. He had also kept a close eye on the deteriorating situation in Laos's neighbor, South Vietnam. Shortly after coming to office Kennedy had read a report on Vietnam that prompted him to tell his advisor Walt Rostow, "This is the worst [problem] we've got" (Newman 1992: 3). Unless support was given urgently, the report predicted that the Communist-backed Viet Cong would topple the American-backed Diem regime. Ngo Dinh Diem, a nationalist with powerful US Catholic backers, had been installed as premier in the South after the French defeat in 1954, to prevent a Communist takeover. A temporary line of division agreed at the 1954 Geneva Conference had separated North and South Vietnam, but instead of the pro-mised elections, which would probably have placed the Northern Communist leader Ho Chi Minh in power, the separation was consolidated by the US support for Diem in Saigon. Ho's Communist forces then resumed their battle to free all of Vietnam, seeking to topple Diem with support from disaffected South Vietnamese, known as the Viet Cong.

Kennedy's initial position on Vietnam

By 1961, the US Embassy in Saigon had concluded that Diem had worsened his situation through nepotism, lack of reform, and alienation of the South Vietnamese people, and that he might be a liability that had to be sacrificed. However other advisors, notably Edward Lansdale, an ambitious general with CIA experience, felt that backing Diem remained the best option. Angling for the embassy post himself, Lansdale argued that extra US help and a change of ambassador would turn the tide. Although Kennedy had spoken in the Senate about how political turmoil in the developing world was fueled by nationalism and acute economic injustice, he chose to define Vietnam primarily as a military issue, and allowed the Defense Department under Robert McNamara, rather than the State Department under Dean Rusk, to be the main engine of policy development. He had dispensed with the Eisenhower committee structure and the regular cabinet meetings that would have debated overall policy, and this led to ad hoc decision making, in which his policy intentions were not always clear to the different agencies involved. Consequently, resources for Vietnam would initially flow to the Military Assistance Advisory Group (MAAG) with no explicit linkage to Diem's pursuit of reform, although in some discussions this was implied.

Assisting McNamara on Vietnam were men who would emerge as "hawks" on other questions, too. Defense Under Secretary Roswell Gilpatric chaired the Vietnam task force with Walt Rostow representing the NSC, and they listened closely to the area field commander General Paul Harkin. Despite being recommended by General Maxwell Taylor, who was known for his advocacy of a more "flexible response" military strategy, Harkin was more traditional in outlook and not familiar with counterinsurgency. He saw the problem primarily as North Vietnamese infiltration, rather than as guerilla warfare by disaffected South Vietnamese peasants.

Kennedy's appointment of a previously European-based diplomat, Frederick Nolting, as ambassador in May 1961 weakened the Saigon embassy, which had been urging Diem to pursue democratic reform. By bypassing Lansdale, a Diem supporter, the new appointment might have renewed the pressure for reform, but instead it transplanted European models of the Cold War to Asia and required Nolting, a NATO specialist, to learn local conditions from scratch. As a result the initial Kennedy measures were military, with a subsidy for Diem to raise a further 20,000 Vietnamese troops and an enlargement of MAAG forces to train local troops in counterinsurgency techniques. Even this increase in advisors (rather than troops per se) underlined the level of Kennedy's concern, since it breached the 1954 Geneva agreement. By September 1961, Diem's military position had not improved, and a month later Kennedy sent Taylor and Rostow on a fact-finding mission.

During the Paris meetings in June 1961, President de Gaulle had warned Kennedy about the perils of fighting in the jungles of Indochina, where France had suffered an ignominious defeat. The Bay of Pigs debacle had already made the president less ready to accept his military advisors' claims, and this skepticism had been reinforced by subsequent discussions of a possible intervention in Laos. Kennedy's questioning had revealed serious logistical flaws: there were only two airfields in Laos capable of receiving large US supply planes and both were only usable in good weather. He had also realized the limited airlift capacity and conventional capabilities bequeathed by Eisenhower's economies, which had led the JCS to include use of nuclear weapons in their contingency plans at a relatively early stage. On the other hand, Eisenhower's reiteration, in the handover meetings, of the domino theory, which posited that a single setback in one country could trigger a cumulative strategic collapse of Western influence in Southeast Asia, had left its mark on Kennedy.

Perceived gains for the Communist bloc in Cuba and Berlin in the course of 1961 left Kennedy feeling that politically he couldn't afford any further international setbacks. He remembered how effective the Republican charge that the Democrats were "soft on Communism" had been in the Truman years. When he addressed the UN in late September 1961, Kennedy ranked Vietnam alongside Berlin as a "threat to peace." In the autumn of his first year, therefore, Kennedy was in two minds: he wanted to halt Communist expansion in Southeast Asia but he also wanted to avoid direct military intervention. At that stage, other officials felt that intervention was essential. Intelligence reports detailed the growth of Viet-Cong forces inside South Vietnam and they also suggested that US intervention would not trigger countermoves by China or the USSR; for hawks, the time was ripe (Newman 1992: 126–27).

Kennedy rejects the troops option

Kennedy was unconvinced and sent two aides to assess the situation. In his directives to General Taylor ahead of his October visit to Vietnam, Kennedy had asked that all recommendations should take as their premise that "effective maintenance of the independence of South Vietnam" should rest with its people and government. He also leaked to the *New York Times* a false story that the Pentagon opposed the commitment of troops (Newman 1992: 129–30). Despite this strong steer from the president, Taylor recommended sending 8,000 combat troops, perhaps deployed under the cover of helping with the chronic flooding in the Mekong Delta. The JCS and the administration hawks favored a more substantial intervention to ensure Viet Cong gains were reversed. They wanted a public US commitment to the preservation of South Vietnam and had contingency plans for sending over 200,000 US personnel. They were already considering air raids against Hanoi; in short, a war. This was not what Kennedy wanted to hear. He believed that once US troops were introduced escalation would be hard to stop. Troop deployments were like a drink, he told one aide, "The effect wears off, and you have to take another" (Rabe 2010: 110).

On November 22, 1962, Kennedy rejected direct intervention, but increased the supply of military advisors and equipment. A few days later, he signaled his dissatisfaction with the advice he was receiving by changing personnel in both the State Department and the CIA. The arrival of veteran diplomat Averell Harriman at the Far Eastern desk, the replacement of the out-of-favor liberal Chester Bowles by George Ball, and the appointment of John McCone as CIA director marked Kennedy's attempt to build his own team, although he remained unwilling to remove Dean Rusk as secretary of state. George Ball, in particular, counseled strongly against sending troops to Vietnam. "Within five years," he told the president, "we'll have three hundred thousand men in the paddies and jungles and never find them again." Less prescient than his advisor, Kennedy said he was crazy to think so (Ball 1982: 366).

Cuba: Operation Mongoose

Gauging Kennedy's intentions in Vietnam is made more difficult by his conduct in other areas of the world. He may not have appointed the flamboyant George Lansdale to the embassy in Saigon, but in November 1961 he did place him in charge of a concerted effort to topple Fidel Castro. With a $50 million budget, Operation Mongoose involved more than 400 CIA employees, a small navy, and thousands of Cuban exiles, guided from its command base in Miami. Underlining the president's personal interest in this mission was the involvement of his brother, Attorney General Bobby Kennedy, who pressed the CIA for greater and greater efforts in Cuba. Speedboats and other vessels delivered agents and exiles to the island for the purposes of sabotage, propaganda, and intelligence gathering.

A popular uprising against Castro, the CIA believed, would justify a US invasion. The Defense Department had elaborate invasion plans and in the spring of 1962 it performed naval and aerial exercises, including an amphibious landing on Vieques Island, Puerto Rico. The exercise was codenamed ORTSAC (Castro spelled backwards). Bobby Kennedy was recorded as suggesting that a staged attack on the US base at Guantanamo could also serve as a pretext for invasion. Bobby was dismayed to learn that the CIA had subcontracted its efforts to assassinate Castro to organized crime figures John Roselli and Sam Giancana. However, rather than the idea of assassination it was the mob involvement that offended him, in the context of his intense efforts to prosecute mobsters as attorney general. The personal anger felt by the Kennedy brothers after the Bay of Pigs amounted to a vendetta against Castro. In their efforts to eliminate what most Americans saw as the threat from Communist Cuba, the death of Fidel, his brother Raul, or close associate Che Guevara would have been seen as a positive development (Rabe 2010: 61–63).

The Alliance for Progress

Kennedy's obsessive desire to eliminate Castroism adversely affected his overall policy towards Latin America. At the outset of his administration, this had seemed the most progressive facet of his foreign policy. On March 31, 1961, he had unveiled his Alliance for Progress, committing the United States to a "vast cooperative effort, unparalleled in magnitude and nobility of purpose, to satisfy the basic needs of Latin American people for homes, work and land, health and schools—*techo, trabajo y tierra, salud y escuela*" (Dallek 2003: 341). At a conference in Punta del Este, Uruguay, Treasury Secretary Dillon told delegates that an influx of $20 billion in US aid and investment would generate growth on a scale that would materially transform the region. The Kennedy administration anticipated that this transformation in health, education, and economic prospects would be matched by political reforms that would eliminate the tax and land laws that perpetuated inequality and authoritarian rule. In Chile, for example, 7 percent of the population owned 80 percent of the land (Rabe 2010: 76–77).

The Alliance program appeared to mark a dramatic change from the Eisenhower years, when the US had applauded figures like Marcos Jimenez of Peru, a notorious tyrant, and had destabilized the popularly elected Guatemalan government of Jacobo Arbenz Guzman. The Alliance proposal hoped to capitalize on the rise of a new generation of progressive political leaders such as Romulo Betancourt of Venezuela, Arturo Frondizi of Argentina, and Juscelino Kubitschek of Brazil. They in turn encouraged the allocation of American aid by arguing that they represented the vital alternative to Communism. After listening to Khrushchev's strategy of Communist expansion via wars of national liberation in January 1961 and hearing him expound his philosophy firsthand in Vienna in June, Kennedy concluded that the USSR intended to target Latin America for subversion. Containment of Communism became a weightier component than ever within the Alliance for Progress's rationale (Rabe 2010: 79–80).

The Alliance assessed

The stark limits of Kennedy's approach in practice were summed up in the aftermath of the CIA-inspired assassination of the Dominican Republic's dictator Rafael Trujillo. According to Arthur Schlesinger, a normally pro-Kennedy chronicler, the president saw three possibilities: a decent democratic regime, a new dictator in the Trujillo mold, or Castro-style Communism. "We ought to aim for the first," he said, "but we really can't renounce the second until we are sure that we can avoid the third" (Schlesinger 1965: 769). In the event, the US remained wedded to the second option in too many countries in Latin America and elsewhere.

The Alliance for Progress fell far short of its brave hopes. It did not generate take-off for the South American economies, and the gains that it secured in terms of education and healthcare were largely overwhelmed by population growth. In the late 1960s, when Lyndon Johnson was accused of abandoning Kennedy's policy, economic growth was higher. Most disappointing of all, reform faltered, and in many Latin American countries military rule returned. Much of this was due to congressional opposition which limited the amount of aid available, but it also reflected Kennedy's priorities. He was more anxious to avoid a second Communist or socialist regime emerging in the Western hemisphere than to secure Alliance goals, and was prepared to back authoritarian regimes and collude in the removal of leaders he suspected of socialistic leanings, as he did in Guyana.

At the same time, the propaganda value of the program should not be ignored. When Richard Nixon toured Latin America in 1958, local people had attacked his car and spat at him as the representative of Yankee imperialism. When Kennedy and his Spanish-speaking wife Jackie visited the continent in 1962 they were cheered fulsomely by massive crowds. Some of this was down to their Catholicism and their media-disseminated glamor, but most of it was the result of changed perceptions. Like African Americans domestically, the general public in the developing world believed that Kennedy cared about them, even though in practice he often disappointed. They believed that initiatives like the Peace Corps and the Alliance for Progress were sincere attempts to improve their lives and they cheered the president on that account. The Peace Corps, in particular, was seen as representing the generosity and compassion of Americans in a new way, and it was an important part of Kennedy's legacy in the developing world. But another part of that legacy was the belief that what was good for America was good for the world.

Europe, burden-sharing, and the economy

Whatever its effect on Berliners, the Berlin Wall had been better than a war in Kennedy's eyes. The Berlin crisis had highlighted the tensions inside the NATO alliance. France's unilateralism remained strong and British anxieties about their position in Europe added to the complexities of the so-called "special relationship" that the Kennedy–Macmillan friendship seemed to symbolize. At the same time, Kennedy wanted to manage all his European allies so that they not only followed US guidance in Cold War matters but also helped him to revive the stumbling American economy. Although he had defeated Nixon primarily by promising greater vigor in the prosecution of the Cold War, Kennedy had also promised to spark economic recovery. In the closing days of the 1960 campaign, Nixon had claimed that the prospect of a Kennedy victory had prompted speculation in gold, driving its London value to $40 an ounce, $5 above the fixed price that the US had agreed to uphold under the Bretton Woods agreement, as the keystone of the postwar financial system. The speculators believed that the Democratic candidate's policies to stimulate the economy would further loosen the money supply and thus force a devaluation of the dollar that would reflect the higher gold price. In response, candidate Kennedy publicly renounced devaluation as an option within his economic policy.

Pushing the possibility of devaluation was the persistent balance of payments problem, rooted in the economic impact of maintaining US military bases overseas, especially in Europe. The immediate advantages of victory in 1945 had disappeared by 1960, and Kennedy was the first postwar president confronted by a decline in US economic power. His advisors believed that he became as obsessed with the balance of payments crisis as he was with the Cold War. It was a dilemma that seemed to confront him at every turn. Military intervention abroad would worsen the situation through transfer payments, while at home an economic stimulus via lower interest rates or tax cuts might be damaging if it grossly weakened the dollar or created an import surge.

When French President de Gaulle countered US pressure by threatening to deplete US gold reserves, Kennedy saw the balance of payments issue as frustrating his foreign policy goals. At the same time, if the US trade deficit were tackled according to the standard International Monetary Fund formula of balanced budgets and higher interest rates, it would seem to ensure that Kennedy's hopes of domestic economic recovery ahead of his 1964 reelection bid would be dashed. Kennedy's options seemed to dwindle to asking European allies to burden-share by making payments to offset the cost of US military defense, as Germany did through arms purchases and aid to developing countries.

Trade policy

Domestically, JFK sought congressional permission to negotiate tariff reductions to promote trade, in the context of a fiscal arrangement that gave US industry tax depreciation allowances to encourage capital investment in new technology. The Trade Expansion Act of 1962 allowed the president to reduce tariffs by up to 50 percent on most goods and to eliminate them entirely in the case of trade with Europe. Commerce Secretary Luther Hodges orchestrated the measure's passage and managed to pacify potentially powerful and hostile lobby groups, such as the textile industry that both Kennedy, from Massachusetts, and Hodges, from North Carolina, knew well. A cartel-like agreement protected US and European textile interests, but other concessions and claims to secure congressional approval enabled European negotiators to argue for sharper cuts in US tariffs in subsequent talks.

The Kennedy administration argued strongly that free trade would inspire American innovation and thus higher productivity, but weak sectors with smaller businesses, such as small metal and textile firms, saw the measure as removing their protection from cheap foreign imports. Cheap labor and mass production would undercut US producers and thus worsen the trade balance. Politicians such as Texan Congressman Bruce Alger warned that if the administration was wrong about the impact of US technological superiority it could discover too late that it had lost American jobs.

Like the Alliance for Progress, liberalized trade agreements did not generate the benefits that Kennedy promised. The European Union's Common Agricultural Policy, for instance, reduced US agricultural exports in 1962–63. Ultimately, by trying to maintain the dollar's value, by entering into multilateral trade talks, and yet increasing defense spending and overseas deployments, Kennedy has been seen as exacerbating the problems he tried to solve.

The steel crisis

More immediately worrying, however, the impact of trade talks on particular lobby groups and of dollar pressures on the stock market fostered the impression that Kennedy was hostile to business.

However erroneous this perception, it grew sharply in the wake of the president's angry clash with the nation's steel producers. From the outset Kennedy had courted big business. Treasury Secretary Dillon was a symbol that JFK was mindful of its needs, and he had spoken of the need to balance wages and prices in industrial sectors where strong unions extracted fuller benefits from large corporate employers like the auto-makers Ford, GM, Chrysler, and American Motors.

Accordingly, Labor Secretary Arthur Goldberg pressurized the steelworkers' union to accept a contract that provided for a 2.5 percent increase in benefits, a rise that fell well within productivity gains. But only days after Kennedy had applauded this restraint, Roger Blough, head of US Steel, announced a 3.5 percent price increase, and other steel producers quickly did the same, flouting the Kennedy policy. An aide, observing Kennedy's reaction to the news, recalled "There should have been a speedometer on his rocking chair"(Giglio 2006: 132).

Kennedy read a statement at his morning press conference condemning the price increase as "a wholly unjustifiable and irresponsible defiance of the public interest." Off the record, his language was far less decorous. "My father always told me that all businessmen were sons of bitches," he fulminated to aides, "but I never believed him until now." To his friend Ben Bradlee, he was even cruder. "Are we supposed to sit here and take a cold deliberate fucking?" he asked rhetorically, before answering with an angry shake of his head: "They fucked us, and we've got to try to fuck them" (Bradlee 1975: 77–78).

Kennedy ordered his brother, the attorney general, to investigate whether the steel executives could be prosecuted using antitrust legislation, and Bobby in turn had FBI agents march into their offices the next day with subpoenas for personal and company records, and made it clear that the Internal Revenue would be auditing the top executives if they didn't reconsider. Bobby himself recalled, "It was a tough way to operate. But under the circumstances, we couldn't afford to lose" (Dallek 2003: 486).

And they won. The split in the steel executives' ranks began, predictably, with a US Steel rival. Joseph Block of Inland Steel declared that he felt strongly that prices should be held down, and the heads of Kaiser and Armco Steel expressed their support.

Fearing lost orders, Bethlehem Steel, the second largest company, also rescinded its price increases, leaving US Steel isolated. When US Steel's crestfallen leader, Roger Blough, privately told Kennedy he would halve his price hikes, the president demanded and got a complete surrender. Talking with historian Arthur Schlesinger, JFK compared the experience to Grant accepting Lee's surrender at the end of the Civil War. "I told him that his men could keep their horses for the spring plowing," he joked (Dallek 2003: 487). Publicly, Kennedy urged conciliation, and spoke of his intention to minimize the role of government in collective bargaining and price decisions. These should be free and private negotiations in America, he felt, but government should protect the public interest.

Business leaders were outraged. Kennedy was compared to Mussolini and the FBI actions were reviled. Businessmen jocularly sported badges identifying themselves as members of the "S.O.B. Club." Bumper stickers declared: "I Miss Ike – Hell, I Even Miss Harry." Less humorously, when Wall Street experienced its largest one-day fall since the crash of 1929, investors blamed Kennedy for damaging business confidence. The standard bearer of the Republican Right, Barry Goldwater, warned that Kennedy was trying to "socialize" America's economy, and in those areas of the country where groups like the John Birch Society thrived, like southern California and Texas, hatred of the president festered (Dallek 2003: 488).

Civil rights and public opinion

Among the groups that continued to back Kennedy strongly were African Americans. Despite his failure to act on key civil rights issues, a *Jet* readers' poll in the summer of 1961 suggested an 87 percent satisfaction rate. Part of this popularity was due to the widely reported inclusion of African American celebrities on the White House guest list, and the resignation of prominent figures like Bobby Kennedy from Washington clubs that operated a color bar. While many African Americans seemed to be swayed by symbolic gestures, the white American mainstream was giving Kennedy no encouragement to go further on civil rights. A June 1961 Gallup poll found that almost two-thirds of the American public disapproved of the Freedom Rides, protests designed to highlight the failure of Southern states to implement the Supreme Court's desegregation of interstate transportation terminals (Bryant 2006: 223–24).

With his approval rating so high with African Americans, Kennedy was unsympathetic to civil rights leaders who scolded him for doing too little. He was largely content to leave the politically explosive issue of desegregation in the hands of Bobby, whose primary mission at times seemed to be not so much upholding the law as the nation's attorney general than protecting his brother as president. Thus Bobby colluded with Alabama and Mississippi state authorities to ensure that the Freedom Rides from Montgomery to Jackson were conducted under military escort, with the Riders quietly arrested on arrival by state authorities. Similarly, during a protest campaign in the southwest Georgia town of Albany that saw Martin Luther King jailed in December 1961 and again in the summer of 1962, Bobby Kennedy praised the local Sherriff Laurie Pritchett for his skillful policing, despite the fact that Pritchett was using his non-brutal tactics to quash African American civil liberties.

In the wake of the Freedom Rides, the Kennedy administration had encouraged a group of liberal philanthropists to pool their grants in order to back a mass voter registration effort, the Voter Education Project. The VEP grants were tempting to all of the cash-strapped civil rights organizations, but the movement's radicals rightly perceived that the administration hoped that a switch away from direct action campaigns against segregated facilities to voter registration work would ensure that the movement generated fewer embarrassing headlines for the president. Radical groups such as the Student Nonviolent Coordinating Committee (SNCC) frustrated this purpose by focusing their efforts not in the towns of the Upper South, where registration efforts might achieve the quickest results, but in the rural districts of the Deep South where white resistance was greatest. SNCC leader Bob Moses characterized one of his field reports from Mississippi as coming from "inside the iceberg" of white supremacy, and SNCC mentor Ella Baker shrewdly assured her protégés that if they undertook voter registration in the Deep South the distinction between direct action and voter registration work would quickly disappear.

The movement remained a problem for the Kennedys, especially as they struggled to find some way of neutralizing the entrenched political power of the white South in Congress so as to pass key elements of their program. Ahead of the 1962 midterm elections, Kennedy wanted to pass tax and tariff reforms and to renew his balked efforts to extend federal aid to education and give senior citizens federally funded health care. Few things would obstruct the achievement of these legislative goals as emphatically as a civil rights bill or enforcement action that antagonized the largely Southern chairmen of key congressional committees. Even long-touted measures such as an executive order to desegregate public housing or the appointment of African American Robert Weaver to a Cabinet post would be postponed if they threatened other priorities.

The crisis at "Ole Miss"

As the Freedom Rides had shown, however, the civil rights movement was driven by a passion and a principle that was not to be suborned to Kennedy-style pragmatism. Certainly no one could shake the determination of James Meredith, a 29-year-old air force veteran who had won a lengthy legal battle to become the first African American to attend the University of Mississippi, his home state's flagship university, known locally as "Ole Miss." On September 10, 1962, the Supreme Court ordered his admission. This made it the Kennedy administration's responsibility to ensure that he was admitted, and the Justice Department strove to negotiate with state authorities to avoid the kind of escalating confrontation that had compelled President Eisenhower to send US troops to Little Rock, Arkansas in 1957. Recognizing how Arkansas Governor Orval Faubus had boosted his political stand-ing at home by resisting federal authority, Mississippi Governor Ross Barnett was determined to do the same. In a televised address he called upon Mississippians to resist. Likening deseg-regation to the destruction of the white race, he declared, "We will not drink from the cup of genocide" (Bryant 2006: 333).

JFK tried as far as possible to leave the matter to his brother, and Bobby, in turn, tried to persuade Barnett that all parties had an interest in maintaining law and order. Believing that they had persuaded the governor to acquiesce in Meredith's quiet, discreet registration, the president arranged a televised address to the nation for the evening of Sunday, September 30, 1962, designed to underline the rule of law. The same weekend Barnett attended an "Ole Miss" football game, giving his own televised speech at half time. Soaking up the home fans' cheers, he boasted of his love and respect for the customs of the great state of Mississippi in a way that played upon white segregationist feelings. Right-wing sympathizers like former General Edwin Walker, whom Kennedy had forced into retirement because of his distribution of John Birch leaflets to enlisted men, were reported at the scene protesting the Meredith enrollment. The administration was compelled to protect Meredith against the growing threat of mob violence.

Just as in the broader area of defense, the Kennedys felt that the previous administration had not pursued policies that allowed for a flexible response. Thus, whereas Eisenhower had used the 101st Airborne Division to protect African American schoolchildren in Little Rock, Kennedy wanted to start in Mississippi with an ad hoc force of federal personnel loosely termed "marshals." Only if they proved insufficient would he use the federalized National Guard, and only if they failed would US troops go in. By late afternoon on September 30 the marshals had taken up position on campus and were facing an angry mob, whose intent was clearly signaled when they beat up a local pastor who pleaded for calm.

At 7.25 p.m. (EST), Kennedy and his advisors learned from the FBI that Governor Barnett had ordered state troopers to withdraw, leaving the marshals to face the growing mob alone. Despite this ominous development, the president went ahead with his address, urging Mississippians to obey the law, even though he knew as he spoke that on the campus rioters had begun to throw Molotov cocktails and stones, and there was sporadic gunfire. Afterwards, he decided that the deteriorating situation required the use of troops, only to discover that the Pentagon had failed to ready them. It took five hours for them to deploy from a base in Memphis, and it took until 5.30 a.m. (EST) the following day for troops and the National Guard to be deployed in sufficient numbers to secure the campus. By that time there had been two deaths, as well as 160 casualties among the marshals.

"I haven't had such an interesting time since the Bay of Pigs," Kennedy observed, with bitter humor, as the hours passed waiting for the army (Dallek 2003: 517). It confirmed his misgivings about the military and represented what he termed "a hell of a problem" for public relations. Kennedy was especially concerned about the international repercussions of the death of a French journalist at the scene, and he knew that politicians in the Deep South would campaign that fall on an anti-Kennedy platform, despite their Democratic label. At the same time, liberal candidates outside the South would seek African American support, and Kennedy's enforcement of desegregation would help them. For civil rights activists, however, including Meredith, the administration's keenness to placate white Southern opinion continued to foster mistrust. It was a balancing act that persisted throughout Kennedy's presidency.

The Cuban Missile Crisis: Origins

President Kennedy's engagement with civil rights as an issue was quickly eclipsed by foreign policy matters, in October 1962. Instability in several Latin American countries, including Argentina and Brazil, dented the hopes for the Alliance for Progress considerably, and more worryingly set the stage for Castro-style uprisings. At the same time, the resumption of atmospheric nuclear testing was symptomatic of the poor state of US–Soviet relations following the Berlin crisis. US proposals for both comprehensive and limited test bans had been rebuffed again in September, and when the Interior Secretary Stewart Udall met Khrushchev in Moscow in the same month, the premier was belligerent. "It's been a long time since you could spank us like a little boy," he declared, presumably alluding to the time when the US was the only nuclear power, "Now we can swat your ass" (Dallek 2003: 533).

Khrushchev's plans

Khrushchev may also have been referring to Operation Anadyr, whereby he had undertaken to install nuclear missiles in Cuba, alongside ILB-28 bombers and nearly 50,000 troops. By placing forty-eight medium-range and thirty-two intermediate-range missiles, as well as bombers capable of carrying atomic bombs, Khrushchev would lessen the strategic imbalance created by the USSR's limited first-strike capability. The missile gap still favored the Americans but the Cuban missiles reduced the likelihood that Kennedy would be swayed by the hawks in the military into a first strike of his own.

Khrushchev saw the missiles as yet another move in the larger game of nuclear deterrence, with the immediate object being to forestall what he perceived to be Kennedy's clear preparations for an invasion of Communist Cuba, which he believed was probably scheduled to happen ahead of the midterm elections to secure maximum political benefit. In a December 1962 speech in the wake of the crisis, he spoke of how he had wanted to make the Americans realize that "Cuba was not defenseless" and thus oblige them "to change their plans" (White 1997: 31).

The expulsion of Cuba from the Organization of American States, the tightening of sanctions, the sabotage efforts of CIA-sponsored teams, and the elaborate military exercises in the Caribbean had certainly convinced Castro that an invasion was imminent, and prompted him to accept Khrushchev's offer of nuclear missiles. Khrushchev was also engaged in a contest within the Communist world, with China, which had grown increasingly critical of Soviet policy. The "gamble" of installing missiles so close to the US mainland would bolster the USSR's claim to be the dominant partner in the increasingly fractious Communist bloc.

Khrushchev's decision was also seen as creating an equivalent to the US missile stations in Turkey and Italy, which were targeted at the USSR. Despite plans to scrap the Jupiter missiles because they were technologically obsolete they had been activated in Turkey in the spring of 1962, mainly as a symbol of Turkey's importance in the NATO alliance. In the context of the Kennedy administration's overall arms build-up, its disclosure of US missile superiority, and Kennedy's acknowledgement in March 1962 that the feasibility of a first-strike strategy had been discussed, Khrushchev's decision can be seen as a reaction rather than as a provocation. He chose to install the missiles clandestinely because he was convinced that an advance public announcement would trigger the US invasion that the missiles were intended to deter (White 1997: 30–55).

The missiles' discovery

The Soviet decision to install the missiles secretly shaped the character of the Kennedy administration's response, since it entailed not simply concealment but defiance of US warnings and face-to-face lying. Ironically, Republican attacks on Kennedy over Cuba played a pivotal role in his uncovering of the Soviet plans and thus ultimately paved the way for his greatest foreign policy success. Led by Senator Kenneth Keating of New York, the Republicans reminded the electorate that Kennedy had complained about Eisenhower's inaction against Castro in 1960, but had failed to back the Bay of Pigs fighters. Now, they claimed, he was allowing the USSR to establish military bases in the Caribbean. Kennedy, urged also by new CIA chief John McCone, ordered U-2 spy plane flights over Cuba, which confirmed that the Soviets had surface-to-air missiles in place on August 29.

In response, Kennedy warned Khrushchev of "grave consequences" if he attempted to intervene in the Western hemisphere, a warning he reinforced on September 13 by declaring that the US would protect the security of its allies and itself in the region by whatever means necessary. The Soviet response was to insist that military assistance to Cuba was limited to defensive capabilities. Soviet ambassador to the US, Anatoly Dobrynin, gave these assurances with conviction because he was not informed of the decision to send nuclear weapons, but others, such as foreign minister Andrei Gromyko, simply lied. After October 16, however, they did so to an administration that, thanks to aerial photography, had proof that they were lying.

Kennedy had been in bed reading the *New York Times*, which carried a page one article headlined "Eisenhower Calls President Weak on Foreign Policy," when his National Security Advisor McGeorge Bundy knocked at his door. On learning that the latest reconnaissance showed medium-range nuclear missile sites under construction in Cuba, Kennedy's immediate response was to splutter, "He can't do this to me." To Bobby, he complained that Khrushchev had behaved like "an immoral gangster ... not as a person with a sense of responsibility." Like his brother, Bobby raged at the personal affront. Studying the photos in Bundy's office, he repeatedly smacked his fist into the palm of his hand in time with the repeated expletive, "Shit," occasionally varied by "Those Russian sons-of-bitches." The Kennedys' anger was shared by most of the Pentagon and national security team. Thus the immediate consensus was in favor of military action to eliminate the missiles. At his only public engagement of October 16, JFK read reporters a Hemingway-esque verse to sum up the burdens of his office and how their commentary rarely comprehended his dilemmas:

> Bullfight critics row on row
> Crowd the enormous plaza full
> But only one is there who knows
> And he is the one who fights the bull

(Dobbs 2009: 15)

Since the Bay of Pigs debacle, Kennedy had mistrusted the claims of both the CIA and the Chiefs of Staff, and so he noted now General Taylor's admission that any air strikes against the missiles were unlikely to be 100 percent effective. Urgency intensified his dilemma, since it was unclear whether the missiles in place were ready for launch. If they were not, swift action might destroy them, whereas delay would permit their completion. If they were ready, however, an attack might trigger their use with escalating, catastrophic consequences, culminating in full-scale nuclear war.

The pressure to attack

Kennedy declared himself mystified by Khrushchev's actions. Defense Secretary McNamara doubted that the Cuban missiles substantially affected the balance of power, but Kennedy saw their elimination as essential because the act was a provocation undertaken despite explicit US warnings. The Cold War was a political struggle in which image and perception were central. If Kennedy acquiesced in the missile deployment, confidence in his leadership would be damaged at home and abroad, while both Castro's and Khrushchev's prestige would be enhanced.

As discussions continued that evening, the symbolic implications of a surprise attack on Cuba reverberated. Bobby Kennedy passed a note to Ted Sorensen which read, "I now know how Tojo felt when he was planning Pearl Harbor." State Under Secretary George Ball opposed the proposed bombing with the same allusion to the Japanese 1941 sneak attack. In talks with Dean Acheson, Kennedy spoke of the proposed raid as a "Pearl Harbor in reverse," an analogy Acheson strongly rejected. But the likelihood that military action would be less than 100 percent effective, and that it would damage US standing in the eyes of the world, shifted the president's judgment towards a blockade, an idea that McNamara had suggested as a means of preventing the delivery of further arms and buying time for a diplomatic settlement. In the meantime, aerial photography might provide a better estimate of the missiles' readiness. Keeping his options open, Kennedy asked CIA Director McCone to make the case for immediate air strikes, while conferring with UN ambassador Adlai Stevenson who favored negotiations (Dallek 2003: 548–50).

Secrecy and the Ex-Comm

On October 18, Kennedy held a prearranged meeting with Soviet Foreign Minister Gromyko. He listened impassively while Gromyko read a prepared statement. Soviet arms shipments to Cuba "were only defensive." Gromyko said "he wanted to stress the word defensive." Kennedy resisted the temptation to show Gromyko the pictures of the missile sites that would have exposed the falseness of the Soviet claims. He did state with unusual deliberateness that the shipments had created "the most dangerous situation since the end of the war." In the background, Gromyko noticed that Secretary of State Rusk was red-faced, "like a crab," but this did not prevent him from reporting to Khrushchev that the general situation was "wholly satisfactory." For his own part, Kennedy had listened, he said, to "more bare-faced lies than I have ever heard in so short a time" (Dallek 2003: 553).

Kennedy had also decided that the best way to ensure that the crisis situation was not leaked prematurely was to limit discussion to a small executive committee of advisors (Ex-Comm). At the same time he was determined to keep to his schedule in order to convey an air of normality to the public. He therefore flew to the Midwest for campaign stops. Behind the scenes he was facing renewed pressure for military action. At a morning meeting he told the Joint Chiefs that an attack on Cuba would probably provoke Soviet action against Berlin. General Taylor responded that inaction would sacrifice American credibility globally and General Curtis LeMay was even more outspoken, declaring the proposed blockade and search for a diplomatic solution to be "as bad as the appeasement at Munich." It was a remark likely to rile Kennedy, given his father's damaging association with Neville Chamberlain's position in 1938, and he asked the general to repeat his comment. LeMay did, stressing his final reflection: "You're in a pretty bad fix." With a derisive laugh, Kennedy observed, "You're in there with me" (Dallek 2003: 555). Unaware of the tape-recording system Kennedy had installed, the other military top brass praised LeMay for his critical comments as soon as their commander-in-chief left the room.

Reflecting on their belief in the merits of a full-scale invasion of Cuba, Kennedy told Ken O'Donnell privately that the military Chiefs' big advantage was that if "we take their advice and it goes wrong, none of us will be alive later to tell them that they were wrong" (Dallek 2003: 556). But however much he wanted to avoid military action because it could escalate to nuclear war, Kennedy recognized that the blockade alone would not remove the offensive weapons that were already in Cuba.

Choosing the quarantine option

With the National Security Council (NSC) on the afternoon of October 20, Kennedy reviewed his options and concluded that the blockade (renamed a "quarantine") would be imposed, alongside a public demand for Moscow to remove the missiles and contingency plans for an air strike if Khrushchev did not comply. Already Kennedy was considering whether it would be necessary to trade; Jupiter missiles in Turkey and Italy could be sacrificed since they were already being superseded by submarine-based Polaris missiles. But his first priority was managing the domestic repercussions of the crisis.

On Monday October 22, Kennedy briefed NSC members on the importance of unity and confidentiality, and phoned past presidents Hoover, Truman, and Eisenhower to alert them. The State

Department was instructed to prepare messages to foreign heads of state, and close aides, especially Sorensen, worked on his televised address. Kennedy spent an hour with congressional leaders and found that they reacted much as he and others had in the first instance; they favored strong military action. Chair of the Senate Armed Services Committee Richard Russell regarded the blockade as too tepid. "We're either a great power or we're not," he said. Chair of the Senate Foreign Relations Committee William Fulbright favored an invasion of Cuba. A blockade would entail a direct confrontation with the USSR, whereas, he declared, "It is not an act of war against Russia to attack Cuba" (Dallek 2003: 557). Republican House Majority Leader Charles Halleck tried to distance his party from the president's actions. He asked pointedly that it be duly recorded that they were informed of the policy decision rather than consulted. Kennedy could only hope that patriotism would ensure their support in the days to come, and he planned to use his speech to the nation to rally popular support. An hour before he spoke, a letter was delivered to Ambassador Dobrynin, insisting that the missile bases and offensive weapons in Cuba be removed and warning of "catastrophic consequences" if war ensued (Dallek 2003: 558).

Over a hundred million Americans heard Kennedy's grave address, which starkly announced that the USSR had created a "nuclear strike capability" in Cuba. He noted that this contradicted repeated Soviet assurances that they would supply their ally only with defensive weapons. He announced the "quarantine" against ships carrying offensive weapons to Cuba to prevent further deployment, and called for the prompt withdrawal of existing weapons under UN supervision. Any missile launched from Cuba, he warned, would constitute "an attack by the Soviet Union" and the United States would retaliate in full. At the same time, the armed forces mobilized in a way that underlined the situation's gravity. Seven thousand marine reinforcements were sent to Guantanamo, an invasion command post was established in Florida, the First Armored Division moved from Texas to Georgia, and one hundred thousand soldiers in the army reserve were placed on full alert. To lessen the impact of any Soviet first strike against US fighters and bombers, an order was issued for them to disperse from their home bases (Giglio 2006: 217).

The crisis escalates

The following morning, the official Soviet news agency denounced Kennedy's breach of international law regarding freedom of navigation and his provocative action. At the United Nations, Adlai Stevenson presented the US case to the Security Council, hoping to build on the diplomatic momentum given by the Organization of American States' unanimous endorsement of Kennedy's demands and actions. The Soviets could veto any resolution offered, but the occasion offered Stevenson a chance to place them in the court of world opinion, which to JFK's surprise he duly did.

Within Ex-Comm, the main discussion was how to enforce the quarantine in a way that did not escalate into wholesale war. Complicating this aim was the resistance of the Navy to clearing their actions with Washington, which led to an angry clash between Admiral George Anderson and Defense Secretary McNamara. The Navy viewed the quarantine as a simple matter of intercepting Soviet vessels using whatever force was necessary, whereas its purpose for the administration was to show determination in a restrained way, and buy time for the Soviets to reconsider. To Anderson's fury, McNamara told him that no vessel was to fire without explicit authorization (Dobbs 2009: 69–72).

Despite their anger at Khrushchev's duplicity, the Kennedy brothers hoped that he would realize the dreadful risks inherent in a confrontation between nuclear superpowers. Bobby Kennedy met privately with Ambassador Dobrynin on the evening of October 23. In a somber exchange, he asked whether Dobrynin knew what instructions had been given to the Soviet vessels. As far as Dobrynin knew they had been told to resist illegal attempts to stop and search them. Gathering his coat to leave, a heavy-eyed Bobby replied, "I don't know how all this will end, but we intend to stop your ships"(Dobbs 2009: 72–73).

By this stage, Bobby's brother Jack was facing mind-numbing choices. Politically, he had to appear resolute and forceful in his demands that the USSR withdraw. The polls showed that Americans had rallied overwhelmingly behind him after his speech. But if he appeared to give way the Republicans would raise the charge that he was "soft on Communism," sweep the Congress in the midterms, and turf Kennedy out after a lackluster single term; making him the first single-term president since Herbert Hoover. He risked being branded a failure as president, a painful blow for such a competitive individual.

Kennedy had recently read Barbara Tuchman's *The Guns of August*, about the beginnings of World War I, and it had left him with a profound fear of being trapped politically in a cycle of escalation towards nuclear war. He had seen men die, and he himself had been on the brink of death several times, due to his recurrent illnesses. Unlike his generals he still saw death as personal, and in contemplating nuclear war he was drawn recurrently to the thought of children whose lives could be obliterated in such a conflict before they had a chance to grow into themselves. It was a thought that haunted him. If he and Khrushchev remained inflexibly committed to a show of strength the confrontation could easily escalate to a war of such immense destruction that it would make past wars, even the carnage of the Western Front or the two nuclear strikes on Japan, seem mere skirmishes. Watching his brother over the next few days, Bobby later recollected, "I felt we were on the edge of a precipice and it was as if there was no way off" (Dallek 2003: 561).

The brink

Fortunately, Khrushchev had also seen war firsthand, and realized the enormity of what nuclear war would mean in reality. On October 24, CIA director McCone reported to Ex-Comm that six Soviet ships inbound for Cuba had either stopped or reversed direction. Recalling a childhood game in which boys would stare at each other at close quarters with the loser being the one who blinked, Secretary Rusk said, "We're eyeball to eyeball, and the other fellow just blinked." The comment entered legend, although in reality Khrushchev had given orders for the change of course the previous day and it came into effect while the nearest Soviet vessels were hundreds of miles away from their potential American interceptors (Dobbs 2009: 86–89).

As the Cuban Missile Crisis unfolded, the greatest dangers grew out of the sheer scale of the operations involved and the myriad individuals whose actions could initiate a fateful escalation. At 10.00 a.m. (EST) the head of the Strategic Air Command, General Thomas Power, ordered his forces to DEFCON 2, a state of alert only one below actual warfare. Concerned that the USSR might respond to the quarantine with a first strike, Kennedy had authorized the move. This was symptomatic of the extraordinary mobilization that the Joint Chiefs were overseeing as the crisis unfolded. In their plans for an invasion of Cuba they concentrated on coordinating massive air strikes, amphibious landings, and paratroop assaults rather than the possibility that their invasion might confront substantial Soviet forces armed with tactical nuclear weapons. They worried about the effect of delay on their troops' morale and urged their commander-in-chief to act before the missile sites were completed.

Khrushchev's first letter

On Friday October 26, Kennedy was shown the latest low-level aerial photography of Cuba. Despite heavy rain, the Soviets were working frantically to complete the missile stations. More significantly, though, reconnaissance had spotted a mobile missile launcher, which, CIA Director McCone realized, raised the possibility that the Soviets had tactical nuclear weapons on the island. "Invading is going to be a much more serious undertaking than most people realize," he told Kennedy. "It's very evil stuff they've got there" (Dobbs 2009: 145–46).

Later that evening, as Kennedy was still pondering whether he would have to authorize an increasingly risky invasion, a message from Nikita Khrushchev arrived. In a long and emotional letter, he urged Kennedy to reconsider, because "if war should indeed break out, then it would not be in our power to stop it, for such is the logic of war." He invoked the appalling Soviet experience of World War II when he spoke of how "war ends when it has rolled through cities and villages, everywhere sowing death and destruction." Towards the end of his letter, Khrushchev compared the crisis to a knot on which both protagonists were pulling and warned that it could become too tight to unfasten. "Consequently, if there is no intention to tighten that knot and thereby doom the world to the catastrophe of thermonuclear war," he wrote, "then let us not only relax the forces pulling on the ends of the rope, let us take measures to untie the knot" (Dobbs 2009: 165).

The letter seemed to offer terms for a settlement. The United States needed to disavow publicly its intention of invading Cuba, and with that promise the Soviet Union would recall its armaments, specialists, and fleet. The offer was seemingly confirmed through a diplomatic back channel, whereby Washington KGB station chief Aleksandr Feklisov told ABC journalist John Scali that the missile bases would be dismantled and Castro would pledge not to accept offensive weapons in return for a US undertaking not to invade the island. But the proposal could have been a ruse designed to buy time while the missile bases were completed, and, as Kennedy confided to British premier Harold Macmillan that evening, he was facing hard choices about further actions to remove the missiles; the quarantine had simply interrupted the supply line (Dallek 2003: 566).

The second letter

Secretary Rusk believed that the Khrushchev letter and Feklisov proposal offered hope, but General Curtis LeMay was predictably dismissive. Even Kennedy declared, on the morning of October 27, that he did not want to become "impaled on a long negotiating hook" while the Cuban missiles became fully operational. Suspicion deepened when a second letter arrived from Moscow, this time demanding removal of the Jupiter missiles from Turkey as well as a noninvasion pledge, and stressing the UN as the diplomatic intermediary.

The new letter disturbed Kennedy because he felt that other nations would see the reciprocal missile withdrawal as "a not unreasonable proposal" (Dobbs 2009: 235). The letter unsettled National Security Advisor Bundy because it would alarm NATO allies by suggesting that in the end the US would trade theirinterests for its own. At the same time, Kennedy had always fretted that the Soviet initiative in Cuba was almost the same as a sacrifice move in chess: it would facilitate their actual objective of seizing Berlin. The USSR would either gain advantage by normalizing the Cuban missile deployment through protracted diplomacy at the UN or it would use an American invasion of Cuba to legitimize a Communist takeover of West Berlin.

Black Saturday: The peak of the crisis

October 27 was known in hindsight as "Black Saturday," the moment in the crisis when the two sides came closest to a nuclear exchange. The risks were revealed by the events of that day, which included the Soviet shooting down of a U-2 plane over Cuba, the tracking of another U-2 by Soviet fighters as it strayed into Soviet airspace while on a monitoring mission over the Arctic, and the receipt in Moscow of a letter from Cuban leader Fidel Castro that urged Khrushchev to preempt the impending US invasion of the island by launching a nuclear first strike. On learning of the missing U-2 over Siberia, Kennedy declared, "There's always some sonofabitch who doesn't get the word," a statement that summed up the perils of escalation due to miscalculation (Dobbs 2009: 270).

Predictably, the downing of a U-2 fueled the Joint Chiefs' demand for a full-scale attack, with mass bombing of Cuba on Monday October 29 in order to prepare the way for an invasion within seven days. News of the presence of tactical nuclear weapons had already prompted the Chiefs to ask for authority to use such weapons themselves. The risks extended to other nations, as the UK placed its nuclear weapons on a fifteen-minute alert alongside the far larger US missile arsenal in Europe, which was already primed under the terms of DEFCON 2.

Since General Issa Pliyev had been unavailable (a chronic gall-bladder condition obliged him to take rest breaks), the decision to shoot down the U-2 had been taken by one of his deputies, Lieutenant General Stephan Grechko. He did so in the context of a concerted mobilization of military forces in Cuba, ahead of what they believed to be an imminent US invasion. The plane's shooting down was greeted jubilantly by Cubans, who had begun to doubt their Soviet allies' resolve. Inevitably, the action increased the pressure on Kennedy to respond. In a conversation with ambassador Dobrynin, while indicating that his brother could remove the Turkish missiles in due course but would have to do so discreetly, Bobby Kennedy warned that time was running out. The president was under great pressure to attack, Bobby said. If the Cubans were shooting down US planes, the Americans "were going to shoot back." Chillingly, he added that Khrushchev needed to understand that "before this was over, while there might be dead Americans there would also be dead Russians" (Dallek 2003: 568–69).

Castro and Khrushchev

Castro was equally pessimistic about the future on Black Saturday. He took it for granted that the Americans would invade, and believed that the scale of US air power meant that they could wipe out the missiles rapidly in a surprise attack. Rather than the dishonor of American occupation, he was ready to die with his comrades in defense of his country, and he wanted the cost of his destruction to be as high as possible for the United States. Accordingly, in his message to Khrushchev he urged the use of nuclear weapons in such a way that it prevented "the imperialists" from carrying out "a first atomic strike against the USSR." In his opinion, "liquidating such a danger forever" was the only option. The salvation of the revolution might necessitate the destruction of Cuba and much of the rest of the world (Dobbs 2009: 204).

Staring into the abyss of nuclear war, Khrushchev told the Soviet Presidium that a tactical retreat was needed, a reality that Dobrynin's report on his meeting with Bobby Kennedy underlined. Khrushchev drafted a letter to be read on Moscow radio, indicating the withdrawal of Soviet missiles in return for a US noninvasion pledge. He also sent a secret communication accepting and promising to keep confidential the agreed removal of the Turkish missiles. While the civilian members of Ex-Comm greeted the Soviet announcement on Sunday with huge relief, the Joint Chiefs saw it as one more trick and recommended that, unless there was irrefutable evidence that the Soviets were removing the missiles, the air strikes should go ahead on Monday with the full-scale invasion to follow.

Defense Secretary McNamara remembered Kennedy as being stunned by their response. Nevertheless, he insisted that he would retain the quarantine until it was certain that Khrushchev had honored his word. To the military officials, who had physically and mentally prepared themselves for a massive attack and invasion, possibly a global nuclear war, it seemed like a monstrous climbdown. While a broader public would praise the president for his restraint during the crisis, there remained those in the military and in the Cuban-American refugee community who doubted his courage and his word from this point onwards.

The crisis recedes

The details of the agreement resolving the crisis were not easy to agree. It was not until November 20 that Kennedy felt able to announce that "all known offensive missile sites in Cuba have been dismantled." He was pleased the crisis had ended peacefully, and hoped that "other outstanding problems" might be open to solution in its wake. To the dismay of Khrushchev and Castro, the American noninvasion pledge was circumscribed, since it was contingent on a US judgment that Cuba was not fomenting Communist insurrection in the Western hemisphere and that Soviet military operations on the island remained minimal. Less publicly, Kennedy's eagerness to see Castro removed was undiminished, although he no longer believed that an invasion of Cuba was viable, no matter what the military said. The removal of Jupiter missiles from Turkey occurred quietly, months later, and was not publicly linked to the settlement of the crisis.

Assessment of JFK's conduct

The genuine possibility of nuclear war had created a profound sense of fear in America and Europe, and in varying degrees around the world. Kennedy therefore profited from the feelings of relief experienced as the confrontation diminished, and in the US especially he was hailed in the press for his masterful leadership. *Newsweek* declared that Americans now had "a sense of deep confidence in their president and the team he had working with him" (Dallek 2003: 575). Insiders like veteran diplomats Dean Acheson and Averell Harriman were quoted elsewhere praising his calmness, resolution, and skill. Later accounts of the crisis, even those that acknowledge that Kennedy's actions towards Cuba helped to precipitate it, tend to acknowledge that he deserves credit for resisting the formidable pressures for military action which could have so easily escalated into a nuclear war.

Kennedy's management of the Missile Crisis remains at the center of any claim made for his greatness as a president. Whereas Washington and Lincoln's heroic status is rooted in their military victories that founded and sustained the American republic, and Franklin Roosevelt's is similarly derived from his leadership of the nation through the acute economic hardship of the Depression years and the trials of World War II, Kennedy's claim to stand within the pantheon rests on his decision not to accept the urgings of his military chiefs to launch bombing raids on Cuba and then invade. He is to be celebrated for what he chose not to do.

The transcripts of the taped Ex-Comm meetings confirm that, while some of his advisors showed strong signs of wilting under the pressure of the thirteen-day crisis, Kennedy himself retained his composure. Yet there is considerable disagreement over the merits of the model he set in his management of the crisis. In particular, critics feel that standard accounts have accepted too readily the idea that Kennedy won through his toughness and self-discipline, being prepared to go to the brink of nuclear war in order to force the USSR to back down. If one gives credence to Khrushchev's claims that his purpose was to protect Cuba from Kennedy's planned invasion and to induce the Americans to reconsider their recent deployment of missiles in Turkey, it needs to be noted that both of these objectives were achieved.

Similarly, Ex-Comm discussions confirm that Kennedy's unwillingness to proceed with military action came primarily from a fear that it could not be as effective as it needed to be, rather than because he was opposed to military action per se. His skepticism towards the military had certainly been boosted by their performances in recent crises. He had learned from their efforts to bounce him into a larger conflict during the Bay of Pigs, and from similar demands for escalation in both Berlin and Laos. He had also been shocked by the gap between their claims and their actual capabilities, most recently in their failure to deliver troops during the Meredith episode in Mississippi.

Kennedy's need to ensure the removal of the Cuban missiles was intrinsically political. He would be damaged politically if he allowed the deployment to occur. The damage would be principally in terms of the advantage such an outcome gave his domestic Republican opponents, but within the zero-sum mindset of the

Cold War it was largely accepted that anything that worked to the advantage of the Communist bloc had to detract from the strength of the West. European allies would fret about irresolute American leadership. Third World countries would perceive the USSR as a more assiduous protector of its allies, and Khrushchev himself would be emboldened to act more forcefully elsewhere, probably, Kennedy felt, in Berlin.

Accordingly, the outcomes for Kennedy were primarily political and they rested on the combined perception that he had been resolute and that Khrushchev had retreated without gaining anything. To preserve this perception, Kennedy insisted on concealing the reality of the reciprocal withdrawal of missiles from Turkey and left his noninvasion pledge of Cuba as vague as possible. More damningly, he allowed later press coverage to present Adlai Stevenson's willingness to pursue diplomacy, including precisely this type of bargaining, as weak and tantamount to appeasement. Stevenson came to represent the limp liberal position that surrendered rather than fought, whereas Kennedy symbolized the tough, calculating position that won through its determination and courage. The symbolism obscured the reality that Stevenson's initial proposal to consider a trade-off was in key respects central to the final settlement. Kennedy's harshest critics would stress that his actions towards Cuba were integral to the crisis, since they gave Castro and Khrushchev ample reason to believe that a US invasion was imminent in 1962. Critics would also see his public, media-focused ultimatum to the USSR as a high-risk propaganda exercise. In their view, Khrushchev's willingness to retreat when it became clear that the crisis could easily get out of control was the real act of courage. Kennedy's defenders, however, would point to the provocative nature of Khrushchev's secret deployment within a larger pattern of impetuous behavior. In their view he misjudged Kennedy and felt that he could present him with a fait accompli. Such a victory would have secured Khrushchev's position at home, where the failing economy was a concern, and abroad, where China was asserting its own leadership claims, as demonstrated by its aggressive actions on the Indian border in October 1962.

In the aftermath of the crisis, US–Soviet relations have been held to improve, with both leaders chastened by the threat of nuclear war that they had faced. Thus, later diplomatic successes such as the nuclear test ban treaty have their origins in the Missile Crisis. At the same time, there are scholars who use Kennedy's conduct during the Missile Crisis, especially his resistance to the military, as proof that he was maturing as a statesman, and who argue that this suggests Kennedy would have followed a markedly different path in Vietnam, where Lyndon Johnson largely accepted the advice of the Pentagon and escalated American involvement. Thus the Missile Crisis has been the lynchpin of Kennedy's reputation.

6   The scale of change

Birmingham, the test ban,
and Vietnam

For scholars who wish to stress the way in which JFK grew in office, the Cuban Missile Crisis is a key milestone. It marks his maturity. But the actual scale of change is debatable, since the October 1962 crisis did not change many things. First and foremost, the defusing of the immediate crisis could not in itself eliminate the profound mistrust of the USSR that the episode fueled on the American side. Consequently, for much of the next nine months there was pressure on Kennedy to ensure that the terms of the agreement over Cuba, specifically the removal of offensive weapons, were met. The crisis had also erupted in the immediate run-up to the midterm congressional elections and Kennedy had worried that any weakness or failing on his part would be punished with Republican gains.

Given the narrowness of his own victory in 1960 and the general tendency of the ruling party to lose seats in the midterms, Kennedy genuinely feared a Republican resurgence that would jeopardize his reelection hopes. Thus he had to appear a resolute Cold Warrior. In the event, the party balance remained the same. Republicans gained two seats in the House, and the Democrats four in the Senate, including Edward Kennedy from Massachusetts. Pollster Lou Harris reported privately that local issues had been the main factor determining outcomes, rather than the international crisis, but the perception was that Kennedy had helped his party.

The successfully managed crisis had seen a significant bounce in the president's personal popularity—up 12 points to 74 percent—but Harris warned Kennedy that behind the reassuring Congressional results were some worrying trends. Many Catholic and Jewish voters who had turned out for JFK in 1960 were disillusioned. There was a marked tendency for ethnic Catholics to vote Republican the longer they lived in suburbia. This was especially the case over the race issue, with most ethnic Catholics in the industrial states as unsympathetic to civil rights reform as white Southerners. While Kennedy's November 20, 1962 executive order integrating federally supported housing was the belated fulfillment of his 1960 electoral promise to African Americans, it was also a source of further mistrust among socially conservative, white Democrats. For many in the white working class, African American gains in relation to housing, employment, education, even political influence, seemed to come directly at their expense. Their hard-won homes lost value. Their prospects of employment or advancement became less certain. Their children's schools faced more challenges, and their political voices appeared to be drowned out by minority demands.

Reelection plans

Kennedy had enjoyed the spectacle of Richard Nixon's defeat to Pat Brown in the governor's race in California, which effectively ended the possibility of a rematch with Nixon in 1964. Nixon's decline, however, only strengthened the position of liberal Republican Nelson Rockefeller, who had comfortably secured re-election as governor of New York, with some African American support. If Kennedy's record was deemed weak by northern liberals and African Americans, Rockefeller might profit. Nixon's fate had also stemmed partly from his right-wing critics within the California Republican Party, and these conservative activists would press hard for Barry Goldwater as the Republican nominee in 1964. If Kennedy's support for liberal causes such as civil rights alienated white Southerners, Goldwater could also be a significant challenger. Despite the praise given to Kennedy after the Missile Crisis, he was shrewd enough to sense that he needed to do more to strengthen his position ahead of the 1964 race. In most cases, this limited his willingness to adopt liberal policies.

Ideally, Kennedy wanted to approach reelection with a buoyant economy, a strong record on national security, and a greater degree of racial calm at home than had been evident in his first two years in office. Thus, at the end of 1962 Kennedy was determined to secure tax reform in order to grow the economy in a way that would ensure a contrast with the recession he had inherited from Eisenhower. The main opposition to this would come from conservative forces within both parties, who believed firmly in a balanced budget and so would not countenance tax cuts before the deficit had been eliminated. To win support, Kennedy couched his proposal in Cold War terms. A growing economy was a vital facet of national security, he argued, because only this kind of prosperity would support the war with Communism, not just in terms of military expenditure but also in terms of the battle to show which system was the more productive. In his 1963 State of the Union address, JFK warned that "our obsolete tax system exerts too heavy a drag on private purchasing power, profits and employment" (Dallek 2003: 585). By cutting rates, he argued, the economy would grow in a way that eliminated temporary deficits in the medium term. Kennedy may have swayed a few who were open to persuasion, but in Congress many key Committee chairmen remained hostile on economic policy, and their hostility deepened in reaction to his civil rights policy.

At the end of 1962, Kennedy gave an influential interview to TV newsmen. In a wide-ranging conversation, he demonstrated his command of his office. He showed a detailed knowledge of key issues and offered a generally sanguine assessment of possibilities and risks. He recognized that Congress remained reluctant to approve federal aid to education, even though the baby boom and the technological revolution had generated pressures on educational budgets that individual states struggled to meet. He also conceded that perhaps the chief lesson of his first two years had been recognition of the limits of American power globally and the president's power domestically. Congress seemed more powerful when viewed from the Oval Office than it had when he was in its ranks.

He gave no indication that the successful outcome of the Missile Crisis had opened up a new era of détente. Instead he stressed the continuing commitment of Communists, perhaps more militantly expressed by the Chinese than the Soviets, to the goal of establishing their totalitarian system around the world. While he hoped that the risk of nuclear war, evident in the recent crisis, had tempered the Soviets' outlook, it had not changed their aims. With increasing support from its prosperous European allies, it was hoped, the United States would continue to oppose and contain the Communist threat in areas of vital interest. Kennedy's message remained couched in the orthodox terms of containment policy, insisting that vigilance and determination had to be maintained because of the continuing threat. He ended the interview by asking Americans to take pride in their country's fight for freedom.

Civil rights

1963 would see continuing celebrations of the centennial of the Civil War, notably the Emancipation Proclamation, and for Kennedy this meant evading the pressures to further the freedom struggle that African Americans still waged. Civil rights leaders had come to realize, over the previous two years, that the Kennedy administration could be forced off the fence by protests that exposed the violence inherent in Southern segregation, but that the president would always seek to placate the white South because of its entrenched position within Congress. Episodes like the Freedom Rides and the integration of the University of Mississippi had shown that the threat of violence and disorder triggered greater federal support than did pressure via institutional channels. The direct action protest groups seemed to get Kennedy's attention more decidedly than did legalistic lobby groups like the National Association for the Advancement of Colored People (NAACP).

Since all the civil rights groups relied upon donations to operate, they needed to act in a way that gained public attention. The Kennedys had hoped that the Voter Education Project, which shared out foundation grants to support registration efforts, might redirect the movement in a way that avoided embarrassing public confrontations. However the most militant groups, such as the Student Nonviolent Coordinating Committee (SNCC) and the Congress of Racial Equality (CORE), which had been at the vanguard of the Freedom Rides into Mississippi in 1961, had chosen to concentrate their registration efforts in the Deep South, where white resistance was fiercest and most prone to resort to violence.

By early 1963 these militants were complaining that they had focused on voter registration because Bobby Kennedy had said that they would receive federal protection, but instead they faced daily intimidation and violence. Phone calls to the Justice Department had some mitigating effect, but this seemed meager compared to the actions of Kennedy-appointed federal judges like Archibald Cox in Mississippi, who labeled civil rights workers "monkeys" before consigning them to jail, or of white Delta, Democratic politicians who cut off food relief to laid-off agricultural workers in the winter of 1962 in a clear attempt to intimidate.

The Birmingham protests

Disappointment in Kennedy's leadership was also evident in the comments of Martin Luther King, who had spent most of the previous two years vainly urging Kennedy to issue a second Emancipation Proclamation ordering desegregation. King's pre-eminence as the public face of the civil rights movement had been damaged by an unsuccessful effort to secure desegregation in the southwest Georgia town of Albany in 1962. To demonstrate that his nonviolent protest tactics were still effective, King was planning to target the much larger and more volatile Alabama industrial center of Birmingham for a mass protest campaign in 1963.

From Kennedy's perspective, this was politically dangerous. It was likely to produce media images that damaged America internationally. It gave the Communists an easy propaganda victory and prompted Western Europeans to criticize America and resist its leadership claims. Domestically, it polarized public opinion in the South, enabling demagogic politicians like Alabama Governor George Wallace to come to the fore. The powerful Southern congressional bloc which had proved such an obstacle to Kennedy's legislative program was likely to be even more resistant if the president was perceived to be backing civil rights militancy. The tax cut that Kennedy saw as crucial to the economy was likely to be blocked. Consequently, it was fairly straightforward for FBI Director J. Edgar Hoover to persuade Bobby Kennedy to approve illegal wiretaps on Martin Luther King and his associates on the grounds that King was acting under the influence of known Communists, a claim that centered on the past activities of King's

New York-based white advisor Stanley Levison. At the start of 1963, the Kennedys saw King and the movement as at best a nuisance and at worst an adversary rather than an ally.

The well-known brutality of Birmingham's Police Commissioner "Bull" Connor, as demonstrated by his collusion in the Klan attack on the Freedom Riders in Birmingham in May 1961, was one reason why King chose Birmingham for his next campaign. However, the negative publicity generated by that incident had prompted local white civic leaders to change the Alabama steel town's system of government. Connor had failed to win the mayoral election against his more moderate segregationist opponent Albert Boutwell in early 1963, but he and his fellow commissioners then sued to be allowed to complete their terms of office. Hence, when King launched his protests, Birmingham, as one local man declared, had a mayor, a council, a commissioner, a King, and a parade every day. The stalled and confused political situation provided grounds for Bobby Kennedy and others to complain that King's action was ill timed and inflammatory.

On Good Friday, April 12, 1963, Martin Luther King led protesters downtown and was arrested by Birmingham police. This generated publicity for his faltering campaign. Kennedy's phone call to Mrs. King during the 1960 campaign had set a precedent, which inevitably caused the media to watch closely how he would react to the latest arrest. He asked Burke Marshall, an assistant within Bobby's Justice Department, if there was anything he could do to help King now, and was told that there was no case for federal involvement. Nevertheless, both Jack and Bobby took an active interest in King's condition. When Coretta King told her husband that the president had phoned her, King remarked: "So that's why everybody is suddenly being so polite" (Bryant 2006: 383–84).

On April 20, white civil rights protester William Moore was found murdered in Gadsden, not far from Birmingham. Without even being asked, President Kennedy mentioned the murder at his next press conference, stressing that, apart from FBI assistance, there was little the federal government could do. King was released the same day and, fearful that other events might draw media attention away from his Birmingham campaign, he accepted colleagues' recommendations that he increase the scale of demonstrations by using the many schoolchildren, some as young as six, who were eager to participate. On Thursday May 2, code-named "D-Day" by King's lieutenants, hundreds of children left the Sixteenth Street Baptist Church and confronted Connor's police in nearby Kelly Ingram Park. Nearly a thousand were arrested. With jails almost full, Connor decided the next day to use water cannon and attack dogs to disperse demonstrators rather than arrest them.

Pictures of the children being bitten or battered by high-velocity water jets appeared in Saturday's newspapers. The *New York Times* called it a "national disgrace." Talking to a delegation from the liberal group Americans for Democratic Action, Kennedy spoke of the "terrible picture in the paper." His comments reflected his uncertainty, flipping from a confident assertion that a bill to pro-tect voting rights would pass this year to a bleaker assessment of the reactionary forces he faced in Congress, which had blocked all of his boldest proposals. Towards the end of the meeting, Kennedy spoke of how the depth of the current crisis reflected dangerous divisions inside the civil rights movement, with groups competing for publicity. The racial situation also threatened many other facets of his program, including his efforts "to prevent this econ-omy from going down again" (Bryant 2006: 388). When a delegate suggested that he address the nation, Kennedy was unenthusiastic. Unsure of his legislative prospects, his main reaction was to step up efforts to get the local parties in Birmingham talking.

Burke Marshall was dispatched to Birmingham to broker a deal between the protest movement and moderate business leaders, who realized that the negative publicity was deeply harmful to the downtown economy. Already stores in the area faced heavy losses, as African Americans boycotted them and white consumers stayed away out of fear that they would get caught up in the violence. Kennedy asked Cabinet members to phone influential business-men with links to the major employers in the area in order to increase the pressure on whites to settle. On Tuesday evening, May 7, Marshall phoned the White House to report that the white Senior Citizens Committee had agreed to negotiate as long as it was not directly with King. At the beginning of his weekly news conference the next day, Kennedy announced that a settlement was imminent and urged "that all bars to equal opportunity and treatment" in America "be removed as promptly as possible" (Bryant 2006: 390).

The Birmingham accord was a fragile one, threatened especially by the anger of hardline segregationists. A local judge nearly torpedoed it by imprisoning King, forcing Bobby Kennedy to raise $5,000 in bail to release him. The even larger sum of $250,000 had to be raised to secure the release of imprisoned schoolchildren. Bobby secured most of this from organized labor, although Nelson Rockefeller dipped into his considerable personal fortune to provide King with a timely donation. On May 11, white terrorists exploded bombs outside the home of King's brother and beneath the hotel room at the Gaston Motel where King had been staying. Angry crowds of local African Americans came onto the streets and rampaged across a twenty-eight block area, torching cars and stores and clashing with police in a scene that foreshadowed the racial disturbances that would shake American cities for most of the decade. Local law enforcement agencies did not regain control until 4.30 a.m., a situation that prompted an Oval Office crisis meeting involving not just Justice Department officials but the defense secretary and army chiefs. Their fear was that African American retaliatory violence in Birmingham would spread to ghettos across the country.

A reluctant leader on civil rights

JFK was persuaded by his staff, especially his brother Bobby, who grasped the moral imperative more fully, that contingency plans that saw troops moved to bases close to Birmingham had to be accompanied by fresh legislative proposals dealing with African American grievances, in order to show that the federal government was working to address them. Over the next week, angry protests in cities as far apart as Jackson, Mississippi, Cambridge, Maryland, and Syracuse, New York confirmed that a new militancy had swept the African American community nationwide.

In his largely critical history of Kennedy's handling of the civil rights question, Nick Bryant underscores the contrast between JFK's demeanor during the Ex-Comm meetings of October 1962 and during the racial crisis meetings of May 1963. In the Missile

Crisis, Kennedy was cool and clearheaded but in the May meetings he was agitated and muddled. During a May 20 meeting, JFK responded to a discussion of the likelihood of increased disorder in the summer by proposing an attempt to legislate a curb on the right to protest. Appalled by this threat to civil liberties, Burke Marshall explained how it would make matters worse. Other Justice Department officials explained how the administration's current civil rights bill, focused on voting rights, would need to be expanded to address desegregation questions. In Bryant's view, "Kennedy's legendary grace under pressure gave way to near panic." In racial matters, JFK was inclined to vacillate and lurch to the right. He relied heavily on Bobby Kennedy and Burke Marshall to guide him (Bryant 2006: 402).

As if to underline this faltering performance, Lyndon Johnson (whose few recorded, bellicose comments during the Missile Crisis have served for some historians as proof of Kennedy's superiority) was quick to realize that a bold civil rights bill was needed, and that the president needed to take a moral stand to galvanize the country and then press Congress into action. On June 1, Johnson, who had won plaudits for an eloquent call for action in a speech at a commemorative event at Gettysburg the previous day, told Kennedy that once his bill was presented he must fight for it relentlessly. It was not the message that Kennedy wanted to hear since he knew that a protracted struggle for a comprehensive civil rights bill would spill into the election year and diminish his popularity. Although persuaded that a bill was unavoidable, he was more intent on restoring order than securing justice. In background briefings, officials spoke of measures as safety valves intended to reduce anger in the black community.

The Justice Department announced that it was targeting Jefferson County (where Birmingham was located) for voting rights litigation and was pressing for public schools to reopen in Prince Edward County, Virginia, where they had been closed since 1959. The Defense Department ordered base commanders to boycott nearby communities that practiced racial discrimination, a significant step given the number of military bases in the South and their economic value to local businesses.

The Pentagon also eliminated segregation in reserve units and began negotiations on the desegregation of National Guard units, thereby completing the military desegregation first ordered by President Truman in 1948. A concerted effort was made to increase the number of African Americans employed by the federal government, against a backdrop of high and persistent joblessness. Labor Secretary Willard Wirtz warned that there could be no quick fix to this problem, given the potent mix of prejudice, poor education, and the loss of unskilled jobs to automation.

A series of White House meetings during June showed that Kennedy wanted to do as much as he possibly could by voluntary means. He urged political leaders across the country to set up biracial councils to discuss community affairs. He asked labor leaders to sponsor apprenticeships and job referral programs, and business leaders to desegregate their businesses voluntarily, ahead of any legislation. He told religious leaders to "recognize the conflict between racial bigotry and the Holy Word" and to preach a gospel of social harmony. He invited lawyers and teachers, too, to play a role in fostering peaceful solutions to racial problems. Most of the meetings were off the record with few details disclosed to the press. They were not aimed at fostering support for legislation but at mobilizing informal networks to mitigate racial discrimination and thereby defuse the explosive racial situation. "Our concern," Kennedy declared, "is that we do not have a battle in the streets of America in the coming months" (Bryant 2006: 415–16).

Kennedy's quest for calm placed him at odds with segregationist politicians like George Wallace, who needed to demonstrate to their followers a willingness to resist court-ordered desegregation. It also placed him in opposition to civil rights leaders like Martin Luther King, who believed in "creative tension": crises that forced the nation to reassess its acceptance of injustice by driving up the cost of maintaining the status quo. On June 2, Governor Wallace renewed his pledge to defy a federal court's order that two African American students be admitted to the University of Alabama at Tuscaloosa. The previous day, wiretaps had recorded King speaking to Stanley Levison about his renewed confidence in the weapon of "mass demonstration." His interest in labor leader A. Philip Randolph's proposed March for Jobs and Freedom in Washington was growing. Even the threat of the March, which Randolph had used against Franklin Roosevelt to press for African American employment in the booming defense industries of 1941,

Plate 1 President Dwight D. Eisenhower and President-elect John F. Kennedy
stand before reporters, December 6, 1960
Photo: Abbie Rowe. White House Photographs. John F. Kennedy
Presidential Library and Museum, Boston

Plate 2 Dinner at Mount Vernon in honor of Muhammad Ayub Khan, president of Pakistan, July 11, 1960
Photo: Abbie Rowe. White House Photographs. John F. Kennedy Presidential Library and Museum, Boston

Plate 3 President John F. Kennedy with Attorney General Robert F. Kennedy, October 3, 1962
Photo: Cecil Stoughton. White House Photographs. John F. Kennedy Presidential Library and Museum, Boston

Plate 4 President John F. Kennedy and First Lady Jacqueline Kennedy greet
Cuban Invasion brigade members, December 29, 1962
Photo: Cecil Stoughton. White House Photographs. John F. Kennedy
Presidential Library and Museum, Boston

Plate 5 The Reverend Thich Quang Duc, a 73-year-old Buddhist monk, is soaked in petrol before setting fire to himself and burning to death in front of thousands of onlookers at a main highway intersection in Saigon, Vietnam, June 11, 1963
Photo: AP-PHOTO/MALCOLM BROWNE

Plate 6 President John F. Kennedy speaks in Rudolph Wilde Platz, June 26, 1963
Photo: Robert Knudsen. White House Photographs. John F. Kennedy Presidential Library and Museum, Boston

Plate 7 President John F. Kennedy and his son, John Junior, 1963
Photo: AP-PHOTO/LOOK MAGAZINE

Plate 8 President John F. Kennedy and First Lady Jacqueline Kennedy arrive in Dallas, November 22, 1963
Photo: Cecil Stoughton. White House Photographs. John F. Kennedy Presidential Library and Museum, Boston

might work again. Kennedy might be so frightened, "he would have to do something" (Bryant 2006: 404).

To neutralize Wallace, the Justice Department lobbied leaders in different areas of Alabama life about the need for law and order and the social, political, and economic costs of disorder. It also secured an injunction circumscribing Wallace's actions in relation to the proposed admission of the students. The governor knew by June 4 that if he did more than stand symbolically in the door, he risked imprisonment. Trying to control the situation, Wallace stationed state troopers around the campus perimeter to keep his hotheaded supporters away. On June 11, Assistant Attorney General Nicholas Katzenbach ensured that the students were safe, and that federal reinforcements were nearby. After an initial, slightly comic encounter between the six-foot-two-inch lawyer and the five-foot-seven-inch Wallace, the Alabama National Guard was federalized and, in response to a direct order from its commander, Wallace stepped aside.

JFK's civil rights address

This successful outcome encouraged Kennedy, who decided to take up his advisors' suggestion that he address the nation. It had been a good couple of days. His "Peace" speech at the American University the previous day had earned favorable press comment and plaudits from Moscow, rather than right-wing denunciations at home. With Sorensen's words to help him, Kennedy may have believed that he could persuade all but the most embittered that racial equality was the fulfillment of America's promise, not the beginning of its decline. By doing so, he might also persuade African Americans to trust him and to refrain from street protests.

When he faced the cameras from his Oval Office desk, however, he held a jumble of hastily typed pages with handwritten revisions. Quickly recounting the day's events in Alabama, he began to make the case for racial reform, moving readily from the centrality of freedom and equality in the nation's founding documents to the contemporary need for America to embody those values before a Cold War audience. The moral case was underlined by the Golden Rule: that one should treat others as one would wish to be treated.

At the heart of the speech was a stark passage explaining how the spiraling racial crisis required a legislative remedy. "The fires of frustration and discord are burning in every city, North and South. Where legal remedies are not at hand," Kennedy said, "redress is sought in the streets, in demonstrations, parades, and protests which create tensions and threaten violence and threaten lives." Legislation was required to remove these tensions, which Kennedy did not regard as creative. His obligation, he declared, was "to make that revolution, that change, peaceful and constructive for all." Having criticized JFK only days earlier for timidity, Martin Luther King praised his eloquence now, as did other civil rights leaders. But senior white Southerners were unmoved. Senator Richard Russell of Georgia said federal regulation of public accommodations was a step towards Communism and added that only the weak-kneed would bow to the president's implicit threat that if the law did not pass, the black community would revolt (Bryant 2006: 422–24).

A harsher measure of the gulf between the president and the segregationists came a few hours later, when the NAACP's Mississippi leader Medgar Evers was assassinated as he placed the key in his front door. Kennedy was informed at breakfast the next day. His dismay at this murderous response grew when House Majority Leader Carl Albert reported that a southern Democratic revolt had blocked the refunding of the Area Redevelopment Administration, which previously had enjoyed comfortable support. "It's overwhelming the whole program," Albert warned (Bryant 2006: 425). A shaken president agreed. New demonstrations in thirty-nine cities, some involving interracial battles, underscored the reality that a single speech could not heal the nation.

On Tuesday June 19, 3,000 mourners in Jackson, Mississippi attended Evers' funeral, with the NAACP's Roy Wilkins reluctantly sharing the spotlight with Martin Luther King, who had enraged Wilkins by announcing a fundraising initiative for the Medgar Evers Memorial Fund. Neither leader was on hand after the service to assist white Justice Department official John Doar in pleading with angry black teenagers to disperse when they started to pelt police with rocks and shout "We want the killer!" Evers, a veteran, was buried with full honors at Arlington National Cemetery the next day. JFK invited the Evers' family to the White House in a show of sympathy, but he worried about the tense mood of the nation (Bryant 2006: 424–27).

On the same day Kennedy sent Congress his civil rights bill. It covered many issues: greater federal oversight of voter registration and the abolition of literacy tests; desegregation of public accommodations such as hotels, lunch counters, and amusement facilities; enhanced litigation power in school desegregation cases; a Community Relations Service to moderate racial disputes; a four-year extension of the investigative Civil Rights Commission; and more power to require nondiscrimination from federal contractors and recipients of federal aid. Overall, Ted Sorensen remarked, the bill was the minimum they could request and the most they could stand behind. Predictably, Deep South politicians characterized the bill as a "blueprint for the totalitarian state," and a crime against liberty (Bryant 2006: 428).

Kennedy had expected this response, but criticisms from civil rights leaders mystified him. On July 28, the main movement organizations issued a statement highlighting the bill's inadequacies, especially its failure to ensure federal protection for civil rights workers in the face of police brutality and vigilante violence. Kennedy had tried to persuade them to exercise restraint, hosting thirty of the leadership, including King, at a White House meeting on June 22.

King had been asked to arrive earlier than the others so that a succession of officials, including Kennedy himself, could press him to break off his relationship with both Stanley Levison and an employee in King's New York-based fundraising office, Jack O'Dell. If the press learned of the two men's Communist links, not only King but the whole cause would be discredited. Referring to the Profumo sex scandal that was threatening to bring down Macmillan's government in England, Kennedy said that Macmillan's loyalty to his friend John Profumo might destroy him. King had to sever ties, he insisted. King replied that he would like to see proof of the allegations. When press reports surfaced a week later, he fired O'Dell and stopped communicating with Levison directly, partly at Levison's insistence.

At the general meeting with the civil rights leadership, Kennedy argued that the overriding priority had to be securing the bill's passage. It faced an uphill battle, he said, reflected in the fact that his own popularity had fallen to 47 percent. "I may lose the next election because of this," he declared, but he claimed that he was determined to fight for the support of roughly 38 moderate senators who could determine the outcome by ending Southern efforts to filibuster. Ensuring that these moderates voted to end debate and pass the bill, in Kennedy's view, required the cancelation or postponement of the March on Washington. "We want success in the Congress, not a big show on the Capitol," was how JFK put it, underlining his suspicion that some civil rights leaders seemed to put their organizational interests ahead of the wider movement's objectives. Moderates would react to a mass demonstration as a form of intimidation and say, "Yes, I'm for the bill—but not at the point of a gun" (Bryant 2006: 432). Lyndon Johnson echoed this point by saying that a protest aimed at the Congress would enrage rather than persuade.

The civil rights leaders did not accept Kennedy's recommendation. They argued that the anger in their community was so great that if it were not channeled constructively into a nonviolent demonstration it would find expression in disorder. Martin Luther King said he had always been told that his protests were ill timed: "Some people thought Birmingham was ill timed." "Including the attorney general," joked JFK, with a glance at his stern-faced brother. At the same meeting Kennedy had startled his guests by remarking that they should not be so hard on Bull Connor, since he had "probably done more for civil rights than anyone else" (Bryant 2006: 432). While this is usually seen as an example of Kennedy's dry wit and his ability to see the irony of unintended consequences, it was also part of his argument against the March. If the African American leaders engaged in militant public action to placate their own supporters at the risk of alienating the moderates, in Kennedy's view they risked being like Bull Connor, with their actions strengthening rather than weakening their opponents.

The leaders did agree to shift the focus of the March from Capitol Hill to the Lincoln Memorial, but they were determined to reassert their leadership through a spectacular public event. The best Kennedy could hope for was that they would be able to keep the demonstration peaceful, in a Washington that in 1963 remained a largely Southern, segregated city. Once the black leaders had departed, Kennedy resumed preparations for a four-country European tour that might incidentally help his goal of dampening the racial situation at home, if only by taking so many of the press corps elsewhere. One of his stops would be Berlin, where he would underline the US commitment to the beleaguered city; others would include Italy and Ireland, places where he could be pictured in ways that reminded ethnic Catholic voters back home that he was their president in particular.

The March on Washington

In the weeks before the March, the Kennedy administration continued to urge calm, but it also took steps to reassure Southern whites that it was not unequivocally committed to African Americans. The Justice Department decision to prosecute nine protesters in Albany, Georgia was the most controversial instance of this balancing act. The Albany Nine had picketed the store of a white man who had been a juror in a court case that saw the acquittal of a notoriously racist and brutal local police officer. Bobby Kennedy decided that federal charges of "retaliation against a juror" would proceed. When this was announced on August 10, wiretaps captured the shock and anger of Martin Luther King, who felt "they [had] really overstepped political and moral boundaries" and who promised to bring "pressures ... from everywhere" unless the decision was reversed (Bryant 2006: 435).

Most of the defendants had links to the SNCC, and its leader, future Congressman John Lewis, was set to give a speech at the March reflecting his group's fury. Many SNCC members had experienced police brutality only to be told that the federal government had no power to prosecute, and now they saw the Justice Department indict civil rights demonstrators for a peaceful protest. Thus the Kennedy administration made it harder for moderates to keep control of the tone of the Washington event.

Chief planner Bayard Rustin had orchestrated the March so that it was no longer a challenging exercise in nonviolent direct action but a strongly biracial and ecumenical mass rally. When Washington's Catholic Archbishop Patrick O'Boyle read an advance copy of Lewis's angry address, which described the Kennedy bill as too little too late, questioned the liberalism of both parties, and threatened to march like Sherman through the South, he threatened to withdraw publicly and thus expose divisions at an event that was striving to make the civil rights movement appear all-American. King, Randolph, Rustin, and others persuaded the SNCC to tone down the speech, although some reporters had already got hold of the unexpurgated version.

On the day of the March itself, August 28, Lewis's revised address was still one of the most militant in the program, but it was overshadowed by the majesty of King's concluding "I Have a Dream" speech. Watching the television coverage at the White House, and relieved that the event was, as the *New York Times* put it, less militant than in the "spirit of a church outing," Kennedy listened to King and told aides, "This guy's good" (Bryant 2006: 436). The leaders of the rally were received at the White House afterwards, where they found the administration's political calculations unchanged. The civil rights bill needed bipartisan, moderate support and that could only be corralled if the president could show that reform would ensure fewer demonstrations. If movement protests continued, Kennedy told them, they would make passage less rather than more likely.

The church bombings

At 10.22 a.m. on Sunday, September 15, dynamite ripped through the northeast door of the Sixteenth Street Baptist Church in Birmingham. Frantically clearing rubble, the congregation recovered the bodies of eleven-year-old Denise McNair and three fourteen-year-olds: Cynthia Wesley, Carole Robertson, and Addie Mae Collins. Addie Mae's twelve-year-old sister Sarah, partially blinded and bearing multiple cuts from the shattered glass of the windows, was pulled alive from the wreckage. The city, already tense because of court-ordered school desegregation, erupted into further violence, which claimed two additional African American victims: sixteen-year-old Johnny Robinson, shot by police, and thirteen-year-old Virgil Ware, murdered by white teenagers returning from a segregationist rally. President Kennedy was in Newport, Rhode Island, spending time with his wife who was still recovering from the loss of their prematurely born son Patrick, who had lived just thirty-six hours after his birth on August 7.

Kennedy's handling of the bombing seems enigmatic. The violent Birmingham clashes of May 1963 and the wave of anger and concern they triggered seemed to have forced him to recognize the urgency of the racial crisis and to commit himself resolutely to reform, but in the aftermath of a day that left African American parents mourning the loss of six children, Kennedy (who is widely reported to have been deeply affected by Patrick's death) showed limited empathy. He returned to the White House and issued a presidential statement, read to reporters by Pierre Salinger. It blamed Governor Wallace for the climate that bred the bombers and announced an FBI investigation, but it rejected calls for federal troops. The safety of black Birmingham was left in the hands of Wallace, who dispatched the state's public safety director Al Lingo, a notorious segregationist, to the scene.

When Kennedy next addressed the nation on radio and television, on Tuesday evening, he spoke about the recently signed nuclear test ban treaty and his hopes for growth through a tax-cutting budget. The bombing went unmentioned and the families were left to bury their dead: there was no national mourning and no presidential representation at the funerals to flag that this was a national tragedy. The apparent indifference incensed black leaders. When he eventually met them on September 19, Kennedy urged them to "keep their nerve," but reiterated that there was no legal basis for his sending troops. He added that they should work to avoid demonstrations and violent confrontations lest the spiral of disorder alienate the white majority. "Once that goes," he declared, "then we're pretty much down to a racial struggle" (Bryant 2006: 443).

Kennedy's disappointing response dismayed civil rights leaders, who sensed that the momentum behind the civil rights bill had faltered as the crises abated. Despite continuing protests in many communities, North and South, Kennedy was now more intent on minimizing white anger and positioning himself to appeal to moderates. When Congressman Emmanuel Celler tried to use public revulsion at the Birmingham killings in September to strengthen the terms of the civil rights bill, Attorney General Bobby Kennedy told the House Judiciary Committee in a private session that augmenting federal authority risked having state authorities forego their policing role, thus creating a vacuum in which racial disorder would flourish. Cellar was obliged to withdraw his proposals. The priority was to retain moderate Republican support to secure passage of a bill that would placate white liberals without fracturing the Democratic Party completely in terms of the South. The president's polling numbers with African Americans remained healthy, especially now that it seemed likely he would face conservative Republican Barry Goldwater in 1964. The votes at risk in his already begun reelection campaign were white and Southern; an anxiety underlined by the sale of bumper stickers in Birmingham that read "Goldwater for President, Kennedy for King" (Bryant 2006: 444–52).

The nuclear test ban

Since May, Kennedy's attention had returned to the area of policy that fascinated him most: international relations. In a key respect he was able to achieve success, with the passage of a nuclear test ban treaty a sign of his new relationship with Khrushchev and the possibilities of détente. In other respects, he continued to be unable to align his European NATO allies behind American leadership as he had envisaged in his "Grand Strategy" and, more fatefully, he had to respond to the deteriorating situation in South Vietnam, where the US policy of backing the Diem regime was becoming unsustainable.

On December 19, 1962, Khrushchev wrote to Kennedy hoping to advance nuclear test ban talks by accepting on-site inspections (no more than four). Unsure that such a light inspection regime would enable a treaty to pass a hawkish Senate ratification process, Kennedy demurred. Ten days later, at the Orange Bowl in Miami, Florida, he accepted the banner of the Brigade which had tried to topple Castro via the Bay of Pigs invasion (see Plate 4). He did so with the words "I can assure you that this flag will be returned to this brigade in a free Havana!" (Beschloss 1991: 572). Such signals were hardly likely to promote détente. Nevertheless, diplomatic soundings on the test ban continued into the New Year. Internal Soviet politics threw up further obstacles, as Khrushchev faced a serious challenge to his leadership from Frol Kozlov, who urged a rapprochement with Mao and increased military spending to prevent further humiliation in confrontations with the West. This threat subsided in April when Kozlov was incapacitated by a stroke, leaving Leonid Brezhnev in line to succeed if Khrushchev stumbled.

Saturday Review editor Norman Cousins arrived in the wake of these events to try to rekindle test ban talks. Khrushchev listened to his explanation as to why Kennedy had rebuffed his December offer. He then said that he could not change his position to accommodate the US and retain the support of his Council of Ministers. When Cousins reported this to Kennedy, JFK remarked that he and Khrushchev were both harassed by hardliners "who feed on one another"(Beschloss 1991: 588). But to maintain momentum for a treaty, he sent veteran diplomat Averell Harriman to Moscow. Ambassador to the USSR during the war, Harriman was a reminder of a time when the two powers were allies. He was also an indication that Kennedy was keen to get a deal in an attempt to slow the pace of nuclear proliferation, with China and France poised to acquire the fateful capability.

The worsening relations with China made Khrushchev sympathetic but wary. To underline the new spirit of cooperation, Kennedy gave his lyrical "Peace" speech at the American University on June 9 and Harriman was named as his special envoy to conclude the treaty. The speech eloquently displayed an understanding of Soviet history, especially the human cost of defeating Nazism for the Soviet people. It argued that progress towards disarmament was essential to protect humanity as a whole. It spoke of how, ultimately, we all share a small planet and wish the best for our children. It strongly reinforced Kennedy's international stature as a man of peace.

By the summer of 1963 Kennedy felt strong enough politically to press ahead with a test ban treaty as a symbol of the new détente. At the same time, he knew that his actions would arouse suspicions in Europe. France would be opposed because of its own nuclear ambitions and Germany would be distrustful. To shore up his standing, Kennedy made his celebrated visit to Berlin on June 26. Nearly a million Berliners cheered as he proclaimed his identification with them on Freedom's front line (see Chapter 8). As Michael Beschloss observes, "Had Khrushchev taken Kennedy's city hall oration as literally as Kennedy had his Wars of Liberation address in 1961, the good done by the American University speech might have been eroded" (Beschloss 1991: 608).

The impasse on the question of inspections ultimately meant that a comprehensive test ban treaty was impossible. However, the two sides were sufficiently keen to achieve a first step that they could agree a more limited treaty prohibiting tests in the atmosphere, oceans, and outer space. Harriman was able to conclude the draft treaty with Khrushchev in just ten days, at the end of July. Kennedy had invited two Republican senators to attend the signing ceremony in Moscow, but none would accept. Warnings of weakness from conservative newspapers sharpened his fear of the treaty's rejection by the Senate. To mobilize public opinion, he addressed the nation on July 26, presenting the agreement as a step away from war which reduced the pollution hazards of atmospheric testing and the pressures of the arms race. Privately, he reassured the military that they would retain ample research facilities to refine and maintain the nuclear arsenal, and he stressed that the treaty was a valuable wedge to widen the increasingly visible Sino–Soviet split.

On September 24, the Senate ratified the treaty overwhelmingly, 80 votes to 19. Kennedy had achieved the first arms limitation treaty of the nuclear age. In the eyes of many Americans the test ban treaty confirmed what the Missile Crisis had shown, namely that JFK was so resolute that the USSR was prepared to back down. Critics have wondered whether he could have achieved a comprehensive ban by accepting Khrushchev's offer of no more than three annual inspections to monitor underground testing, but hawks in the US would certainly have bridled at this, and their Soviet counterparts would certainly have tried to elude such inspections in order to narrow the missile gap that favored the US. In practice, the treaty proved an ineffectual measure against nuclear proliferation: China, France, India, Israel, and Pakistan all joined the "nuclear club" in the coming years, with little impediment from the treaty's strictures. Nevertheless, the *Bulletin of Atomic Scientists* which had dramatized the dangers of the Cold War with a doomsday clock that was set at seven minutes to midnight moved the minute hand back to show twelve minutes remaining, as a sign of the added security the treaty offered humanity. The perception grew of JFK the peacemaker, the president who would keep America out of war.

Vietnam: What did Kennedy plan to do?

Given that his successor Lyndon Johnson presided over the worst military defeat in US history, the question is regularly asked: Had he lived, would JFK have avoided the quagmire of Vietnam? What makes this question so tantalizing is the fact that one can point to documents that outline a plan of military withdrawal, but one that is clearly predicated on specific political considerations: not until after US elections in 1964 and only when the internal stability of the South Vietnamese government is assured. What is far clearer in the archival record is the reality that, in the summer and autumn of 1963, Vietnam became a foreign policy concern that preoccupied the Kennedy administration in a way that only Berlin and Cuba had done previously. For most of 1962, Kennedy had been content to believe that the additional resources he had committed in 1961 had turned the tide.

Kennedy's supporters have noted that he resisted the commitment of American combat troops even in 1961, despite strong recommendations from the military chiefs and others. Instead, he had greatly boosted the level of military assistance and weaponry, and part of the success reported in 1962 against the South Vietnamese insurgents was due to the arrival of helicopter gunships and more American advisors. At the same time, advocates of the view that Kennedy might have withdrawn from Vietnam seem to pay too little attention to his dissatisfaction with the neutralization solution attempted in neighboring Laos. Far from ensuring a stable pro-Western regime, neutrality seemed to maintain instability, with the Communist forces remaining active and the territory continuing to be used as a supply line into Vietnam. Had Kennedy been satisfied with the Laotian situation, one could make a stronger case that he would have been willing to accept a similar settlement in Vietnam.

For critics of Kennedy, his escalating commitment to South Vietnam between 1961 and 1963 was symptomatic of his approach to the developing world. Modernization needed to be directed in ways that ensured new nations resisted the Communist model, and instead saw the American-style market economy as the path to progress. In theory this meant that American aid and support should ensure popular reform as well as Communist containment, but in practice the US became allied to authoritarian regimes that used US support to bolster their own positions while resisting key measures such as land reform. Evident in Latin America, despite the Alliance for Progress's promises, the same pattern was equally visible in the Diem regime in South Vietnam, and in the course of 1963 the autocratic nature of Diem's rule became so flagrant that it created a series of crises.

The counterinsurgency strategy

Vietnam was also the testing ground for Kennedy's new kind of warfare: counterinsurgency. Believing that guerilla wars would become a key facet of Communist efforts to expand their global influence, Kennedy began a major effort to prepare US forces to fight against this new enemy. The "Green Berets," as these commando-style units were nicknamed, were very much JFK's "pet project." Kennedy courted counterinsurgency experts, including those involved in the British campaigns against Communists in Malaya. They had used fortified encampments to provide security for peasant communities in the combat zone, and improved living conditions in these consolidated settlements had helped to win popular support. Modeled on this, the "strategic hamlets" scheme that relocated South Vietnamese peasants from their native villages to better-protected locations had ostensibly slowed the success of the insurgency in the countryside in 1962.

Negative reports about the scheme's deep unpopularity and the government corruption and intimidation that accompanied it did not gain credence until the following year. Reporters such as David Halberstam, who sent back accounts of military failure and a regime out of touch with its own people, came to be regarded as giving comfort to the enemy. Kennedy, to his discredit, unsuccessfully urged editors to restrain them. Nevertheless, in February 1963, Kennedy officials Roger Hilsman and Michael Forrestal returned from a fact-finding mission and struggled to sound upbeat. "We are probably winning," they wrote, "but more slowly than we had hoped." They were also unsure how far the "inevitable accidents" from air strikes and heavy weaponry were breeding "resentment among persuadable villagers" (Young 1991: 93).

Internal divisions over Vietnam

Forrestal recalled years later that their report made JFK extremely nervous, since he believed that the weapons being used profligately by the South Vietnamese army (ARVN) were alienating the very people whose loyalty would determine the war's outcome. At the same time, the military chiefs argued in favor of what would later be termed a "surge": an expansion of operations and forces intended to batter the enemy in order to prepare the ground for American withdrawal.

In the report's conclusion, Forrestal and Hilsman declared that "No matter how one twisted and turned the problem, it always came back to Ngo Dinh Diem" (Young 1991: 94–95). The South Vietnamese premier had become an alarming disappointment to his American allies. Obstinate in his refusal to reform, he had fallen increasingly under the sway of his brother Ngo Dinh Nhu and Nhu's outspoken wife. It was often the violence and corruption associated with Nhu that so troubled journalists reporting on Vietnam. The Diem regime seemed intent on surviving as a dynasty rather than developing into a modern democratic state. It did not seem worthy of US support. At the same time, the regime was growing uneasy with the scale of US military involvement in the country. It undercut Diem's anticolonial credentials and confronted him with calls that he tolerate political opposition and engage in reform. By the spring of 1963 Diem was complaining that the US was infringing on Vietnamese sovereignty and declaring that he would not tolerate any further increase in US advisors, numbers of whom by this stage had reached 16,000.

The Buddhist crisis

In the fight against Godless Communism, Diem's Catholicism had been deemed an asset by his American sponsors in the 1950s. By 1963, however, it served to underline the gulf between the regime and the largely Buddhist Vietnamese people. Diem's brother, Ngo Dinh Thuc, was Archbishop of Hue, a city towards South Vietnam's northern border. It was there on May 8, 1963 that government troops opened fire on crowds celebrating the anniversary of the Buddha's birth. When an estimated 10,000 marched in protest at this brutality, Diem imprisoned Buddhist leaders, and other officials denounced the religion as a Communist front and sealed off the most politically active pagodas with armed guards.

By May 23, the White House was considering a contingency plan should the regime fall.

Kennedy was too preoccupied with the attacks on children in Birmingham, Alabama, to pay much attention to the immediate crisis in Vietnam in May. When asked about it at press conferences, he responded that a reduction in US forces was sought, but vacillated over whether this would come immediately, at Saigon's request, or over time, as ARVN forces became trained to meet the Communist threat. On June 11, however, the self-immolation of elderly Buddhist monk Quang Duc, at a busy Saigon intersection with invited press in attendance, produced a story and an image that dramatized for Americans the intensity of Buddhist resistance to the Diem regime (see Plate 5). If Kennedy had decided to withdraw from Vietnam, as he is reported to have told Senator Mike Mansfield, he needed to leave behind a regime with a semblance of legitimacy to lend credibility to the retreat. The photo of the burning monk shredded Diem's legitimacy.

More immediately, if Vietnam's deterioration was not to become as threatening to Kennedy's re-election chances as Castro's conversion to Communism had been to Nixon's hopes in 1960, action needed to be taken to steady the situation in Saigon. Diem's sister-in-law, Madame Nhu, herself a convert from Buddhism to Catholicism, underscored the difficulty of sticking with Diem for Kennedy by mocking Buddhist self-immolation as a "barbecue" and offering to supply gasoline for future burnings. Secretary of State Rusk warned the Saigon embassy that unless Diem resolved the crisis quickly and acceptably, the administration would no longer associate itself with his regime, the implication being that the US would countenance Diem's fall.

Appointment of Lodge and the August telegrams

The Buddhist revolt, coming at the same time as the African American nonviolent protests, shocked Kennedy. His immediate response was to change personnel at the Saigon embassy, and typically he chose a high-profile Republican, Henry Cabot Lodge, in a move that transparently sought to ensure bipartisanship and a measure of political cover if things went wrong. Kennedy was receiving contradictory reports from Vietnam. The military continued to stress that new operations were successful and promised to end the insurgency, but civilian sources had been so alienated by the Buddhist revolt that they saw Diem as a US liability. Alarmed by the continuing crisis in July, Kennedy brought forward Lodge's posting to Saigon. By the time Lodge was ready to depart, Kennedy was reading negative press reports on the military situation and receiving protest petitions urging him to break with an "unjust, undemocratic and unstable regime" (Jones 2003: 295).

Arriving August 22, Lodge quickly concluded that Diem was irredeemable, since he had ignored calls for him to repudiate his controversial brother and sister-in-law, the Nhus. The regime's crack-down against Buddhist dissidents continued to embarrass the US, and so Lodge began actively encouraging a military coup. On August 24, the local staff received a telegram appearing to give a green light from Washington for Diem's overthrow, but it later emerged that the telegram had been drafted and approved while Kennedy and other senior figures like Bundy and McNamara were out of town. Assistant Secretary of State Roger Hilsman had been outraged by the pagoda raids, and the new under secretary for political affairs, Averell Harriman, endorsed his view that Diem had become a liability. They drafted a telegram that asked Lodge to give Diem an ultimatum: get rid of the Nhus or the US would withdraw its support. The embassy should prepare plans for Diem's replacement.

With the draft prepared, NSC staffer Michael Forrestal called the president, who was in Hyannis Port helping his family recover from the shock of baby Patrick Kennedy's death. Under Secretary George Ball also talked to Kennedy about the proposed telegram and was told that if Secretary Rusk and Deputy Defense Secretary Gilpatric agreed the text it could be sent. Assuming that Ball had already got the president's approval, Rusk signed off, and Gilpatric also felt that Defense should not block a State Department docu-ment that had JFK's consent. The CIA's deputy director for plan-ning, Richard Helms, was emphatically in support. "It's about time we bit this bullet," he said, feeling no need to confer with his vacationing boss John McCone. With these endorsements, Kennedy confirmed that the telegram should be sent (Rust 1985: 116).

Lodge believed that warning Diem that any failure to remove his brother would end US support would only serve to alert him to the threat of an imminent coup. Since Lodge believed Diem would never break with Nhu, he told the State Department that, instead, he was going to talk directly to the Vietnamese generals who would have to stage the coup. But before he could do so a "Voice of America" radio broadcast exonerating Vietnam's military leaders for the pagoda raids and blaming Nhu for the mass arrests alerted the Diem regime to Washington's new position. Confronted by the anger of Robert McNamara, Maxwell Taylor, and John McCone, who felt that a major policy move had been made deliberately in their absence, Kennedy presided over a stormy White House meeting on Monday that ultimately accepted the telegram as a fait accompli.

A further meeting with former Ambassador Nolting, however, raised unsettling questions about the solidarity of the military plotters involved. Kennedy vacillated, fearing that a coup might either fail, or fail to improve the situation. He sent Lodge further instructions on August 28, saying that the coup plan could be delayed or changed according to Lodge's on-the-spot assessment. When Lodge complained that this was no time for second thoughts, Kennedy responded that "failure is more destructive than the appearance of indecision ... . When we go, we must go to win, but it will be better to change our minds than fail" (Young 1991: 97). This, for him, had been the lesson of the Bay of Pigs fiasco. The mixed signals from Washington and the countermeasures taken by the Diem regime made the Vietnamese generals wary, and by the end of the August it was clear that coup plans were on hold.

JFK's position on Vietnam in September 1963

Interviewed by Walter Cronkite on CBS news on September 2, Kennedy sent a clear message that Diem needed to break with Nhu and reach out for popular support. He reaffirmed his position that popular backing was crucial in the war against communism. "In the final analysis," he declared, "it is their war. ... We can help them. ... But they have to win it, the people of Vietnam, against the Communists." At the same time, he stressed again that this "is a very important struggle even though it is far away." He disagreed with those who favored withdrawal (Rabe 2010: 120).

The lack of clear and accurate information appalled Kennedy. The problem was epitomized by the Krulak–Mendenhall mission in early September. Major General Victor Krulak visited rural areas and talked to eighty US advisors before concluding that the ARVN was fighting the Communists hard and well. Joseph Mendenhall from the State Department's Vietnam desk visited the central coastal provinces and talked to American and Vietnamese civilian officials in urban areas worst affected by the recent Buddhist crisis. He concluded that Diem was hated and that as long as he was in power the war was doomed. Listening to their contrasting reports, Kennedy asked whether the two men had visited the same country, but as the debate continued his impatience was evident. "We can't run a policy," he declared angrily, "when there are such divergent views on the same set of facts" (Newman 1992: 375).

The McNamara–Taylor Mission: A final attempt at clarity

September also brought another alarming possibility. Sensing that American support was fading, the Diem regime, and especially Nhu, began to talk about negotiating directly with the Communist North and requiring the Americans to withdraw. With his advisers divided and his policy adrift, JFK sent two of his most trusted advisors, Defense Secretary McNamara and head of the Joint Chiefs General Maxwell Taylor, to evaluate the situation in Vietnam. Their report was strongly in favor of increased pressure on Diem to break with the Nhus and pass reforms. The outcome of tactical cutbacks in US aid would be either reconciliation with Diem under more favorable circumstances or encouragement of a military coup. At the same time, the report acknowledged some apparent military success, sufficient to proceed with plans for a troop reduction of 1,000 by year's end. At an October 2 NSC meeting a relieved Kennedy urged a united front behind the McNamara–Taylor proposals. Reports of disagreement had appeared in the press to the detriment of policy. Everyone, he said, should stay united.

Fresh coup plans

Unfortunately for JFK, his team in Vietnam was not of one mind. Lodge in particular believed that getting rid of Diem was the only way forward, and was not prepared to wait and see whether the aid cut would bring him into line. Instead, he welcomed fresh feelers from Vietnamese generals that the Americans would not thwart any coup attempt nor deny a new regime economic or military assistance. General Harkins, on the other hand, believed that the war was being won and that Diem remained the best option available. He warned one of the conspirators, General Tran Van Don, that the US would not support a coup and this interrupted its planning. Lodge, meanwhile, reported that Diem remained obdurately resistant to American pressures for reform.

Kennedy's instructions to Lodge became more demanding as the likelihood of a coup grew. He wanted a shrewd assessment of the rebels' chances, with the option to discourage any attempt that was likely to fail with negative consequences for US policy in the region. Lodge did not think this was possible or wise and disagreed with General Harkins' warnings that a change of government might damage the military situation. On November 1, despite growing misgivings among senior officials in Washington, the Vietnamese military plotters overthrew the Diem regime. Kennedy had sent his personal friend Torby Macdonald to Saigon to advise Diem to seek asylum in the US Embassy, but before they could escape Diem and his brother were murdered.

Assessment of JFK's policy on Vietnam

If Kennedy is judged mainly on the effect of the coup, the verdict has to be negative. As some of his advisers had warned, the military junta that succeeded Diem did not provide stability. There were seven different governments in 1964 alone. Predictably, the North Vietnamese and Viet Cong stepped up their operations, thus confronting Lyndon Johnson and the Defense and National Security team that he largely inherited from Kennedy with the dilemma of escalating US involvement or allowing Vietnam, Laos, and Cambodia to fall rapidly to insurgent forces with Communist ties. The general scholarly consensus is that the fall of Diem made the survival of South Vietnam less likely, and made the likelihood of increased US involvement greater. At the same time, Kennedy's own murder, barely three weeks after Diem's, also made it far harder for his successor to withdraw from Vietnam.

Nevertheless, it has become an integral part of the Kennedy story among loyalists that he was planning to withdraw from Vietnam; in other words, the tragedy of Vietnam grew from the tragedy in Dallas. Longtime Kennedy aide Ken O'Donnell recalls that Kennedy told him that after the 1964 election he intended to get out of Vietnam by the simple stratagem of installing a government that would ask the US to leave. Senate Majority Leader Mike Mansfield, an advocate of withdrawal, also remembers Kennedy assuring him that once he had secured re-election he would maneuver for a speedy exit. Camelot chronicler Arthur Schlesinger emphasizes that the de-escalation strategy which would see a thousand troops withdrawn by the end of 1963 was concrete evidence that JFK would never have Americanized the war the way that Lyndon Johnson did.

More recently, Frederick Logevall has argued that the best opportunity for withdrawal came during the summer and fall of 1963, when allies saw little reason for the US to deepen its involvement, when North Vietnam was suggesting that it might be willing to participate in coalition politics, and when the revulsion of the US public with the Diem regime's treatment of Buddhist dissent had made continuing support of the South a more open question. He concludes that Kennedy's record suggests that he would not have escalated US involvement to the same extent or at the same speed as Johnson did in 1965, but he also believes that Kennedy would have been anxious to have a government in place in the South that could last long enough to provide cover for an American exit, given the inevitable charges a Communist victory would bring (Logevall 2001).

The political dangers that made JFK anxious about Vietnam ahead of his reelection bid would not have disappeared with victory. The crisis that Lyndon Johnson faced in 1965 would have presented JFK with the possibility that he would mark his second term with a foreign policy catastrophe as grave as the Bay of Pigs had been in his first. Thus speculation about Kennedy's intentions needs to give due weight to his desire for political protection, as well as to his reluctance to commit combat troops. As James Giglio concludes: "If one is seeking examples of presidential growth in Kennedy's last year, one should look elsewhere rather than to Southeast Asia" (Giglio 2006: 253–54).

7 The mysteries of November 22, 1963

The question that most people ask about John F. Kennedy is: Who killed him? Fifty years after the traumatic events of November 22, the details of his death are more widely known than any other aspect of his life. In this chapter, we will look at the events surrounding the murder, and then review the main theories that have developed about the nature of the assassination. In its 1964 report, the initial investigation by President Johnson's Warren Commission identified Lee Harvey Oswald as the lone gunman. Despite the singular nature of Oswald's background as a former Marine who had defected to the USSR and then returned, the Warren Commission was at pains to stress that this was a crime motivated more by a personality disorder than by ideological imperatives. The murder of Oswald by Jack Ruby preempted Oswald's trial and added to the suspicions of skeptics about the Warren Commission's findings.

In the 1970s, the assassination was investigated again by congressional committees established in the aftermath of the Watergate scandal, which had severely dented the prestige and credibility of the presidency and the federal government more generally. While no individual was identified as an assassin, the overall finding was that it was likely that Kennedy had been killed by a conspiracy, and the most likely parties were organized crime figures and anti-Castro Cubans. In 1991, Hollywood director Oliver Stone made *JFK*, a film largely based on the efforts of flamboyant New Orleans district attorney Jim Garrison to try a local businessman, Clay Shaw, for his role in the conspiracy that killed the president. Shaw, it was alleged, had been part of a larger CIA plot. The publicity surrounding the movie was an important factor in prompting Congress to pass the 1992 JFK Assassination Records Review Act, which called upon all federal agencies to release all relevant documents.

The Assassination Records Review Board was set up to oversee the processing of records from agencies such as the CIA and FBI, where quite commonly documents were classified as secret for reasons of national security. The Board also tried to establish the accuracy of medical records related to JFK's wounds, since contradictory statements had fed the debate over whether there was more than one gunman and fueled the larger belief that the American people had been lied to about the nature of Kennedy's murder in 1963. Thus, at the century's end, the precise nature of the assassination was unresolved, and November 22, 1963 remained a day of mystery as well as horror.

Time distorts the Kennedy image

To understand the events in Dallas, it is important to break away from many assumptions that have taken root due to the increased popularity of JFK in death. Polls taken since his death have regularly found at least 70 percent of people claiming that they voted for Kennedy, even though in 1960 he received less than 50 percent of the votes cast. Kennedy's posthumous veneration and Lyndon Johnson's landslide victory in 1964 have prompted many people to assume that Kennedy would have defeated Barry Goldwater by a similarly wide margin had he lived. But in the weeks prior to the assassination this was not obvious. On the contrary, the political challenges facing the incumbent president were much more evident, and so too were the strengths of his Republican challenger.

To understand the context of the assassination, it is valuable to review the vexed politics of the period. First and foremost, they explain why the president was in Texas, a key swing state which had been essential to his narrow victory in 1960 but was very much in doubt in November 1963. At the same time, a re-examination also highlights the strength of conservatism in the politics of the period, and questions the assumption that, if Kennedy had survived, the Great Society reforms would have proceeded, but without the negative consequences of an escalating Vietnam War. To review the politics of 1963 is to be reminded of how radical the civil rights movement seemed within the politics of the time, and how the pragmatic Kennedy, eager to court powerful white Southern congressional interests, may have retreated from the battle over comprehensive civil rights legislation. Other elements of liberal reform, from Medicare/Medicaid to immigration reform and community action programs, were by no means an assured part of a Kennedy second-term program, especially if the elections of 1964 had produced a far less dramatic swing in favor of liberals in Congress.

Kennedy's Republican rivals

Barry Goldwater was far more assured of the Republican nomination in late 1963 than Kennedy was of a second term. Goldwater's liberal rivals, New York's Nelson Rockefeller and to a lesser extent Michigan Governor George Romney, faced an uphill battle to be competitive, since early signs were that support for the Arizona senator was so strong among party activists that he was assured of at least 500 delegate votes even before the formal nomination contest began. The *New York Times* reported at the start of October that a *Time* magazine poll had found that in a contest with Goldwater, Kennedy faced "a breathtakingly close race." Goldwater could combine Western and Southern voters in a way that eroded the usual foundations for Democratic presidential success. Pennsylvania's GOP governor, William Scranton, added to Democratic anxieties when he declared that, if the election were held right away, JFK would equally struggle to retain Pennsylvania, given Republican midterm gains. James Reston, a syndicated columnist whom the president read diligently, summed up the situation in an October *Times* column on why Kennedy was right to worry about Goldwater. In addition to the Southern white revolt on civil rights, Reston declared, Kennedy faced "an anti-high taxation, anti-integrated housing, anti-job equality movement in the North, even among pro-Democratic labor union members." This was the kind of coalition that ultimately voted for Richard Nixon and third-party candidate

George Wallace in 1968, and when Wallace was effectively removed from the 1972 race by an assassination attempt that wounded but did not kill him, Nixon won a landslide victory over George McGovern on the basis of this emergent conservative majority.

Goldwater had been the vital precursor of this shift, representing a conservative social movement that believed the Eisenhower years had seen a betrayal of their values, a period when the Republican Party had offered an "echo" rather than a "choice." When Goldwater spoke of Kennedy as being dangerously committed to the growth of government, he articulated a free market philosophy that would ultimately form the core of the Republican resurgence under Ronald Reagan in 1980 and beyond. The mystery of the 1963 murder diminishes a little, once one recognizes that Kennedy was not the nation's sweetheart; he was detested by some, and mistrusted by many more, especially in the South.

Although there were signs that Kennedy's conduct during the Cuban Missile Crisis and his subsequent negotiation of an atmospheric test ban treaty with the Soviet Union had produced a "peace issue" for voters who might be alarmed by Goldwater's aggressively anti-Soviet stance, there remained a countervailing fear that Republicans could effectively portray Kennedy as "soft on Communism," in much the same way as they had attacked Truman in Joe McCarthy's time. A foretaste of this approach was offered by Richard Nixon, an influential figure although not an active candidate in 1964. Defending freedom, he told reporters, had been JFK's stated position in 1960, "but it has been watered down and wrapped in double talk from the time negotiations for the test ban began."

The public debate over proposed wheat sales to the USSR further illustrated the strength of public suspicion. The Kennedy administration defended the sale for its positive benefits to Midwestern farmers and the overall US trade balance, as well as its role as a trust-building mechanism in the new era of peaceful coexistence. Hardline Cold Warriors countered that, by alleviating the food crisis inside the Communist system, the sales sustained an immoral regime. Pundits added that the measure was electorally damaging. The grain farmers of Nebraska or the Dakotas might welcome the sales but they would still vote Republican in the next election, whereas the Polish, Hungarian, and Slovak-American communities in urban centers, who had voted for Kennedy in 1960, might be alienated by his seeming acceptance of Soviet domination of their homelands.

Kennedy and the white South

Kennedy's generally frustrated relationship with Congress was still apparent with just twelve months to go before the election. He himself recognized that he needed to pass his tax reduction bill in order to spur economic growth, but that at the same time it would be better if he could pass his controversial civil rights legislation and thus boost black voter turnout in the North. The latter consideration had become even more salient, as the electoral calculus suggested strongly that in 1964 Kennedy would have to offset lost Southern votes with African American ones in Northern metropolises.

Unfortunately the two goals were at odds with each other, since progress on the tax bill required the cooperation of mainly Southern congressional leaders incensed by the administration's proposed racial reforms. The situation was captured during the president's visit to Arkansas in October. His visit to mark the completion of a federal dam project was widely seen as an effort to court the state's powerful congressional delegation, including the House "Ways and Means" Committee chairman Wilbur Mills, whose opposition could block tax legislation. The occasion, however, placed Kennedy on the same platform as Arkansas Governor Orval Faubus, best remembered for his defiance of court-ordered school desegregation in Little Rock in 1957. Attuned to the mood of his constituents, Faubus showed no reluctance to denounce the civil rights bill even as he introduced the president. Faubus's comments were greeted with more surprise than applause, but reporters noted that scattered among the largely Kennedy-friendly crowd were placards that read: "Kennedy for King; Goldwater for President." The allusion to civil rights leader Martin Luther King underlined how racial reform stirred white opposition and made Southern politicians wary of tying themselves too closely to JFK's re-election bid.

The radical Right

Kennedy was also preparing for his reelection fight by learning more about his likely opponent, Barry Goldwater, the champion of the Republican Right. White House counsel Myer Feldman presented an assessment of the radical Right in August, stressing that it was well-funded by influential companies and individuals. In over 150 congressional races where its influence was evident, the Right had been successful. Thus Kennedy was warned that he should not underestimate the threat, which can be likened to that posed by the "Tea Party" to President Barack Obama's re-election hopes in 2012. Alert to the danger, Kennedy nevertheless believed that the Right's doctrinaire opposition to governmental programs like Social Security, plus their rashness in foreign affairs, alarmed more Americans than it attracted. By the same token, he hoped that within the Southern states there were more voters interested in economic development than there were hardline segregationists. If he could highlight how they were better off than they had been four years earlier, he would win following a strategy that would later work for Ronald Reagan, in 1980, and Bill Clinton, in 1992. The state of the economy has frequently been a powerful election issue.

A necessary but risky visit to Texas

In part, JFK's trip to Texas in late November had a simple financial motivation: to raise money for the cash-strapped Democratic Party nationally. He had hoped to persuade Texan Governor John Connally to host a series of dinners in August, but had been rebuffed. Connally had publicly opposed Kennedy's civil rights bill and was involved in a bitter feud with his liberal Texan rival, Senator Ralph Yarborough. He feared that being linked to JFK would alienate some of his conservative supporters and give encouragement to liberal and minority voters, who backed the Yarborough faction. The two-day visit in late November represented a compromise, with Connally agreeing to host a single fundraising dinner but with no clear role assigned to his rival, Senator Yarborough. Everything about the visit also served to spotlight the diminished political stature of Lyndon Johnson, whose protégé Connally had once been. Whereas in 1960 Johnson had been vital to Kennedy's victory in Texas and elsewhere in the South, three years later he was seen as a spent force, with some speculating that Kennedy might even dump him in favor of a more advantageous figure.

In the weeks prior to the trip both Johnson and Connally tried to discourage the president from anything other than a perfunctory visit to Dallas, which was a notorious center for right-wing activity. Profiling Texan political divisions for the *New York Times*, journalist Ronnie Dugger noted that the level of political acrimony in the state might be gauged from the fact that someone had fired a shotgun into the Democratic Party headquarters in Dallas that summer. The city ranked alongside Orange County in southern California as a center for the John Birch Society (JBS) and other extremist groups. On October 24, when UN Ambassador Adlai Stevenson addressed a Dallas rally celebrating the anniversary of the UN's formation, he had to run the gauntlet of a spitting mob of radical Right and anti-Castro groups as he left the building, and was struck on the head with a placard by a female demonstrator.

When the Dallas Chamber of Commerce sought to minimize the public relations damage done by this assault through a press statement condemning the perpetrators, a local right-wing leader, former Major General Edwin Walker, denounced the Chamber, telling reporters that Kennedy had "assisted Khrushchev in taking over Cuba and establishing it as a base for subversion." The Kennedy administration had pushed Walker into retirement when an internal investigation proved that he had been propagandizing for the John Birch Society on military bases. One of the mysteries surrounding the political background of Lee Harvey Oswald is the fact that, according to his wife Marina, on the night of April 10 he fired a shot at General Walker while he was seated in his Dallas home. The bullet was deflected by the window glass and narrowly missed its target. While there was no investigation at the time, the FBI subsequently concluded that the bullet retrieved was similar to those fired by Oswald's Mannlicher-Carcano rifle, which he had ordered from a Chicago mail order house in mid-March (Kaiser 2008: 182–83). The limited investigation into the Walker shooting suggests that police and secret service officials devoted more resources to the threat from radical Right groups in Dallas than to someone like Oswald, whose two years' defection to the USSR, subscription to Trotskyite publications, and apparent involvement with pro-Castro groups in New Orleans suggested a left- rather than right-wing political allegiance. As we shall see, the tangle of associations around Oswald makes him an almost perfect figure for numerous conspiracy theories, involving the CIA, FBI, and organized crime.

In his profile of Texan politics, Dugger indicated that Senator Yarborough's liberal faction was resting its hopes partly on an early November referendum on the repeal of the state's poll tax requirements. Prospective voters had to prove that they had paid the tax, which thereby deterred electoral participation among poorer citizens, including blacks and Hispanics, who were typically followers of Yarborough rather than Connally. As a sign of how the political tide was running in Texas, the proposal was defeated, 303,763 to 237,524, on November 10. In Dallas, the rightward tilt was reflected more emphatically by Republican victories in two special elections for vacated seats. Little wonder that Republican Senator John Tower expressed the hope that Texas, where Kennedy's approval rating was barely 40 percent, could become the power base for the Goldwater movement's efforts to recapture the GOP, or that an alarmed Democratic committeeman tried vainly to persuade the president to scratch Dallas from his itinerary on the eve of his departure.

JFK and Jackie draw rapturous Texan crowds

The first day of the Texan visit, November 21, went encouragingly, with enthusiastic crowds greeting the president and his wife in San Antonio, Houston and Fort Worth. Jackie's presence, in particular, seemed to boost the crowds, giving substance to Republican fears that Kennedy might win reelection more through the power of his image than the popularity of his policies. Richard Nixon had been telling reporters that, from the point of view of public relations, the Kennedy administration had been "the most successful in the history of the country. It has taken a bad case and sold it well." Visiting Dallas just a day ahead of

Kennedy, he charged that the image was tremendous but the actual performance was poor. As an experienced campaigner, Kennedy sensed that direct personal contact was valuable in mobilizing support and that his glamorous wife enhanced his appeal. He insisted on motorcades in all cities, including Dallas. Speaking to a crowd outside his Fort Worth hotel on the morning of November 22, he sparked laughter by remarking that the first lady was still getting ready upstairs. "It takes her a little longer," he grinned, "but, of course, she looks better than we do when she does it" (Manchester 1967: 114).

As if to demonstrate the president's words, Jackie Kennedy eventually appeared wearing an elegantly tailored rose pink suit with a navy collar over a matching blue blouse. Her outfit was completed by a pink pillbox hat and white gloves. The nearly two thousand businessmen and their wives gave her a standing ovation as she entered the hotel ballroom. A delighted JFK joked that no one ever wondered what he and LBJ would be wearing, and then skillfully dodged calls for him to put on the ten-gallon hat which Fort Worth's mayor had just presented. In jovial spirits, the presidential party moved out to Carswell Air Force Base for the short flight to Dallas. Conscious of negative press comments about party in-fighting the previous day, Senator Yarborough was told to ride in the Vice President's car and he complied. By the time they reached Dallas, Governor Connally had similarly yielded to Kennedy's demand that Yarborough had to be at that evening's fundraising dinner. An outward show of unity had been created, and the early morning drizzle had evaporated. The weather would be good for the Dallas crowds. Governor Connally's wife Nellie, who had greater reason than most to remember the details of that day, recalled how good it felt as the two couples strode down the stairs from Air Force One onto the tarmac of Dallas's Love Field airport. Referring to her and Jackie's smiles, she declared: "We were two women, so proud of the men we loved" (Connally and Herskowitz 2003: 2).

Dallas

Mayor Cabell's wife presented the first lady with a brilliant bouquet of red roses; at all their other stops the roses had been the predictably yellow roses of Texas (see Plate 8). Watching the rapturously cheering reception from the press pack, *Los Angeles Times* reporter Robert Donovan caught himself thinking how the presidential couple looked straight out of Hollywood's central casting: beautiful, glamorous stars. Eventually, after shaking hands with members of the crowd through the perimeter fence, the president and his wife took their seats in the rear of an open-top limousine. Governor Connally was seated in front of JFK, although slightly to his right. Jackie sat to the right of her husband, ready to wave to the crowds on her side, while JFK waved to those on the driver's side. Nellie Connally was seated in front of Jackie and Secret Service Agent Roy Kellerman was next to presidential driver Bill Greer. The third car in the motorcade, the presidential limousine was flanked by four police motorcycle escorts, with Secret Service agents riding on the running boards of the car immediately behind. On Kennedy's orders, the agents were not to ride on the running boards or rear step of the limousine itself. Their presence made him uncomfortable and obscured the spectators' view. Of course, they would also have obscured an assassin's aim.

Having flirted with death from natural causes for most of his life, Kennedy had a cavalier attitude to security. If someone is intent on killing me, they will, he had been known to say. That morning in Fort Worth, he had repeated the phrase to staff. On the outskirts of Dallas, he spotted children with a placard reading "MR PRESIDENT, PLEASE STOP AND SHAKE OUR HANDS." He ordered the limousine to stop and was mobbed by the delighted kids. A few blocks later he stopped the car again for a group of small children under the care of a Catholic nun. The Secret Service reacted to these unscheduled stops as best they could. Once they were in the downtown area, the size of the crowd would, it was hoped, make such pauses impractical (Manchester 1967: 135–36).

As each block passed the crowds thickened, and Governor Connally and the other Texans in the motorcade relaxed at the unexpectedly warm and friendly reception. It was plain to them that the president was enjoying himself. Kennedy aides Kenny O'Donnell and Dave Powers felt that the Dallas crowds were the most enthusiastic they'd seen in Texas and remembered the roar of their cheers. Jackie Kennedy recalled afterwards that her husband repeatedly told her to take off her sunglasses, as they diminished the rapport she could establish with the crowd, and that he had always stressed that she needed to concentrate on her side of the street so that the optimum number of spectators would get a sense of connection to the First Couple as they passed. In the downtown area the crowds were so large that they surged into the street despite the police lines, and the motorcade dropped its speed to barely ten miles an hour.

Dealey Plaza

Ahead, at the corner of Elm and Houston, directly across the street from the Texas School Book Depository, two men waited for the motorcade. One of them glanced up to the sixth floor and saw a thin, young white man seated or kneeling uncomfortably amidst boxes. Oddly, the eyewitness recalled, the man was not looking in the direction of the motorcade, which was drawing roaring cheers as it moved along. Instead he was gazing across Dealey Plaza, down towards the Triple Underpass. At that moment, nearing 12.30, the head of the motorcade rounded the corner of Main Street onto Houston, to be greeted by loud cheers. Soon the presidential limousine was making a slow turn. The open space of Dealey Plaza after the tall building-lined canyon of Main Street produced convection currents and a strong breeze made Jackie Kennedy reach up to steady her hat. Delighted by the reception, Nellie Connally turned to the grinning president and declared that now he had to believe that there were "some in Dallas who love you and appreciate you" (Bugliosi 2007: 56).

From the lead car, Police Chief Jesse Curry radioed that they were approaching the Triple Underpass and agents at the Trade Mart could expect the president in five minutes. The clock on the Hertz sign on top of the Book Depository read exactly 12:30. Perched on a large abutment on one side of an ornamental pergola, a Dallas dressmaker, Abraham Zapruder, began filming the presidential party as it came down from Houston and Elm towards the Triple Underpass on his right. His receptionist, Marilyn Sitzman, stood behind him to steady him as he gazed through the lens of his new 8-millimeter movie camera. In the next few seconds he would film JFK's murder. Motorcycle patrolman H.B. McClain had a faulty microphone which was locked in the open position, thus providing a recording of noises in the motorcade.

Oswald and the Book Depository

In the Book Depository, employees usually took a 45-minute lunch break at noon and, given their location, most had decided on November 22 to watch their president. Lee Harvey Oswald had worked there since early October and was certainly there that day. The poorly paid Oswald had unexpectedly visited his estranged Russian wife, Marina, the previous evening, and had surprised her by giving her $170 to buy whatever she and their two baby daughters might need. Later she discovered that he had also left his wedding ring, which normally he always wore, concealed in a china cup. Lee's co-worker Wesley Frazier, who lived near Marina, had driven Oswald back to work in the morning and noticed that he had a package, which he took into the Depository. Lee had told him it contained curtain rods. At the Depository, Oswald's job was to fill orders: collecting books and bringing them downstairs for collection or shipment. He tended to work alone, visiting any of the building's floors. He did not join the group of workers who gathered on the fifth floor to watch the motorcade. They later reported that loose plaster fell from the ceiling when shots rang out above them and eyewitnesses outside also claimed to have seen shots come from the Depository.

The assassination

A sign for the Stemmons Freeway interrupted the view from Zapruder's movie camera as the president's car came towards him. But frames 225 and 226 showed both Kennedy and Connally reacting to being hit. The president's hands were shown moving up to his throat and Jackie had turned towards him. Less than six seconds later the camera caught the moment when another shot caused the right side of Kennedy's head to explode. Patrolman Bobby Hargis, at the rear of the limousine on the driver's side, was splattered with blood and brain matter; so too was the first lady as the president fell into her lap. Governor Connally had wounds to his chest, wrist, and thigh, but was still conscious when he heard Jackie cry, "They've killed my husband; I have his brains in my hand"(Bugliosi 2007: 64).

Seconds too late in his attempt to save the president, Agent Clint Hill bounded from the Secret Service car and threw himself onto the trunk of the limousine, pushing the first lady back into her seat as the car accelerated. He saw the gaping wound in the president's head and Connally's blood-soaked shirt. In the Vice President's car, Agent Rufus Youngblood had pinned Lyndon Johnson to the floor as soon as the shots rang out, ordering him to lie still. In chaotic scenes, the cars hurtled away from Dealey Plaza. Some people were pointing in the direction of the Book Depository but others felt that shots had been fired from the fenced area on top of a grassy knoll above a railroad track to the left of where Zapruder was standing.

Police Chief Curry shouted into his radio: "We're going to the hospital ... . Have Parkland stand by." With his knees still on Johnson's back, Agent Youngblood explained that on arrival he would be taking LBJ and his wife to a separate secure area. He recalled being impressed by the Vice President's calmness. The race to Parkland Hospital was so fast that there was no one to meet them at the emergency entrance, but two gurneys with stretchers for the president and governor were quickly found. Reluctantly, Jackie Kennedy released her hold on the shattered head of her husband, once Agent Hill had discreetly covered him with his coat to shield his head from sight. Parkland records log the arrival of John F. Kennedy at 12:38 p.m. Although he was probably effectively dead on arrival, doctors worked desperately for twenty-two minutes to save him, making an incision for a tracheotomy in his throat that overlaid a gunshot wound.

Officer Tippit's murder

Even before Kennedy had arrived at Parkland Hospital, Dallas police officer Marrion Baker had begun searching the Depository, where he encountered Lee Harvey Oswald nonchalantly standing in the second floor lunchroom. Building superintendent Roy Truly identified Oswald as an employee and Baker hurried to continue his search of the upper floors. Oswald was next seen crossing the second floor, taking his jacket and scarf, and heading down the stairs to the front entrance. According to his landlady he was back at his rented room on North Beckley Avenue shortly after one o'clock, although he left again almost immediately.

Driving his patrol car in the same neighborhood, Dallas Police Officer J.D. Tippit spotted a suspicious-looking white male walking erratically and decided to tail him. According to eyewitnesses, Tippit stopped his car, talked briefly to the suspect through the passenger-side window, and then got out. As Tippit walked around his patrol car, the man, later identified as Oswald, shot the officer repeatedly in the chest. Calmly, he stood over the body and fired a final shot to the head before he took off. Meanwhile, Dallas police had found three spent rifle cartridges by the window on the sixth floor of the Book Depository. As they continued their search, they found a rifle and a brown paper bag that they believed may have been used to carry it. There was one live cartridge still in the rifle chamber.

JFK's death announced

At 2.38 p.m. Eastern Standard Time (1:38 in Dallas), veteran newscaster Walter Cronkite read the bulletin that announced that John F. Kennedy had died from his wounds. Across the country, men and women wept. Motorists pulled over. Telephone networks collapsed under the volume of calls, and total strangers spoke to one another of their shock and disbelief. Modern media ensured that rapidly the entire nation was stricken with grief. In some parts of Texas, and elsewhere, however, there was sick jubilation. In Dallas, fourth grade pupils at one school burst into spontaneous applause at the news, while in Amarillo a group of high school students partied. Southern newspaper offices received calls praising the shooter of the man they called a "nigger lover." Notorious Teamsters' union leader Jimmy Hoffa allegedly told attorney Frank Ragano over the phone of his delight at the death of "the son of a bitch," since he expected this would end Bobby Kennedy's tenure as attorney general. Later on November 22, Ragano recalled, there were numerous toasts in celebration at a party thrown by mobster Santos Trafficante.

Oswald's arrest

In Dallas, at 1.50 p.m. local time, police converged on the Texas movie theater in search of a suspect in the murder of their colleague J.D. Tippit. After a struggle, Oswald was disarmed and handcuffed, to the consternation of the dozen or so people in the theater. In the patrol car, his wallet contained ID in the name of both Lee Harvey Oswald and A.J. Hidell. By 2.00 p.m. he had been taken to police headquarters, and it was becoming clear that the real identity of Tippit's suspected killer was Oswald, a man who worked at the Book Depository where officers had found what they believed to be the assassin's sniper's nest. Thus, even before Air Force One had left Love Field carrying the new president and the slain JFK and his shocked and grieving entourage, the Dallas police had in custody a man who they believed had killed twice that day.

Release of JFK's body

At Parkland Hospital a dispute arose over the release of Kennedy's body, since legally the local medical examiner was required to perform an autopsy on any victim of a violent or suspicious death. Angrily, Kennedy's staffers demanded that they be allowed to take their leader home. The dispute meant that the body did not arrive at the airport until 2: 14 p.m., by which time Kennedy's aides assumed that Lyndon Johnson would have already left for Washington in his plane, leaving Air Force One to bring home the murdered president's body, his widow, and his grieving staff. They were therefore shocked to find Johnson on board Air Force One. The pilot told them he had been instructed to wait because Johnson wanted to return to the White House with the entire party after he had been sworn in as president. At 2.30 p.m., just ninety minutes after JFK was pronounced dead, an old friend of Johnson's, federal district judge Sarah Hughes, presided over the brief cere-mony in the overcrowded cabin, surrounded by press. At Johnson's invitation, Jackie Kennedy was present, still wearing the now bloodstained suit.

Johnson's initial concerns

At the time, Johnson believed the photographed swearing-in would reassure Americans that their government continued, even in the face of such horror. Subsequently his haste to take the oath, his insensitive phoning of Bobby Kennedy to establish the oath's precise wording, and his inclusion of the deeply shocked widow in the event were all cited as evidence of his crassness. Johnson knew that he did not have the respect of Kennedy's close associates, and even though key figures like Robert McNamara, McGeorge Bundy, and Dean Rusk stayed on, ultimately it became an important part of the Camelot legend that the Johnson succession constituted a descent from glory.

Late that night Johnson heard on the television that there was speculation that Oswald was part of a larger Communist conspiracy. He told longtime associate Horace Busby that such talk had to be curbed. "We must not start making accusations without evidence," he declared (Bugliosi 2007: 284). Johnson's anxieties over the international ramifications of the assassination did not abate. As early as November 23, agent James Hosty in the Dallas FBI office was being instructed to keep a lid on foreign dimensions to the investigation. On November 29, while trying to persuade Senator Richard Russell to join a presidential commission to investigate the crime, LBJ indicated that he was anxious to squash dangerous speculation. "We've got to take this out of the arena where they're testifying that Khrushchev and Castro did this and did that," he warned, adding with chilling effect, "and kicking us into a war that can kill forty million Americans in half an hour." Russell agreed to serve (Kaiser 2008: 270).

Dallas police, FBI, and CIA squabble

In Dallas, however, on November 22, Police Chief Curry was still confirming to reporters that the investigation had found "a great, great amount of Communist literature" in Oswald's room. He also disclosed that the FBI were aware of Oswald as a potential subversive in the Dallas area but had not shared this information with his department. As soon as this was reported, FBI Director Hoover demanded and got a retraction. A predictable turf war between different agencies became evident, with local police, the Secret Service, the FBI, and ultimately the CIA all anxious to ensure that the death of the president was not ascribed to their negligence (Bugliosi 2007: 335–36).

International reaction

All three US television networks canceled their regular programs and filled the hours not only with news coverage from Dallas, Washington, and other American cities, but with scenes of mourning from around the world. In Berlin, where Kennedy had delivered his rousing "Ich bin ein Berliner" speech in June, Mayor Willy Brandt had asked people to light candles in their darkened windows. Within minutes, the homes of the city were flickering with candlelight. In Tokyo harbor, Japanese fishing vessels sailed beside American warships with flags at half-mast as a sign of respect. In London, the bells of St. Paul's Cathedral tolled in mourning. In Paris, where the presidential couple had drawn lavish praise in 1961, the cameras showed crowds of people standing in weeping tribute, despite heavy rain. "From Madrid to Manila," one reporter wrote, "churches filled and American embassies were thronged with people who wanted to sign memorial books" (Bugliosi 2007: 339). The grief spilled behind the Iron Curtain, with thousands of Poles lining up to sign the book of condolence in Warsaw. Premier Khrushchev himself visited the Moscow embassy to pay his respects. Everyone, it seemed, was at one in sadness. The significant exception was Communist China, whose official newsagency did not pause in its almost daily denunciation of American imperialism.

Oswald's murder

While news of the assassination circulated around the world on Saturday November 23, the Dallas police conducted a series of largely fruitless interviews with an uncooperative Oswald, even confronting him at one point with an enlarged picture of him standing proudly with both rifle and pistol, from a negative they had found when they visited his wife Marina. Since he would need to appear before a grand jury to be arraigned on the charges against him, they knew that he would have to be transferred from the city to the county jail. In the early hours of November 24, the Dallas FBI office received an anonymous phone call threatening to kill Oswald. The police were alerted and additional steps were supposedly taken to ensure the transfer could be done safely. These measures did not, however, include the barring of the media, who had covered much of the investigation from inside police headquarters.

There were about seventy officers in the basement garage, to ensure Oswald's safe transfer. The police even decided, at the last minute, to use an armored car they had ordered as a decoy, while transferring their prisoner in an unmarked car with armed officers. Astonishingly, they had failed to secure the ramp leading down to the basement from Main Street and a Dallas nightclub owner, Jack Ruby, strolled inside. Well known to the police and given to visiting their headquarters, he had mingled with reporters the previous day, and so now he aroused no suspicion. TV networks had cameras set to film Oswald's departure, and at 11.20 a.m. they broadcast the chaotic scenes in the garage as the press surged forward to get close to the accused, who was handcuffed between two detectives. Suddenly, Ruby lunged through the crowd of shouting reporters and fired into Oswald's stomach at point-blank range. A national audience witnessed America's first live murder. NBC showed the shooting live, while CBS used a slow motion replay to reveal the enormity of what had happened. For a nation already in shock, it was a further blow to their faith in law and order.

The shock

The entire episode did not make sense. The most powerful man in the world, who was widely believed to be the most protected man in the world, had apparently been killed by a lone gunman, and then the suspect supposedly at the center of what appeared to be the crime of the century had himself been killed live on television. What was America coming to? The televised murder of Oswald deepened the trauma Americans felt and sharpened the feeling that they were participants in an unforgettable moment of history. The continuing controversy over the assassination has its roots in this unsettling disorder. But later events, notably the war in Vietnam, the violent racial disturbances in American cities, and the growing cultural clashes within the nation, climaxing in some respects in the summer of 1968 when Kennedy's brother Robert was similarly gunned down, strengthened a popular sense that JFK's murder was the tragic turning point.

At the same time, the rejection of the official version promulgated in 1964 by President Johnson's Warren Commission—that Lee Harvey Oswald acted alone and that Jack Ruby killed him because he was so outraged at the assassination—grew out of a profound urge on the part of many Americans to find a more satisfying explanation; more satisfying both in the sense that it incorporated details that proponents felt had been unjustly ignored and in the sense that it made the actors and the motivation more proportionate to the enormity of the crime. Coupled to this was a broader cultural trend of delegitimation, whereby popular mistrust of government grew, while alongside it a powerful residual belief persisted that it was possible to uncover the whole truth, to tell the whole story. Through these potent cultural processes, investigative mistakes ceased to be simple errors and became instead acts of collusion and concealment.

Failings of the police and others

The failure of the Dallas police force to investigate adequately reports of shots from the grassy knoll, the failure of the post-mortem to trace the tracks of the bullets through JFK's body and thus establish points of exit and entry, the failure to protect Oswald—all have fed the conspiracy mill, which took hold first in Europe, where the killing was almost instantly seen as a political act, and then in the United States. Currently only a minority of Americans accepts the Warren Commission's findings, and subsequent official investigations by the House Select Committee on Assassinations in the 1970s and by the Assassination Records Review Board in the 1990s have largely destroyed its credibility. It seems fair, therefore, to state categorically that there was a cover-up in relation to the assassination, but this conspiracy to give a quick and simple answer to the American people in

1964 does not in itself prove that the assassination was the work of a conspiracy, and certainly does not clarify who were the conspirators.

If the Dallas police had taken greater care to investigate the claims of onlookers that shots came from the grassy knoll, and had found evidence of gunshots fired from that location, they would have obtained proof that Oswald did not act alone. Their negligence gives credence to claims that the lethal shot (the second to hit Kennedy) did not come from Oswald in the Book Depository behind the motorcade. Their failure to investigate eyewitness testimony related to other locations can be ascribed to the speed with which searches at the Book Depository yielded compelling evidence, in the form of three gun cartridges and the sniper position by the sixth floor window that corroborated some eyewitness testimony. Alternatively, it can be seen as deliberate neglect, or as marking the successful laying of a false trail. Similarly, their failure to protect Oswald can be seen as human error stemming from a willingness to allow the press full access to their activities, or it can be seen as collusion in the elimination of an Oswald whose role and value within a larger conspiracy had ended.

But not all the failings were in Dallas. At Bethesda Naval Hospital, the failure of the autopsy to establish definitively whether the president's wounds were consistent with gunfire from a single location can be ascribed to a desire to expedite the process, in order to allow the grieving first lady and her entourage the earliest possible opportunity to bury the president, and to minimize the mutilation of his corpse; or it can be viewed as yet another measure to conceal the reality that he was caught in a cross fire. If the latter is true, the scale of the conspiracy is staggering.

A left-wing or a right-wing plot?

The initial disclosures about Oswald's Communist connections fed rumors of a "Red" plot that understandably alarmed Soviet officials, who in their own coverage insisted that Kennedy was the victim of a right-wing coup. They noted accurately that JFK had been virulently attacked for signing the test ban treaty and that

Dallas was a center for right-wing forces. Liberal Americans similarly linked the murder to the violent segregationist opposition to civil rights legislation, since the murder occurred in the South, and Southerners in turn pointed in their own defense to Oswald, the Communist defector with his Russian wife and stash of leftist literature.

For many Americans in 1964, the Warren Commission's verdict that Oswald acted alone and did so more for personal self-aggrandizement than for broader political objectives was reassuring. At the same time, even though it was implicated by the Warren Commission, the radical Right suffered a devastating blow to its electoral hopes, as demonstrated by the landslide defeat suffered a year later by its standard bearer Barry Goldwater at the hands of Lyndon Johnson. Americans voted for LBJ as the man who was continuing the work of the fallen president; for some it seemed that to vote Republican in 1964 was in some sense sacrilegious.

The growth of disbelief

While the political establishment and most of the media accepted the Warren Commission's findings, there remained a vocal minority who did not. Their claims raised doubt by insisting that the original investigation was inadequate in terms of establishing that there was only one gunman. As we shall see, they also amplified the tangled web of connections that linked Oswald to both the FBI and the CIA, and that also linked his murderer Jack Ruby to organized crime. Flamboyant district attorney Jim Garrison created a stir in the late 1960s by trying to implicate local New Orleans business figures in collusion with the CIA, and his accusations ultimately gained a mass audience through the popular success of Oliver Stone's 1991 movie *JFK*.

By the 1970s, the Pentagon Papers had disclosed the failure of the US government to keep its own people informed about the escalation of US engagement in Vietnam and the progress of the war. This was followed rapidly by the Watergate scandal, with its revelation of "secret operations" by the imperial presidency, and the subsequent congressional investigations that unearthed the clandestine operations of the CIA, notably in relation to Cuba, and those of the FBI in relation to domestic dissent, all of which added to public cynicism about the Warren Commission's and indeed all of Washington's probity.

Revelations about President Kennedy's personal life and the vexed relationship between the CIA, organized crime, and Bobby Kennedy's crusade against mobsters and racketeers extended the range of potential conspirators behind his death, particularly since individuals came forward to testify alarmingly. The CIA had negotiated with crime figures to have Castro assassinated. The Justice Department's campaign against figures like Teamsters' leader Jimmy Hoffa and crime kingpins Sam Giancana, Carlos Marcello, John Roselli, and Santos Trafficante had prompted each of these demonstrably dangerous men to speak openly of the need to eliminate Kennedy. Investigators believed that they could place both Oswald and Ruby within a common, tangled web of covert operations and criminality in Dallas, New Orleans, and Miami. All these disclosures and assertions combined to ensure that the assassination was increasingly seen as a carefully planned act rather than the work of a bizarre "loner."

In the pages that follow, we will review the main conspiracy theories. While a few theories—such as those that argue that Oswald was actually trying to kill Governor Connally (who had been secretary of the navy when Oswald received a dishonorable discharge from the Marines), or that Johnson plotted the murder (and casually mentioned his plans to get rid of the Kennedys to a mistress the night before), or that Kennedy's fate was sealed once he asked to see further details of the Roswell UFO incident (and indeed any that involve extraterrestrials)—will receive scant attention, the plausible possibilities will be reviewed.

Oswald's ties to the USSR and Cuba

The murder of Officer Tippit is a key circumstantial event in persuading many people that Oswald had a role in the assassination. He denied both crimes but eyewitness identification and the pistol found on him at the time of his arrest form the basis for concluding that he did murder Tippit. Why would he have done so unless he had reason to fear arrest barely an hour after the assassination? Even if one gives Oswald a role in the assassination, however, it is not clear that he was cognizant of who was really sponsoring his action.

Lyndon Johnson's fear that the assassination might be linked to Cuba and the USSR (and thus produce a potentially catastrophic clamor for war) grew out of the revelation that Oswald, whose defection to the USSR in 1959 and return to America in June 1962 was a matter of public record, had visited both the Cuban and Soviet Consulates in Mexico City in late September 1963. The person handling visa applications at the Cuban Consulate, Silvia Duran, a Mexican, told the House Select Committee in 1978 that when Oswald disclosed that he wanted to go to Cuba as a transit point to the USSR she advised him that he would need to get a Soviet visa first. At the Soviet Consulate, according to Oleg Nechiporenko's 1993 memoir, Oswald told officials that FBI surveillance of him now included a campaign of intimidation against his wife Marina, and that to escape this he wanted to return to the USSR. He wanted to go to Cuba first, just in case the USSR would not admit him, he said. To his dismay, he was told that he would have to apply to the Soviet Embassy in Washington. Clearly agitated, Oswald had told Nechiporenko that this wouldn't do, and declared, "For me, it's all going to end in tragedy" (Nechiporenko 1993: 66–71).

Oswald then foolishly tried to bluff a visa out of the Cuban Consulate by falsely claiming to have already obtained the Soviet one. Sensibly, Silvia Duran phoned the Soviet Consulate to check Oswald's story, and since the CIA had wiretaps on the Soviet Consulate phones, when Valery Kostikov phoned her back they had a record of the conversation. While both Kostikov and Duran were sympathetic to Oswald's predicament, both felt that he had to follow the customary procedures and seek a visa for the USSR in his home country. While the substance of the exchange seemed to imply only that Oswald was seeking to go back with his Russian wife to the USSR, and hoped to do so via Cuba, the mere fact of contact could be used in the agitated climate of November 1963. Conservative "hawks" could easily suggest that this proved Oswald had been commissioned to assassinate Kennedy by America's archenemies, especially since Kostikov, the consular official involved, was actually a KGB agent, active in its Department 13, which handled "black ops," including assassinations. With their own axes to grind, such people were less likely to reveal that Oswald had left the Cuban Consulate after an angry shouting match (Kaiser 2008: 269–71).

With hindsight, the only possibility of a Soviet mission to kill JFK would arise in the context of a maverick operation by Kremlin hardliners eager to create international tensions that would undercut Khrushchev's efforts to develop détente. In much the same way, it would have been illogical for the Cubans to license such a mission. The revelations concerning Operation Mongoose, the CIA's plan to assassinate Fidel Castro and foment instability within Cuba, gave the Cuban leader ample personal reason for retaliation. On September 7, 1963 Castro allegedly told an Associated Press reporter that "United States leaders should know that if they are aiding plans to eliminate Cuban leaders, they themselves will not be safe." But it was equally clear that, were JFK's assassination revealed to be of Cuban origin, the logical consequence would be an American invasion. The latter had been an imminent threat up until the Missile Crisis, and the crisis's most positive outcome from Castro's point of view was to reduce this possibility. He would be unlikely to jeopardize his country, and while rumors persist that Oswald boasted to Cuban officials that he would kill Kennedy during his visit to the Mexico City consulate, they are not corroborated by other documents related to his visit. Despite troubling evidence, conspiracy theories that link Oswald to foreign powers have less credibility than those that tie the assassination to Kennedy's internal enemies, although among these must be listed anti-Castro Cubans residing in the US.

The importance of institutional self-defense

It is clear that the knowledge that the CIA and to some extent the FBI had about Oswald became an embarrassment to them in the aftermath of the assassination. Given that they and the Secret Service had failed to protect the president by neutralizing Oswald as a potential threat ahead of Kennedy's visit to Dallas, all agencies had a vested interest in minimizing revelations that suggested they knew of Oswald and yet did little to monitor or control his movements. Whereas most people would assume that there was an imperative to discover the truth behind Kennedy's murder and apprehend the perpetrators, in reality as soon as the assassination succeeded most of the agencies entrusted with national security were largely concerned with damage limitation to themselves, and this instinct for self-defense, alongside a political judgment that it was important to calm the people, led to a cover-up. Once the cover-up was exposed, it generated further suspicions of official involvement.

The suspicious conduct of the CIA

In the context of the Cold War, it seems inconceivable that an American citizen who had served in the Marines could defect to the Soviet Union, then return after nearly three years of living there, and yet draw no official attention. At the same time, it is evident that the FBI and CIA did not cooperate well, and that their obsession with protecting their own activities greatly inhibited their cooperation with local police forces. It is reported that on the afternoon of the assassination the FBI's legal counsel in Mexico City was appalled to learn that the CIA had not informed the FBI of Oswald's visits to the Cuban and Soviet embassies. Worse still, after listening to taped phone conversations and reviewing photographs the FBI had to report to the new president and the Secret Service that the person depicted in the CIA photos was not the Oswald their agents had interviewed but an imposter.

Given that the person on the phone spoke only very broken Russian, it was not Oswald, and certainly the figure in the photographs did not look like him. Some suspect, therefore, that this was a CIA operation intended to conceal Oswald's real association with them. Initially they may have made the phone calls and staged a further visit to the consulates in an attempt to elicit information about Oswald from consulate officials, but they then used the materials they had to sow confusion in the wake of the assassination.

Shortly thereafter, on November 26, the CIA forwarded a report from a Nicaraguan agent, Gilberto Alvarado, who claimed to have seen Oswald receive $6,500 in cash at the Cuban Embassy at a meeting on September 18. The Warren Commission quickly established that this was a hoax, since they had evidence that Lee Harvey Oswald was seen by multiple witnesses in New Orleans on the day in question, and Alvarado himself subsequently confessed that he had invented the story in an attempt to incite hostilities between the US and Cuba. Thus we have evidence that the CIA conveyed information to the government which was likely to support calls for dramatic action against the Castro regime, and that this was in line with the policy advocated by significant figures within the Agency who regarded the Bay of Pigs fiasco as an unjust stain on the CIA's reputation.

The anti-Castro Cubans and Oswald

During the Eisenhower era, the CIA, under its then director Allen Dulles, had emerged as a formidable force within US foreign policy. It had aided the rise of the Shah in Iran in 1953 and toppled the democratically elected government of Jacobo Arbenz in Guatemala in 1954. It was predictable that, when by 1959 Fidel Castro signaled that his new regime was moving into the Communist sphere of influence, the CIA would develop plans to replace him with a pro-American leader. Thus Dulles and his lieutenant Richard Bissell were behind the Bay of Pigs, and seemed to have proceeded on the assumption that ultimately the anti-Castro forces could rely on US armed support if their own efforts faltered. They certainly created this impression within the Cuban refugee community. As a result, when JFK refused to commit US forces to save the Cuban Brigade in 1961, it was seen as a betrayal. In the years that followed, as the CIA continued to support efforts to overthrow Castro, they inevitably came into contact with a variety of anti-Castro Cubans, who had established themselves in various cities, notably Miami and New Orleans.

In addition to groups who received CIA support, there were many others who were sponsored by wealthy conservative Americans and Cuban exiles anxious to take up the fight against Castroism. By 1962 the Cuban Revolutionary Council (CRC), the Revolutionary Junta in Exile (JURE), the Cuban Student Directorate (DRE), and the Insurrectional Movement for Revolutionary Recovery (MIRR) were some of the leading anti-Castro groups in the US. Some of these groups worked with the CIA to spread anti-Castro propaganda, while others staged various kinds of attacks, including sabotage raids on the island of Cuba itself. The latter sometimes also involved American mercenaries, notably Gerry Hemming and Frank Sturgis. On August 24, 1962, for instance, two DRE vessels shelled the Sierra Maestra Hotel in Havana, where numerous Soviet and Czech advisors were staying. These attacks were technically a breach of the US Neutrality Act and of international law, and the State Department worried over the ramifications, asking the CIA to rein in its associates.

Despite worries that these paramilitary groups might trigger open warfare, the reality was that the DRE raid brought the group unprecedented publicity and, equally important, financial support from figures such as *Time* magnate Henry Luce. This enabled DRE to establish branches in other cities, including New Orleans, where one of its leaders, Carlos Bringuier, met Lee Harvey Oswald in early August 1963. The CRC also had offices in New Orleans, at 544 Camp Street, a location it found with the assistance of Guy Banister, a former FBI agent and local police officer who was working as a private investigator and sometime CIA operative out of the same building. Oswald's handbills, distributed supposedly on behalf of his New Orleans chapter of the Fair Play for Cuba Committee, gave 544 Camp Street as the organization's address. It was while handing out these leaflets that Oswald became involved in a street altercation with Bringuier and two other DRE members. Arrested for disturbing the peace and lacking the means to post bail immediately, Oswald was held in jail, during which time he asked to speak to an FBI agent. This has prompted some authors to suggest that Oswald's FPCC (of which he seems to have been the only known member) was a front operation funded by the CIA as an agent provocateur exercise to enable them to monitor pro-Cuban sympathizers. Thus, while on the surface Oswald was pro-Castro, in reality he was working for the CIA as part of its anti-Castro operations (Kaiser 2008: 220–34).

What has become known as the Odio Incident is also cited as evidence for Oswald's involvement with anti-Castro groups. A Cuban refugee from Castro, Silvia Odio, who had been a founding member of JURE, had moved to Dallas following her divorce. She told FBI agents that sometime in late September or early October two men claiming to be JURE members came to her house, with another man whom they introduced as Leon Oswald. They wanted her assistance in preparing a fundraising letter for JURE to selected Dallas businesses. Miss Odio said that she told them she could not assist since she had curtailed her political activities for fear of reprisals against her parents, who were in one of Castro's prisons following a failed assassination plot.

The next day one of the two men phoned Odio and asked her what she thought of the American, Leon. He said that Leon was an ex-marine, a terrific guy interested in helping Cubans. But when he sensed that Odio was unenthusiastic, he added that Leon, an expert marksman, was *loco* (crazy), capable of anything, even killing Castro. In the same conversation this man, whom Odio knew only as Leopoldo, said that Leon had complained that the Cubans lacked guts, that they should have assassinated Kennedy for what he did during the Bay of Pigs invasion. In Miami, Odio's sister Annie, who had been visiting at the time of the men's visit, told FBI agents that she was "almost certain" that Leon was Oswald.

Odio's testimony did not make it easy for the Bureau to follow its director's orders to guide the Warren Commission as smoothly as possible to the clear conclusion that Oswald was a lone gunman. Her evidence was therefore suppressed, although subsequent investigations have strongly suggested that Odio did indeed meet Oswald, but probably in the company of Spanish-speaking American mercenaries rather than Cubans, namely Loran Eugene Hall and Larry Howard. The latter two's contact with anti-Castro Cubans, extreme right-wing groups such as the Minutemen, and organized crime figures certainly did not help the FBI's efforts to bolster the lone gunman hypothesis, and unsurprisingly their names did not feature in the Warren Commission report, which dismissed Odio's claims (Kaiser 2008: 255–56).

As gunrunners, Hall and Howard operated in Miami and Los Angeles as well as New Orleans and Dallas. In addition to participating in raids on Cuba, their arms smuggling was a crucial part of their involvement with anti-Castro groups. The ability of Cuban groups to arm themselves while in the US aggravated the control problems that the Kennedy administration had. There were occasional seizures and prosecutions, but they seemed almost token gestures and did little to end the armed attacks on Cuba, which for many of these groups were vital for publicity and fundraising.

JFK's mixed messages

By 1963, the dominant element within Kennedy's Cuban policy (in the larger context of the Alliance for Progress as a program to deter Communist expansion in Latin America) was propaganda. Accordingly, the administration wanted Latin Americans generally and Cubans on the island in particular to see the United States as principally backing social democratic exile groups such as MIRR, under Manuel Artime, and JURE, led by Manuel Ray, rather than groups that could be linked back to the Batista regime or to American business interests. The administration was actually divided on how to proceed.

Secretary of State Dean Rusk no longer believed that sabotage operations would trigger Castro's downfall, and National Security Advisor McGeorge Bundy was even prepared to consider a diplomatic rapprochement that would entice Castro away from his Soviet paymasters. President Kennedy and his brother Robert, however, still hoped to topple the regime, as this would be the most politically advantageous outcome, and this goal had ardent supporters inside the CIA. This gave the Agency the complicated task of stirring groups to act against Castro at the same time as it also tried to prevent them from triggering fresh international embarrassment. In the last high-level meeting he attended on Cuba, on November 12, President Kennedy heard CIA director McCone and one of the Agency's Cuban operations directors, Desmond Fitzgerald, defend the sabotage program. An assassination plot involving Rolando Cubela, a close associate of Castro, was also believed to be imminent.

However mixed Kennedy's intentions and policies were towards Castro, the perception among anti-Castro Cubans was that he was doing too little and was actually a traitor to their cause. There was strong competition among the different groups, and this fueled their courtship of nongovernmental backers, including right-wing groups and organized crime, from whom they obtained money and weapons. By the autumn of 1963 the most troublesome group in the eyes of the CIA was probably the DRE. Its leaders had issued repeated denunciations of official American efforts as a justification for their own radical proposals for independent military action. Aware that more support was being given to JURE efforts to establish operational bases in Central America, the DRE warned its CIA contact that it planned to establish a military base on a Caribbean island, and later commentators have linked this to a surge of confidence born of private financial backing.

By mid-October, the DRE was actively in the market for weapons, and among its suppliers was a Dallas gun dealer, John Thomas Masen, who contacted Colonel George Nonte of the Fort Hood Armory to assist. Masen was arrested by the Bureau of Alcohol, Tobacco, and Firearms agents on November 21. Some writers claim that Masen also bore a passing resemblance to Lee Harvey Oswald, prompting at least one person to tell the FBI in the wake of the assassination that Oswald had attended a DRE meeting in late October. (The photos of Masen in the public domain don't bolster this claim.) But the overall contention thus emerges that, at the time of the assassination, Dallas had become a site of active anti-Castro activity, where the refugees' frustration and resentment against what they perceived to be JFK's betrayal may have spurred the movement's associates to murderous action.

Organized crime's involvement

Before concluding that the assassination was linked to the disaffection of anti-Castro Cubans with Kennedy, it is important to consider another strong possibility. Just as Oswald's murder of Officer Tippit provides evidence that on November 22 he was desperate to avoid arrest, so his murder two days later by Jack Ruby sparks the obvious suspicion that he was killed to prevent him from divulging the identity of his sponsors. Accordingly, commentators have turned their attention to Ruby, seeking to overturn his contention that he killed Oswald out of patriotic anger and to shorten the ordeal of the Kennedy family, particularly Mrs. Kennedy and her young children. This requires them to discount the testimony of his close relatives and associates, who reported that Ruby was profoundly affected by the assassination and displayed acute psychological agitation in the days leading up to Oswald's shooting. His conduct on the morning of the shooting seems remarkably composed. He sends a money order and then calmly enters police headquarters. Most importantly, an examination of Ruby's background reveals links to organized crime that certainly warranted more investigation than they received in 1963–64.

In June 1964 two eminent members of the Warren Commission, Chief Justice Earl Warren and future President Gerald Ford, then a Republican congressman, visited the Dallas County jail to interview Jack Ruby. "I want to tell the truth, and I can't tell it here," Ruby declared, pleading with them to order his transfer to protective custody in Washington (Kurtz 2006: 196). They refused his request. Anxious to conclude their investigation and publish their report, they ignored the obvious ties that Ruby (born Jacob Rubenstein in Chicago in 1911) had to organized crime. A teenager in Chicago in the 1920s, Ruby had lived in a neighborhood known for gangster activity, and enjoyed pastimes, particularly gambling, that were likely to strengthen these links. He had been active in a local branch (number 20467) of the Scrap Iron and Junk Handlers Union, whose founder was murdered in 1939 as part of a mob takeover.

Investigating the role of organized crime in the labor movement, often referred to as racketeering, became a political cause in the 1950s, providing a platform for both John and Bobby Kennedy. Bobby in particular became known for his efforts to secure evidence against Teamsters' leader Jimmy Hoffa, an objective that he pursued vigorously as attorney general. While the Kennedy brothers moved up in the world of politics in the 1950s, Jack Ruby was establishing himself with other members of his family as a nightclub owner in Dallas specializing in striptease shows and illegal gambling. He cultivated his relations with members of the Dallas Police Department, and his meager finances and dubious activities strongly suggest that he was a minion within a network of organized crime. Thus the Warren Commission's dismissal of his links is unpersuasive.

In contrast, the congressional committee investigation of the 1970s documented Jack Ruby's close relationship with numerous organized crime figures. One of his Dallas friends was Joseph Civello, who had attended a notorious meeting of organized crime leaders at Apalachin, New York in 1957. Civello was accompanied to that meeting by Joseph Marcello, whose brother Carlos was the leading mobster in New Orleans and by 1963 a major target of Justice Department efforts. As early as April 1961, Bobby Kennedy had ordered Immigration officers to seize Marcello and deport him to Guatemala. Marcello angrily returned to Louisiana, and his hatred of the attorney general deepened when the Justice Department charged him not only with illegal reentry to the United States but with perjury and fraud. Talking to friends over drinks at his home near New Orleans in the fall of 1962, Marcello's anger at Bobby Kennedy was obvious. Referring to Bobby as the "tail" and JFK as the "head," he said that if you cut off a dog's tail it can still bite you, but if you cut off the head it can't. What he needed, he concluded, was some "nut" to carry out the assassination (Kurtz 2006: 208).

By the time Congress was holding its hearings in 1975, stories of the CIA's efforts to recruit organized crime figures as part of Operation Mongoose (the code name for their efforts to topple Castro) had a wide circulation. Among the individuals contacted by the Agency was Sam Giancana. He was one of the first organized crime figures to be linked by conspiracy theorists to the Kennedy assassination, partly because his showbiz relationship with Frank Sinatra and the fact that President Kennedy and Giancana shared a mistress, Judith Exner, added spice to the telling. Another figure involved in the Mongoose plots was Giancana's sometime associate, Las Vegas gangland boss John Roselli.

Since the main CIA station engaged in Operation Mongoose plots was in Miami, the Florida mobster Santos Trafficante was also strongly implicated in the story because of his past links to Cuba. He had owned casinos in Havana and in 1959 had been imprisoned for a time by Castro. Significantly, the House Select Committee on Assassinations (HSCA) in its final report explicitly stated that police intelligence on both Marcello and Trafficante was inadequate, since, unlike Giancana and others, they had not been subject to FBI electronic surveillance (much of it technically illegal) in the crucial period from January 1963 to June 1964. The final report quoted an FBI official conceding that they had been unable "to get very far" with Marcello. "He was too smart," the official had told the Committee (US HSCA 1979).

During the congressional hearings of the mid-1970s, a suspicious number of witnesses and potential witnesses met violent or sudden deaths. On the night of June 20, 1975, for example, Sam

Giancana was shot to death in his Chicago home. His murderer fired repeated rounds into the area around his mouth, sending the message that this was what happened if you did not keep your mouth shut. On the afternoon of July 30, Jimmy Hoffa, having served five years in prison, left his house for a meeting with Teamster officials and was never seen again (Kaiser 2008: 406–7).

A less conspicuous figure, but potentially a valuable witness, was John Martino, who had worked in Santos Trafficante's Havana casino and had been imprisoned in Cuba until 1962. Witnesses had seen him in Guy Banister's office at 544 Camp Street New Orleans in the summer of 1963 and at Curley's Corner, an illegal betting hangout, where he spent time with Dutz Murrett and Emile Bruneau. Murrett was Oswald's uncle and it was Bruneau who eventually got Oswald out of jail after his street clash with DRE members. Writer Anthony Summers has reported that Martino told a Texas business associate that "Oswald didn't know who he was working for" and that, once he was arrested, the mob "had Ruby kill him" (Kurtz 2006: 209–11). Although he was not on the HSCA's list of scheduled witnesses, for those anxious about what he might reveal under questioning, Martino died conveniently, of an apparent heart attack, in August 1975.

Having already appeared before one congressional committee in 1975 to discuss mob involvement in CIA plots against Castro, John Roselli was called to testify before another in April 1976. Clearly nervous, he provided less detail about the efforts to kill Castro than he had previously given to journalists, including Edward Morgan, who had already testified that JFK may well have been killed in retaliation for the repeated attempts on Castro's life. Although he denied directly that Carlos Marcello was involved in anti-Castro operations, Roselli did suggest, however vaguely, that Santos Trafficante had been, and this proved a fatal mistake. He went missing in Florida on July 27, 1976, and his dismembered body was found inside an oil drum floating in the sea near Miami.

After Giancana's death, Trafficante and Marcello were the prime remaining suspects for complicity in the assassination among organized crime figures. Trafficante was subpoenaed but, in the wake of the Roselli murder, he was able to persuade the Committee to allow him to testify off the record. While showing an impressive knowledge of Lee Harvey Oswald, in the opinion of one onlooker, Trafficante confirmed that he knew of Roselli's efforts to land assassination teams in Cuba, and said that he too had wondered whether Castro might have retaliated. Despite evidence that Jack Ruby paid a brief visit to Cuba in 1959, when Trafficante was trying to access money from the US to buy his release from prison, and that Ruby knew members of Trafficante's organization in Cuba, the committee accepted the wily drug lord's categorical denials that he ever knew Ruby. Later writers have speculated that Castro had allowed Trafficante to continue to use Cuba as a base for his drug trade operations in return for a percentage of the profits, and that the gangster could have further strengthened his relations with the dictator by alerting him to the Mongoose assassination plots the CIA had encouraged. Trafficante died a free man in March 1987, despite repeated federal attempts to entrap him.

Carlos Marcello fought deportation from the United States for thirty years through a variety of legal loopholes, but unlike Trafficante he was eventually prosecuted successfully, in 1981, for racketeering and attempted bribery of a judge. Bizarrely, while in a prison hospital in February 1989 he suffered hallucinations that convinced him he was at home among trusted associates. On three occasions over a two-day period he spoke of how he was going to get, or fix, "Kennedy in Dallas." When the FBI investigated his comments, however, the recovered Marcello stated that "this was crazy talk." A year after Marcello's death in 1993, Frank Ragano, a lawyer well acquainted with both Marcello and Trafficante, published a book in which he recounted how he had told the two mobsters in the spring of 1963 that Jimmy Hoffa wanted them to kill the president, and that their reaction had led him to believe that such a plot was already in the making. A few days after the deaths of Kennedy and Oswald, Ragano claimed, Marcello had told him: Hoffa "owes me, and he owes me big" (Kurtz 2006: 216–17).

The CIA's role

In the half century since the assassination, a myriad of theories and disclosures has emerged. The most politically charged has been the theory that a coalition of hardline military figures and CIA operatives had concluded by November 1963 that Kennedy was too soft on Communism. They believed he was about to prove this by reneging on commitments in Vietnam, just as he had backed away from the invasion of Cuba they had expected him to authorize in 1961. The murky world of national security and intelligence provides fertile soil for speculation because it is fed by an intrinsic secrecy and the presence of individuals who believe that their work necessarily straddles ethical boundaries, as they operate in a state of undeclared war.

In addition, a key part of the Agency's work is misinformation and deceit. Once the assassination occurred, the CIA, like the FBI, was most likely going to respond by concealing information that might be used against the Agency. A key part of this damaging information documented the Agency's prior relationship with Oswald and Oswald's relationship to numerous individuals with intelligence connections. And once elements of this cover-up were exposed it was inevitable that investigators would ponder the motivation behind the withholding of information. Suspicions of CIA involvement then extended not only to covering up information about individuals like Oswald but also to inventing and planting information to provide false trails and support false conclusions.

The so-called Lopez Report to the House Select Committee on Assassinations, for example, documented (as explained earlier) that at least one person impersonating Lee Harvey Oswald visited and rang the Soviet Embassy in Mexico City, and that the CIA had deliberately sought to steer the Warren Commission away from evidence that linked Oswald to the Agency. As critics of the Commission probed Oswald's background, they soon discovered individuals who knew Oswald and had CIA links. Jim Garrison, for instance, in his sensational investigation of Oswald's links to anti-Castro groups in southern Louisiana in 1963, tied his prime suspect Clay Shaw to Oswald via figures such as Guy Banister and David Ferrie. Sightings of Banister and Oswald together, at a time when Oswald was supposed to be recruiting for the pro-Castro Fair Play for Cuba Committee, have prompted the theory that in reality Oswald was working for the CIA to expose Castro sympathizers in New Orleans. Banister employed airplane pilot David

Ferrie to smuggle arms, fly dangerous missions into Cuba, and train recruits at training camps for would-be guerillas along the northern shore of Lake Pontchartrain (Kurtz 2006: 186–88).

Conspiracy theorists who are entirely convinced that Oswald was a CIA operative believe that his defection to the USSR was either an attempt to plant him as a potential double agent or to test and learn more about Soviet counterintelligence procedures. Others believe that he was recruited on his return through a mixture of disillusionment with Soviet Communism and financial incentives. Certainly, in Dallas, his family received important support from the enigmatic figure of George de Mohrenschildt, a Russian émigré and petroleum geologist who befriended Oswald not long after the latter's return from the USSR with his wife Marina in the summer of 1962. He helped Lee find work, gave the young couple money, and introduced Marina to a circle of Russian-speaking friends.

It has since emerged that at the same time as he came to the aid of Oswald and his family, de Mohrenschildt was assisting CIA efforts to topple Haitian dictator "Papa Doc" Duvalier. The sophisticated de Mohrenschildt had moved in elevated social circles. In New York he had socialized with Igor Cassini, brother of Jackie Kennedy's dress designer. He knew Jackie's parents, and had even met the young Jackie herself. Predictably, given his work, de Mohrenschildt knew several oil barons, including Edwin Pauley of California, who had been a key figure in Democratic fundraising circles since the 1930s, protecting the generous tax breaks that oil companies received. By the early 1960s Pauley was a conservative who would become a significant supporter of Ronald Reagan. In Dallas de Mohrenschildt knew millionaire oilmen Clint Murchison and H.L. Hunt, and members of the right-wing Crusade for Freedom, all of whom could be fairly described as extremely hostile to JFK.

De Mohrenschildt had worked for the intelligence services in Yugoslavia, and in Central America and the Caribbean. His wife Jeanne numbered among her friends future CIA director Richard Helms, and the head of the CIA's Western Hemisphere operations in 1963, David Atlee Philips, who operated largely out of Mexico City. De Mohrenschildt told the Warren Commission in 1964 that he had reported to J. Walton Moore, head of the Dallas Domestic

Contacts Office of the CIA, although he was uncertain for which government department Moore worked. In 1976, while waiting to be interviewed by congressional committee, de Mohrenschildt committed suicide with a shotgun.

It is clear that de Mohrenschildt helped Oswald find work and helped Oswald's wife Marina acclimatize in Dallas's Russian-speaking community. Given Oswald's documented contacts with the Communist Party USA, the Trotskyite Socialist Workers' Party, and the Fair Play for Cuba Committee in New York, his relationship with the clearly anti-Communist de Mohrenschildt requires explanation. The argument that he was only pretending to be pro-Castro while working for the CIA on anti-Castro operations offers one.

To the more ardent conspiracy theorists, Oswald is not the main focus for their story of the CIA's involvement in the Kennedy assassination. Mark Lane, one of the leading and earliest critics of the Warren Commission, has taken the view that there is ample evidence that the gunshot that killed Kennedy did not originate from the sixth floor of the Book Depository but from the grassy knoll. Kennedy was assassinated by a CIA team positioned behind the fence at the top of the knoll. Three tramps arrested in that vicinity allegedly used security connections to secure their release without interrogation by Dallas police. Conspiracy theorists have identified E. Howard Hunt and Frank Sturgis, who were involved in Mongoose operations against Castro prior to Dallas, but who would gain far greater notoriety for their involvement in the Watergate scandal, as two of the three men. But assessment of these allegations was greatly complicated in 1999 by statements from a KGB source, Vasily Mitrokhin. He stated that the KGB had forged a letter from Oswald to Hunt in 1975 and circulated it to active JFK assassination investigators in order to discredit the CIA. Thus, the suppression and fabrication of evidence by US intelligence in relation to the assassination is compounded by concurrent activities by foreign intelligence services.

Was it a coup?

A vital element in the claim that the CIA was involved in JFK's death is the argument that he was seen as a threat to the Agency, and more generally as a president who could not be trusted to back the national security agencies and armed forces in their efforts to win the Cold War. In this respect, some of the conspiracy theories offer a version of the Camelot legend, insisting that the negative events of the post-Kennedy era would not have occurred if he had been spared, and elevating Kennedy's death by making him the victim of malign forces that ultimately bear responsibility for Vietnam and Watergate. Thus the unresolved debate about the assassination has become an integral part of the historical assessment of JFK.

Some theories present Kennedy as ultimately the victim of his own misguided policies, in terms of his illegal efforts to kill Castro, and others see him as the murdered hero, slain by organized crime or by a "hidden government" that he was seeking to overturn. The continuing public debate over the assassination, which prompted passage of the Assassination Records Act in 1992 and the long process of records review, testifies to the way in which the murder has continued to have political overtones. Oliver Stone's movie *JFK* may have been the catalyst for the release of additional materials but by the time the review board completed its work, in 1998, the politically polarized climate of the late Clinton era found Americans even more deeply entrenched within a conspiratorial mindset.

The Warren Commission cover-up

The conflicting evidence about the number and directionality of the shots fired, about the nature of the wounds that Kennedy suffered, and about the conduct of the police, FBI, and CIA at the time of the assassination present the historian with a profoundly difficult problem in terms of establishing the reliability of basic evidence. This problem has been compounded by the growing evidence that the first investigation of the crime, namely the Warren Commission, was indeed a cover-up, designed to provide a reassuring conclusion that benefitted the perceived interests of the new president, and the security services. Lyndon Johnson feared a witch hunt against Communists, which, even if it did not set in train an international crisis that culminated in nuclear war, would, like the McCarthyite Red Scare before it, operate to the advantage of the Republicans in the 1964 election. He did not want the full character of Oswald's trip to Mexico City to be dissected, and nor did the CIA.

At the same time, Johnson quickly recognized that his strongest political lever in the aftermath of the assassination was public sympathy for the slain president. For this reason, he was also content to draw a veil over the extent to which the administration's operations against Castro's Cuba may have engendered the assassination itself. A president who has tried to murder other world leaders commands less sympathy than one who is murdered by a mentally troubled, lone gunman.

FBI complicity

If Johnson had good reason for pressing the Warren Commission to a quick judgment against Oswald, so too did both the CIA and the FBI. If the Commission had exposed Oswald's connections to the Agency, and with them the scale of the CIA's nefarious operations, not simply abroad but within the United States, the public outcry would surely have jeopardized the Agency's future, or at the very least cast doubt on the competence of its leadership: What should be done with a group incapable of assassinating Castro, despite numerous attempts, but able to facilitate the murder of its own commander-in-chief?

By the same token, the assassination was a crisis for the FBI. Its long-serving director, J. Edgar Hoover, had built the Bureau into a formidable institution through a mixture of adept public relations and political hardball. The public image of the FBI, developed during the 1930s, was that it had broken the power of gangsterism, which was why the congressional investigations of the 1950s exposing the extent of organized crime in the US had been so threatening to Hoover's Bureau. During the 1940s and 1950s Hoover had strengthened the FBI by expanding its anti-subversive operations within the Cold War context. The Communist Party of the US had been thoroughly infiltrated and Americans had come to believe that the FBI was an effective bulwark against internal threats.

In the early 1960s the Bureau was beginning to monitor the upsurge in militant conservative groups, including racist groups like the Ku Klux Klan and extreme libertarian groups like the

Minutemen. However it did so reluctantly. In 1963, its efforts to infiltrate the Klan seemed hard to distinguish from efforts to support it, given the racism prevalent among not just local agents but Hoover himself. He believed that the nation was threatened by Martin Luther King's campaigns, to such an extent that he was intent on destroying King by exposing the civil rights leader's sexual promiscuity and alleged Communist links. More generally, FBI agents were viewed as sympathetic to groups like the John Birch Society, which warned of a conspiracy against America, and hostile to civil rights groups like the American Civil Liberties Union, which they believed to be at best Communist "fellow travelers." If the assassination could have been rapidly connected to organized crime or right-wing groups as well as to Oswald, an individual whose Communist links had been known to the Bureau, then the future of the FBI, like that of the CIA, would have been called into question.

Ironically, the Secret Service, the governmental agency most directly charged with presidential safety, would ultimately emerge from the Warren Commission investigation with a series of recommendations that would strengthen its role and resources. Admittedly, the wilder fringes of the conspiracy theory movement have conjured up ideas about either deliberate or accidental complicity of the Secret Service detail in Kennedy's death, but they do not enjoy the same popularity as those other narratives that give JFK's murder greater meaning. Thus, the various threads of conspiracy that subsequently have been stressed by investigators—involving anti-Castro operations, organized crime, right-wing hate groups, the CIA, and the FBI—have grown in credibility as the cover-up attempt has been exposed.

An open verdict

The Assassination Records Review has not so far produced a body of evidence that can decisively end speculation about the answer to the question: Who shot JFK? Its efforts to clarify medical testimony relating to the autopsy, for example, have, in its own words, produced a situation where "witnesses contradict not only each other, but themselves" (ARRB 1998: 122). Unsurprisingly, the most secretive agencies, the CIA, the FBI and the Defense

Department, have all either divulged that no written record exists or have indicated that they wish to contest release on continuing grounds that the documents could adversely affect national security, current relations with foreign powers, or other concerns. They have also found instances of documents having been destroyed or "lost." When the Review Board did secure the release of records that assassination investigators had sought to obtain, such as transcripts of FBI electronic surveillance of Carlos Marcello, the evidence did not contain what previous writers had claimed, namely an open confession of involvement in the assassination.

In the absence of credible confessions, conclusive evidence, and demonstrable proof, the historian is left to conclude that he is unable to say definitively who murdered John F. Kennedy. The failings of the Warren Commission have become more obvious over time and the credible list of people with means and motive has also increased well beyond a lone gunman. What is self-evident is that Kennedy had many enemies in 1963, ranging across the political spectrum from General Walker's Minutemen to Castro's agents, from organized crime leaders to CIA figures, each of whom saw the president as a threat to their continued operations. As long as Oswald remains in the equation as an agent within the assassination, it seems most likely that those who sponsored him were tied to the Cuban question, either pro- or anti-Castro, but with the strong likelihood of an organized crime connection. His murder by Jack Ruby strengthens this contention.

The House Select Committee hesitated to conclude that the assassination was a mob hit because it said that, historically, organized crime figures have felt that the risks of murdering political figures outweighed the certain benefits. They preferred blackmail, corruption, or intimidation to assassination. Nevertheless, organized crime would certainly have had the expertise for the job. The same might also be said of the CIA, but if that was clearly so, why did they turn to the mob in their efforts to get Castro? By the same token, why did the mob use Jack Ruby, a man with a reputation for garrulous chatter, especially about himself and his role in the world? Previously eager to share any claim to prominence that came his way, Ruby died in prison in 1967 without divulging secrets.

John F. Kennedy died brutally in Dallas, but, in another sense, he sprang to life. He became the iconic figure who is now remembered, the president of eternal promise. Historically, the assassin's bullet made Kennedy's reputation more compellingly than did his achievements in office. For fifty years, he has been cherished in the popular memory even while his historical significance has been debated among scholars, with relatively little interaction between the two activities. It is to that process of memorialization that we now turn.

8   Images and actions

John F. Kennedy's memory has grown from the rich iconography of his life, so it is fitting to begin with his public image. In terms of media management, John F. Kennedy had a major impact on the presidency. He was, of course, not the first president to cultivate an image. Franklin Roosevelt had understood its power: projecting his jaunty, self-confident persona through controlled photo opportunities (deliberately avoiding the reality of his paralysis due to polio) and personal appeals via radio broadcasts ("fireside chats"). Hiding his actually tight and astute oversight of policy, Eisenhower attracted broad support through a radiant smile and genial manner that reassured Americans they were in safe hands. However, by 1961, television had become a much more dominant medium than it had been when Eisenhower took office in 1953, and the Kennedy White House deliberately played to it. As a result, the norms and motifs of the televised presidency were largely established by the Kennedys, not just Jack but in almost equal measure his wife Jackie and their two young children, as well as his brother Bobby and similarly youthful Cabinet members (the so-called "best and brightest"). JFK would establish the live press conference and the special TV broadcast to the nation as features of American life, and his wife would demonstrate how the first lady could be a cultural trend-setter and arbiter of taste. In myriad ways, JFK has served as the challenging template for his successors, and few have matched him.

The "Jackie" phenomenon

Even before the new First Family entered the White House in 1961, the planning of Jackie's image had begun, after a shaky start. During the transition, her social secretary caused consternation by indicating that Jackie felt that the White House needed a "makeover." Alarm bells rang because critics mistakenly feared that the new first lady would extend her love of Parisian fashion to a preference for modern European furnishings. In fact, she wanted a historic restoration. Given her role as a national symbol, Jackie's attachment to French couture, notably Givenchy, was seen as potentially unpatriotic, so the emergence of the New York-based Oleg Cassini as her designer of choice was an early, shrewd maneuver. In practice, she conferred with Cassini to develop designs that mirrored European trends, regularly identified by her fashion scouts in Rome and Paris. Cassini became part of her management of the press, whom she feared were set on making her "the Marie Antoinette of the 1960s" (Bradford 2000: 193–98).

Her husband's anger at her lavish expenditure on clothes gave Jackie further reason to avoid signs of extravagance. But her secretiveness also piqued press interest. While JFK's West Wing became fabled for its easy accessibility, the first lady and the children remained largely out of bounds. Discussion of Jackie's cultural projects was encouraged, her press secretary Pamela Turnure knew, but the children were off limits. To understand the mystique of Jackie, therefore, one needs to appreciate how much she protected her privacy, and in doing so made news and images about her, captured on foreign trips or formal engagements with the president, all the more valuable as a media commodity. Jackie's attitude to the press stood in contrast to her husband. When asked what she would feed her new German shepherd puppy, she replied, "Reporters" (Bradford 2000: 200)!

Despite this antipathy for the press, Jackie was in key respects the principal architect of the Kennedys' "Camelot." She entered the White House determined to make it "a grand house," as part of a larger effort to give her husband's presidency an aura and a glamor never seen before. Her White House would be a fitting residence for a head of state and a cultural *salon* in the French tradition, a place where witty and elegant people met to share culture at its best. This would underline the arrival of a "new generation." Paradoxically, the new generation's style would be linked to a physical process of historic restoration, since the White House mansion was in a depleted state, with furnishings that were at best described as characterless. Journalist Joseph Alsop more acerbically recalled "the peculiar combination of vomit green and rose pink that Mrs. Eisenhower had chosen for her bedroom and bathroom" (Bradford 2000: 227–28).

By the time the Kennedys moved into the White House, Jackie had plans for each of the seven family rooms on the second floor. As soon as a room was remodeled, rugs, furniture, and pictures completed the transformation. Within two weeks, she had spent the entire $50,000 appropriation for redecoration, and the State Rooms had not yet been touched. For these rooms, a more elaborate restoration process ensued that had political ramifications. A federal Fine Arts Committee was set up to locate period furniture and legislation was passed making the White House a museum to ensure that items donated would be retained as national treasures. Adding vital legitimacy to the project, prominent Republican and establishment connoisseur Henry Du Pont was appointed as committee chairman. Without him, the scheme could have been dismissed as the flighty extravagance of Joe Kennedy's daughter-in-law. Behind the scenes, however, Jackie was apt to listen more to the French expert, Stéphane Boudin, than to Du Pont, and only considerable diplomacy quieted his misgivings. But the project's prestige lured wealthy donors, and more money was raised through the success of Jackie's White House guidebook. The Kennedys gave the presidency a new cultural cachet.

In justifying the project's costs, Jackie proved a shrewd publicist. With journalist Hugh Sidey, she collaborated on a *Life* feature article in the summer of 1961 that described plans to make the White House a genuine national treasure. At the end of the year she hosted a televised tour of the White House which was seen by nearly 60 million Americans. Despite caustic criticism of her performance from Norman Mailer in *Esquire* magazine, the program was a huge success, confirming Jackie's status as a genuine political asset for Kennedy. Subsequent first ladies have not equaled her cultural influence. Recent Democratic ones—Rosalynn Carter, Hillary Clinton, and Michelle Obama—have tended to be policy advocates in their own right, while Republican ones—Nancy Reagan and both Barbara and Laura Bush—have been more presidential helpmates and subdued symbols of home life. None has been an icon quite like Jackie (Bradford 2000: 255–56; Klein 1996: 293).

The change of tone made by the Kennedys is more consistently admired with hindsight than it was at the time. On Sunday January 29, 1961, they gave a reception for Cabinet members and their families to which the press were invited. The stiff, teetotal, smoke-free gatherings of the Eisenhower era were gone, the press noted, and the sad-looking potted palms and the martial spittoons had also vanished. Fires glowed in reception room fireplaces. Flowers adorned tables. Hosts and guests drank and smoked in relaxed fashion. While the press corps enthused, the public relations tightrope to be walked was quickly demonstrated when Protestant clerics rebuked the Irish Catholic Kennedy for serving alcohol on the Sabbath, a sign that religious tensions persisted.

Nevertheless, the tone of stylish informality remained the dominant media message. Even formal state occasions seemed more imaginative under the Kennedys, as when Jackie held an al fresco dinner for Pakistan's president Ayub Khan at George Washington's Mount Vernon in July 1961 (see Plate 2). Boats ferried guests up the Potomac to the former plantation home, where they were treated to a Revolutionary War re-enactment before dining in an elegant marquee on the lawn. The grace of this event was part of the larger emergence of the White House as a cultural center. Jackie admittedly had to browbeat her husband into having more concerts at the White House, but positive press coverage resulted; in November 1961, for instance, when Spanish cellist Pablo Casals, after more than three decades of boycotting America for its support of the Fascist dictator Franco, performed there to rapturous applause. While no fan of recitals, JFK was more willing to host dinners for writers and scholars. He famously declared at a dinner for Nobel laureates in April 1962 that this was the most intellectually talented group to dine at the White House, with the possible exception of those occasions when Thomas Jefferson dined there alone. At such events, the shimmering glamour of the First Couple was not merely noted but widely reported, making the liberal intelligentsia far more enamored of Kennedy in 1963 than they had been in 1960.

Jackie's celebrity status boosted the president's reputation on the international as well as the domestic stage. Prior to 1960, US presidents did not travel the world as readily as they do today, so there was a novelty value to their trips abroad. In early June 1961,

Kennedy made his first European trip. En route to his Vienna Summit with Khrushchev, he paid a state visit to France. Franco–American relations at the time were delicate due to President Charles de Gaulle's deep-seated suspicion that NATO was largely an Anglo–American attempt to preempt France's natural hegemony over postwar Europe following the division of Germany. The recent Bay of Pigs fiasco had enraged French radicals and deepened fears that American power was in inexperienced hands. Given this inauspicious context, Jackie's ability to charm became a diplomatic asset.

Being of French ancestry himself, press secretary Pierre Salinger made sure that Jackie's Bouvier ancestry, her haute couture clothes, cultural interests, and knowledge of French life (she had spent a year at the Sorbonne in Paris) were widely publicized ahead of the visit. During the trip itself, commentators observed how Jackie's fluent French enabled her to act as her husband's interpreter in a way that entranced de Gaulle. British observers acknowledged that the General had been impressed with Kennedy; "no mean achievement," they declared. Jackie's largely Givenchy-designed wardrobe was for once seen as simply adept diplomacy. The American press proudly reprinted the praise lavished upon the first lady by the French newspapers, and the happily eclipsed president summed up his wife's impact by telling a press conference that it seemed necessary at this point to introduce himself: he had enjoyed being "the man who accompanied Jacqueline Kennedy to Paris" (Bradford 2000: 263–65).

The Vienna Summit did not go as Kennedy hoped, but as a style offensive the European trip firmly established the First Couple's glamour. On the way home from the bruising and dispiriting meeting with the Soviet premier, the presidential party stopped in London for a visit that gilded the Kennedys with the aristocratic English style that Americans esteem. A lunch with Prime Minister Harold Macmillan underlined how Jack's late sister Kathleen's marriage to Billy Hartington had brought the Kennedys into the heart of the British establishment. Macmillan's wife, Dorothy, was Hartington's sister and David Ormsby-Gore (later Lord Harlech) was the brother of the wife of Macmillan's eldest son. Ormsby-Gore had known Jack during Ambassador Kennedy's time in London and would shortly come to Washington as

Britain's ambassador. Press coverage of the visit strengthened a growing sense of change felt in the early 1960s, with the stylish Jack and Jackie underlining the generational shift from the old guard: Eisenhower, Macmillan, and de Gaulle. Jackie became a new kind of international superstar, whose every change of clothes was reported. Even behind the Iron Curtain, advertisements referred to the "Jackie look." Polish magazine *Swait* declared: "The face and silhouette of Jackie are known to all people all over the civilized world." In a Cold War context, such influence had political significance, and Jack Kennedy was obliged to treat his wife with a new degree of respect (Bradford 2000: 268–71).

Domestically, however, the impact of Jackie's public image was not constantly positive. The American public enjoyed having a glamorous first lady, and were fascinated with her wardrobe, but there remained those who took a more puritanical view. Her many trips away from the White House began to draw negative comment. Photos of her waterskiing on a day when she had ducked out of an official reception were damaging. As her travels increased, a columnist suggested that newscasters sign off their programs with the words "Good night, Mrs. Kennedy, wherever you are" (Klein 1996: 292). Her time away also called into question her dutifulness as a wife and a mother in the eyes of more traditional Americans. There had always been people who resented the Kennedys' wealth and Jackie's lavish lifestyle bolstered accusations of extravagance, the subtext being that a family that was loose with its own money might be foolish with public funds as well.

Jack Kennedy did not approve of his wife's shopping sprees or her tendency to acquire homes, like Glen Ora in Virginia, which she would expensively refurbish and then leave. But media coverage of both habits reinforced the view that with the Kennedys money was no object. The perception of a first lady as self-indulgent grew during 1962, as Jackie visited the Indian subcontinent and moved among the European jet-set in London and Rome. While the Indian trip, like her presence on JFK's trip to Mexico, had positive diplomatic effects, it underlined her globetrotting tendency. More clearly damaging politically were the pictures that came back from her August stay in Italy in the company of Fiat heir, Gianni Agnelli, an elegant man of the world with a reputation. As reports grew more critical, Kennedy felt obliged to send his wife a brusque cable reminding her that photos with their daughter Caroline would be more tactful. The telegram read: "More Caroline, less Agnelli" (Bradford 2000: 307–11).

Tragedy has largely obliterated the reality of doubts about the first lady that circulated when 1963 began. The first tragedy was the death of her newborn son, born nearly six weeks premature on August 7. In the early hours of August 9, the tiny Patrick died from respiratory failure; Jack held his baby son's hand and cried in a way that close associates had never seen. During the ensuing wave of public sympathy, the White House announced that Mrs. Kennedy would undertake no official duties until the end of the year. Aware that his wife needed time to recuperate, Kennedy agreed that Jackie could join her sister Lee as guests of the Greek shipping magnate Aristotle Onassis. He knew that he risked negative publicity from the inevitable photos of his wife sunbathing on a millionaire's yacht and Jackie appreciated that he was putting her needs first. Later revelations of the full extent of JFK's promiscuity have tended to underscore his insensitivity towards his wife. She appeared to "look the other way" with regard to his many dalliances. But their close friends felt that the relationship deepened in the summer of 1963, especially after Patrick's death. This made the November scenes, of first glamor and then horror, all the more poignant (see Plate 8).

When Jackie returned from Europe in late October she agreed to campaign with her husband, almost by way of recompense for his consideration. Kennedy was delighted by this news, since experience had shown that his wife not only attracted bigger crowds but in some ways took the partisan edge off what were clearly campaign visits to cities like Dallas. Such calculations placed Jackie next to her husband in the open-top limousine on November 22, and that night, in her bloodstained clothes, her image was captured for the nation as she stood beside Lyndon Johnson as he took the oath aboard Air Force One. With remarkable composure, Jackie Kennedy helped to organize the funeral for her husband, adapting state funeral practice to her own sense of pageantry. She resisted family pressure to take him home to Boston for burial, and instead orchestrated the nation's mourning, adding touches such as the family walking behind the funeral cortege, and, most touchingly, preparing her son John to give a farewell salute. It is overstating the case that she planned the funeral, since there was an established procedure and, ironically, rehearsals for a state funeral had been taking place discreetly at the time due to the deteriorating health of former President Herbert Hoover (he died in October 1964). Nevertheless, Jackie's poise at the funeral cemented her place in the iconography of the Kennedy era as the brave, loving, and above all stylish widow. As we have noted elsewhere, in her first postfuneral interview, with sympathetic journalist Theodore White, she planted the idea of the Kennedy White House as a latter-day Camelot. In all these ways, Jackie nurtured the mystique of the Kennedy years.

The "family man" image

Equally potent in its appeal to everyday Americans in the midst of the baby boom was the image of the president as a youthful family man. John F. Kennedy, Jr. was born on November 25, 1960. When the Kennedys moved in, "John John" was a baby of four months, while his sister Caroline had only just turned three. Not since Theodore Roosevelt stepped into the presidency on McKinley's assassination in 1901 had the White House been a home for young children. The voracious press appetite for family stories simply horrified Jackie Kennedy. She complained that they wanted to chase Caroline around with their flashbulbs and turn her into "a ghastly Shirley Temple if I'd let them." But while Jackie tried to shield the children from the press, Jack was ready to use their charm. During his 1958 Senate re-election campaign, *Life* photographers had been admitted to Caroline's nursery. The practicalities of having children in the White House, given security as well as press concerns, produced arrangements that were likely to excite public curiosity. A nursery school with ten pupils met there, complete with sandbox and a menagerie of rabbits, guinea pigs, and goldfish. There was a hatchery for chicks, a tree-house, a swing, slide, trampoline, and two ponies. All of this, Kennedy knew, constituted a human interest story that few editors could ignore (Bradford 2000: 181, 161, 251).

Proof that the place of the Kennedy children in the visual symbolism of the dynasty was a product of Jack's political judgment lies in the fact that the celebrated images of John and Caroline in the Oval Office, including the one of John peeping out from under his father's massive desk, were taken while Jackie was abroad in the autumn of 1963 (see Plate 7). JFK called *Life* photographer Stanley Tretick with the invitation, saying, "Things get kind of sticky around here when Mrs. Kennedy's around. But Mrs. Kennedy is away. So now's the time to do some of those pictures you've been asking for of John and Caroline." Trelick was allowed to take pictures over a five-day period and he and the president selected the best. Jack singled out the one of John playing under his desk. "With this one, you can't lose," he said (Klein 1996: 339–40).

JFK's physical appeal

While acknowledging the significance of media coverage of Kennedy's wife and children in forging a public image that gave the Kennedy presidency a special place in the national and international consciousness, one cannot ignore the charisma of Kennedy himself. Despite his many health problems, he appeared publicly to be a paragon of strength, wit, and vigor. The thick head of hair, the gleaming smile, the deep tan, the quietly stylish suits were essential ingredients in his appeal. They contributed to his electoral victory over Nixon, symbolized the end of the Eisenhower era, and underpinned his use of other devices, such as his live press conferences, televised addresses, and international visits. During the 1960 campaign reporters started to talk about the growing number of "jumpers," young women so keen and excited at the prospect of seeing JFK that they would leap high in the air amidst the roadside crowds. Commenting on the unanimity with which Irish people who met Jack during his triumphant visit in June 1963 spoke about his tanned face, thick hair, exceptionally white teeth, and piercing blue eyes, Ryan Tubridy notes that Kennedy made a deep physical impression in a postwar world that for many had been overwhelmingly dour, dull, and dreary. Kennedy came to Ireland hot on the heels of his historic visit to Berlin and he remarked to aide Ted Sorensen that he had been struck by the difference between the pretty girls who lined the streets in Dublin and those in Berlin. "In Dublin," he said, "he could see them mouth the words 'God bless you!' In Berlin, he felt they were

mouthing something much more earthy which I won't repeat"
(Tubridy 2010: 104, 278).

The brothers

Augmenting Jack's appeal, his brothers Robert, and to a lesser
extent Edward, attracted growing press attention. Despite the
predictable charges of nepotism that were made at the time of his
appointment as attorney general, by 1963 Bobby Kennedy was a
substantial political figure in his own right (see Plate 3). His
public stature had grown due to positive press coverage of his
energetic and determined leadership of the Justice Department,
his wider role within the administration as his brother's con-
fidante, and his newsworthy personal life, as the loving father of
seven children who also found time to make his Virginia home a
key center of "Camelot."

The house at Hickory Hill was regarded by many as the true
social center of the Kennedy administration because of its legendary
parties, presided over by Bobby and his wife Ethel. The press enjoyed
reporting how Ethel provided a table centerpiece of live bullfrogs
one St Patrick's Day, and especially how she and other formally
dressed partygoers ended up in the swimming pool fully clothed.
Among high-ranking officials who experienced this Kennedy
baptism were Defense Secretary Robert McNamara, press secretary
Pierre Salinger, and aide, historian Arthur Schlesinger; the last
was immersed while wearing "an impeccable light-blue dinner
jacket." Hickory Hill also hosted its famous seminars, where
intellectuals such as philosophers A.J. Ayer and Isaiah Berlin and
pioneer environmentalist Rachel Carson spoke. Both the parties
and the seminars served to glamorize the administration, and in the
media hothouse of Washington to validate those who were invited
to such gatherings as genuine "insiders" (Heymann 1998: 337–41).

Sex addiction

The later revelations about JFK's reckless sex life partly retain
their fascination because of the power of the initial image of Jackie
and Jack as the ideal couple. At the same time, the discovery that

the outwardly perfect marriage concealed a more sordid reality has reinforced the larger mystery narrative pattern on which conspiracy theories feed; things are not what they seem. Given Kennedy's many illnesses included a hormonal component addressed by injections of artificial hormone, there is a possibility that his relentless sex drive (he told a shocked British premier Harold Macmillan that if he didn't have sex at least once a day, he felt ill) was partly due to physiological factors. Since reports about his father's and brothers' affairs are also extensive there were also psychological and indeed cultural elements, of seeing sex as a sport in which women were trophies to be "bagged." Certainly, JFK was reported as more interested in the chase than its aftermath.

Jack's need for casual sexual encounters was accommodated by the first lady's desire to escape the limits of Washington. She even seems to have ignored his ongoing affair with her press secretary Pamela Turnure. Her insistence that they acquire a country residence in Virginia where she could ride was resented as a needless expense by Jack (he would have preferred a seaside retreat where he could sail) but it did ensure that she was away. The Secret Service details of first lady and president grew accustomed to liaising with each other to ensure that the president was alerted before the first lady returned. Rumors that Jackie took lovers herself certainly surfaced in relation to her visits to Europe. Jackie's subsequent marriage to Aristotle Onassis grew out of her prior friendship with him and her belief that his money could insulate her and her children from the demands of an intrusive public.

Jack Kennedy was well aware that Americans, especially in the heartland, would take a dim view of a president who cheated on his wife with mistresses and prostitutes. However, like his father before him, he believed that the male-dominated culture of America's media would enforce a code of silence. During the 1960 campaign, Turnure's landlady, Mrs. Kater, became obsessed with Kennedy's adulterous relationship with her tenant, and the threat of public exposure became palpable. Mrs. Kater and her husband picketed the White House on Inauguration Day with a placard denouncing the president, but the loyal Washington press corps ignored them. The threat of exposure came also from J. Edgar Hoover's FBI. Hoover kept files on political figures in his personal office and was known to use them in bargaining sessions. In Jack's case, the considerable dossier went back as far as his relationship with Inga Arvad in 1941, but also detailed more recent events, including his affair with Marilyn Monroe and sex parties with Frank Sinatra in Palm Springs, Las Vegas, and New York. Through Sinatra, too, JFK had social contact with known organized crime leaders. Jack's appointment of his brother Bobby as attorney general had several motives, but one was certainly to ensure that the attorney general (technically Hoover's boss) would be alert to FBI scheming. Whether Bobby ensured that there were no incriminating materials about Jack's involvement with Marilyn Monroe to be found in the star's home after her apparent suicide in August 1962 has been a source of much speculation for many writers.

Just as Jackie's public standing oscillated from her rise to stardom in 1961 through criticism in 1962, to tragic redemption as the nation's symbolic widow in 1963, so the threat represented by any exposure of Kennedy's infidelities was clear on Inauguration Day, lurked quietly for his first year, and then in the months before his death grew stronger. When Marilyn Monroe, dressed in a shimmering skin-tight backless gown, breathlessly sang "Happy Birthday" to JFK in May 1962 at a birthday tribute held in his honor, few doubted that her performance suggested a close relationship. Pictures of Kennedy at the event, laughing and smoking a cigar in roguish fashion, praising Monroe for singing in such a sweet and wholesome way, certainly capture Kennedy's machismo.

The Profumo scandal in Great Britain had generated global headlines and in late June 1963 a New York newspaper reported that two call girls linked to the scandal in London had also sold their services to "a high-ranking US aide." When interviewed by Bobby Kennedy the reporters confirmed that the aide in question was the president. Only days later the FBI informed Bobby that they had learned that an East German woman, Ellen Rometsch, one of the many call girls that Texan Bobby Baker provided for the entertainment of high-ranking officials via the Senate's Quorum Club, was believed to have espionage connections. The parallels to the Profumo affair were worrying. On August 21 Rometsch was deported. However, a Senate investigation into Baker's nefarious operations in October 1963 revived the possibility that Rometsch might be recalled to testify. The approaching election would increase the risk of disclosure as Kennedy faced a contest with a Republican Party that had turned towards its conservative wing. Given the later furor over Bill Clinton's affair with White House intern Monica Lewinsky, JFK's casualness in sexual matters was a risky venture. Posthumously, it probably adds to the interest he excites.

Hidden health problems

Another secret to be concealed from the public was the true state of Kennedy's health and the complex pharmaceutical regimen he followed. Persistent back problems required him to wear a lower back brace at all times, except when bathing. He found that a rocking chair eased discomfort when working, and that a hard mattress with a bed-board beneath was essential for sleeping. He also required a boost inside his left shoe to compensate for a general asymmetry, and had to undertake daily exercises, in addition to swimming, to strengthen his core muscles. Nevertheless, during the exhausting 1960 campaign, which had resulted in weight gain, Kennedy experienced increasingly severe muscle spasms in the back. His personal physician, Dr. Janet Travell, treated these with Novocain, but Kennedy also received injections of an amphetamine-based concoction from maverick practitioner Dr. Max Jacobson.

Jacobson's amphetamine-laced cocktail of painkillers and stimulants was on top of the regular dosage of cortisone that Kennedy took to counteract his adrenal insufficiency. Such drug use, which in the case of the steroid medications has been linked to a predisposition to psychotic delusions, was blatantly concealed by medical professionals, who were prepared to state publicly that the president was in excellent health. The pictures of JFK aboard his yacht, or of the Kennedy brothers throwing a football, or of Jack playing with his children bolstered the overall exercise in misinformation. A more accurate sign of his physical state was the fact that, when Kennedy was asked to plant a ceremonial tree on a visit to Canada in mid-May 1961, his back jarred so badly that he needed crutches to walk from Air Force One to his limousine. Later presidents have faced more rigorous scrutiny as a result.

The Kennedy speech-making style

The Kennedy White House set a public image standard that his successors have tried to match, not just in terms of visual imagery but also in terms of speeches and soundbites. Jack Kennedy worked hard to improve his speech-making, as he was far from naturally gifted in vocal delivery, and at times his Boston accent grated on listeners. Nevertheless, several of his set speeches have become classics of American oratory. Kennedy's main speechwriter was Theodore Sorensen, who was often assisted by Dick Goodwin, Mike Fellman, and occasionally Harris Wofford. Court intellectuals Arthur Schlesinger, Kenneth Galbraith, and Walter Rostow also contributed. Nevertheless the key figure in setting the Kennedy oratorical tone was Sorensen. All of Kennedy's immediate predecessors—FDR, Truman, and Eisenhower—had speechwriters, but none were Sorensen's equal.

There were several markers of the Sorensen style, which he always saw as simply the embodiment of Kennedy's own preferences. Reading copies of the major addresses confirms that Kennedy edited right up to the moment of delivery, and underlined to guide his delivery in terms of intonation. The most obvious Sorensen "signature" was the contrapuntal phrase, such as, "Let us never negotiate out of fear, but let us never fear to negotiate," and more famously, "ask not what your country can do for you—ask what you can do for your country" (* see Note page 245). Both phrases come from the celebrated inaugural address. Other traits were short, direct sentences and nicely calibrated repetition. In his first State of the Union address, for example, Kennedy was keen to emphasize the problems he inherited, saying, "Each day the crises multiply. Each day their solution grows more difficult. Each day we draw nearer the hour of maximum danger, as weapons spread and hostile forces grow stronger." As if to transmit the sense of mounting burdens, the sentences lengthen, with added poignancy given by the balanced final phrase. The somber tone and solemn cadences were intended to persuade Congress to support his increases in conventional military expenditures in a manner that contradicted Eisenhower's equally dark warnings in his 1961 farewell address about the threat of the military–industrial complex to American democracy.

In January 1963, when he gave his final State of the Union, Kennedy faced the difficult task of marrying his call for continuing sacrifice and effort with a public celebration of Democratic achievements in line with the midterm election victories, and acclaim for his management of the Cuban Missile Crisis. Hence, he declared: "The mere absence of war is not peace. The mere absence of recession is not growth. We have made a beginning—but we have only begun."

Sorensen's use of repetition, counterpoint, and short phrases remain evident, but it was by this stage geared towards the more positive task of translating "the renewal of our national strength into the achievement of our national purpose." Central to that purpose remained the defeat of Communism, although greater care was now taken simultaneously to signal that the United States realized that the "modern globe is too small, its weapons too destructive, and its disorders too contagious" to permit either side total victory. Kennedy's speechwriting team consistently achieved eloquence in the rhetorical showpieces of the presidential calendar, and they rose to the harsher challenge of unexpected crises. In particular, they were able to provide Kennedy with the words for special televised addresses, essential moments that locked his administration in the popular imagination. Kennedy was an astute performer on television, taking the trouble on occasion to check how the studio lighting presented him to the nation, and having it adjusted to best effect (Watson 1994: 75).

The space program as a Kennedy symbol

On May 25, 1961, Kennedy addressed a special session of Congress. The bulk of this so-called "second State of the Union" speech was focused on the economy, but another key theme was the need for the US to appear strong in the eyes of the rest of the world. Kennedy reminded his listeners of the Cold War context for space exploration. "If we are to win the battle that is now going on around the world between freedom and tyranny," he declared, "the dramatic achievements in space which occurred in recent weeks should have made clear to us all, as did Sputnik in 1957, the impact of this adventure on the minds of men everywhere." He was alluding to cosmonaut Yuri Gagarin's successful orbit around the Earth on April 12 and US astronaut Alan Shepard's first flight into space on May 4, which underlined the Soviet lead in the space race but indicated the possibility that the US could catch up. Kennedy therefore asked Congress to commit America to the goal of landing a man on the Moon before the end of the decade.

This costly commitment seemed a strange ingredient in a speech largely devoted to policies aimed at promoting economic recovery within a generally conservative framework. Kennedy couched his announcement in terms of asking the nation to make a positive choice, and embrace an ambitious goal, rather than simply rallying in the face of adversity. Over time, the successful Moon mission became part of the myth of the Kennedy presidency, symbolizing a time when Americans were confident enough to reach for the stars. At the time, his announcement represented more mundane political realities. Several congressional leaders hailed from places set to benefit as centers for NASA-related research and development. When liberals complained that he secured money for space projects and defense but not for schools and healthcare, Kennedy replied bluntly that Congress would never vote for the latter as they would for defense.

The foreign policy speeches

The rhetoric of the Kennedy presidency, while serving to establish the high ideals of the administration, also used the classic pattern of emphasizing the enormity of the external threat, to promote national unity and justify increased defense spending. Kennedy's televised address of July 25, 1961, like his inaugural, spoke starkly of the burdens the American people must bear because of the perils they faced. To defend Berlin, he proposed boosting the army's strength to over a million, and doubled and tripled draft call-ups for reservists. He controversially urged a private as well as a public fallout shelter construction program. Khrushchev responded by terming the speech a preliminary declaration of war, a reaction that reinforces the charge that, in trying to rally domestic support, Kennedy risked deepening international crises.

In October 1962, "the hour of maximum danger" that Kennedy had alluded to in his speeches seemed to arrive with the Cuban

Missile Crisis, and Kennedy's enhanced popularity after the crisis was due to the skillful way in which he presented the facts to the American people. In key respects, his previous televised speeches had set the stage for the special October 20 newscast in which he informed Americans that "a series of offensive missile sites" were under construction on what he termed "that imprisoned island." He had been warning Americans that the threat they faced was growing and that it needed to be met vigorously, and the Cuban developments appeared to confirm his stance. Significantly, he presented the missiles as a threat to the nations of Latin America as well as the US, thus beginning the diplomatic task of securing their support for any action the US might undertake. He also warned the Soviets explicitly that aggression against Berlin would be seen as an act of war.

Drafts of his speech show that it was revised to tone down its condemnation of Soviet action so as to ensure scope for negotiation. In this respect, his speech was designed for more than a domestic audience. For those familiar with his father's reputation as ambassador in London at the time of the Munich Crisis, there was a certain irony in Kennedy's reference to the lessons of appeasement to justify his strong stance. Listing the steps he had authorized, he demanded the withdrawal of the missiles, and after appealing directly to the freedom-loving people of Cuba he concluded by reiterating the determination with which Americans must face the risks of the nuclear crisis. Compared to other speeches, this address was muted and somber, and Kennedy's delivery reflected this, becoming a template for future presidents when they chose to address the nation. Even when the influence is not conscious or direct, presidents and their advisors know that it is seen as positive if their performance is likened to Kennedy's. Equally, audiences know that when a special broadcast shows the president seated at his desk in the Oval Office and begins solemnly with the words "My fellow Americans … " the news is rarely good.

The civil rights speeches

Three weeks before the missile speech, on September 30, Kennedy had addressed the nation because of a racial rather than international crisis. He spoke to explain why he had sent US marshals onto the campus of the University of Mississippi to enforce the registration of its first African American student, James Meredith. He reminded his audience that "Americans were free to disagree with the law but not to disobey it." The speech had been crafted to include a range of patriotic appeals to the university's students and other Mississippians, and it labored the point that the integration order had not been instigated by the administration but issued by Southern judges at a time when other Southern universities had already complied with similar orders. Yet, even in this context, Kennedy spoke of the global threat. Healing the wounds within the nation, he concluded, would ensure the unity needed to withstand "the greater crises that are without." As he spoke, the situation at the Mississippi campus deteriorated, and the mob attacked the federal marshals, illustrating that rhetoric alone could not change minds. However, in some respects the Southern reaction underlined one of the purposes of the address: namely, to align moderate Americans across the nation behind their president and against extremism. Kennedy's rhetoric on civil rights, and his actions, even more so, were carefully calibrated. His posthumous reputation as a civil rights champion is supported more by the escalating tone of his rhetoric than by the compelling force of his actions, although even here his willingness to act was greater in the summer of 1963 than it had been in 1960.

Kennedy's June 11 address signaling that he would ask Congress to pass a comprehensive civil rights bill is usually seen as the high-water mark. Coming in the wake of the dramatic images of children being swept off their feet by water cannon or bitten by police dogs in Birmingham, his speech marked an attempt to pull the nation back from the brink of racial warfare, and to corral the divisive civil rights issue within the more stable sphere of formal politics. Ultimately, Kennedy averred that the nation faced "a moral issue," and in an unprecedented show of empathy for the African American cause he detailed the disadvantages they faced and asked white Americans to consider how they would react to the same mistreatment. "The events in Birmingham and elsewhere," he declared, "have so increased the cries for equality that no city or state or legislative body can prudently choose to ignore them." At the same time, Kennedy linked the issue to the larger Cold War conflict, reminding his listeners that African Americans were defending their country in Berlin and Vietnam and that all those who were working to develop racial tolerance were, like soldiers and sailors, "meeting freedom's challenge on the firing line." The immediate Southern response to this address, as with the Meredith speech, came in Mississippi and was a violent one. A leading African American activist in the state, Medgar Evers, was murdered on the doorstep of his home.

Kennedy's use of the so-called "bully pulpit" of the presidency to rally support for civil rights reform was slow in coming, largely reactive, and of dubious efficacy. Southern violence in 1963 claimed more lives, notably with the church bombing in Birmingham in September. The president's own death in Dallas, a city known for its conservative views, reinforced the image of the South as a region of extremists, but it certainly assisted his Southern successor, Lyndon Johnson, in his political battle to get Congress to pass substantive legislation. Posthumously, the cause of civil rights became that of the martyred president, but his speeches on the topic were few and his commitment was limited. He spoke more eloquently and effectively on the issue of disarmament and US–Soviet relations.

The American University "Peace" speech of 1963

Only ten days before his June address to the nation on civil rights, Kennedy spoke at the commencement ceremony of the American University in Washington, DC. The address he gave there is frequently seen as a measure of how far he had traveled from the bellicose Cold Warrior stance of the 1960 campaign. In this speech, he spoke of the need for a practical peace and asked Americans to "re-examine their attitudes to the Soviet Union." For a figure whose family had once been close supporters of Senator Joe McCarthy, it was startling to hear him urge Americans to empathize with the Russian people. He became the first postwar president to acknowledge publicly the enormous human cost of World War II for the Soviets and to conclude that a shared humanity transcended ideological differences; the rival superpowers were inhabitants of the same planet, with similar hopes for their children, and so needed to strive for coexistence. While Kennedy was disappointed by the speech's immediate impact at home, its importance was evident in the USSR, where it was broadcast and published in full. Thus, while Kennedy's speech-making resonated most strongly at home, in the call for national unity, preparedness, and sacrifice at the outset of his presidency, by 1963 his addresses spoke effectively to his Soviet adversary about the need for peaceful coexistence, a posture that Khrushchev himself had publicized and for which he had been attacked by his Communist rival, Mao Ze Dong of China.

The Berlin speech

The success of Kennedy's international speech-making, however, did not lie in any consistent pattern of evolution, but in its skillful sense of audience response. From the standpoint of calming East–West relations and cultivating détente, Kennedy's Berlin speech of June 1963 was ill judged. Having privately admitted that a wall was better than a war, Kennedy used the symbol of the Berlin Wall to expound Communism's failures, as in the declaration: "We have never had to put a wall up to keep our people in." Freedom-loving people everywhere, he proclaimed, identified with the heroic people of Berlin in a way that made the phrase "Ich bin ein Berliner" a boast of freedom (see Plate 6). The speech at the Berlin Rauhaus was the centerpiece of a triumphal visit that served to underline American commitment to Berlin and to its German allies, at a time when rapprochement with the Soviets stirred Europeans' doubts over the sincerity of American promises. Taken together, the American University and Berlin speeches reflect a presidency that was still struggling to adapt its tone to divergent constituencies; the strong, anti-Communist feeling in the US, particularly, was hard to diffuse, and would only become more so in the coming election year.

JFK and the media

Kennedy's widely broadcast public addresses created a paradigm for the TV presidency, etching into the national consciousness a set of expectations regarding the manner in which the president would address the people in times of crisis. Kennedy was the first to use television extensively in this way, largely because the widespread ownership of televisions and syndication of broadcasts across networks came of age in his time. In moments like the Cuban Missile Crisis, he used the medium well. However, it was not the formally attired Kennedy solemnly seated behind a desk and speaking directly to camera that captured the nation's affections. The informal images of family and friends were more important in this respect.

Amplifying this process was Kennedy's relationship with both the press and television reporters. Kennedy cultivated them. He was close to *Washington Post* publisher Philip Graham, *Newsweek* editor Ben Bradlee, syndicated columnist Joseph Alsop, and Hugh Sidey of *Time* magazine. His press secretary Pierre Salinger made a conscious effort to ensure that the wire services, like Associated Press, United Press, and Reuters, and the networks were guaranteed spots at formal events. In addition, the White House press corps received invitations to state dinners and private parties. Kennedy extended numerous perks to the journalists covering him and they, consciously or not, repaid him by giving him largely sympathetic coverage, although he did not always see it that way. Reporters who were deemed "unfriendly" quickly found the White House less accessible and no longer received social invitations. The pressure on reporters to retain the Administration's favor was increased by the realization among newspaper editors that television was eating into their market share as a news source. The *Chicago Tribune*'s reaction to the announcement that Kennedy was to televise his press conferences was to complain about the onset of "government by public relations" (Liebovich 2001: 16).

The press conferences

The "live" televised press conference was a major innovation. Eisenhower had held usually weekly press conferences, and his comment at his December 2, 1953 conference captured his attitude: "I will mount the usual weekly cross and let you drive the nails." (Joynt Kumar 2006: 221). Kennedy, in contrast, seemed to relish the challenge, and prepare for the event like an actor for a first night. The event was moved to the large State Department Auditorium, a change that drew complaints from the press that they were no longer close to the president. The *Chicago Daily News*'s Peter Lisagor complained that "we were props in a show." The reporters might be further away, but the cameras in the new location brought the public up close to the president, allowing them to register his expression and gesture as seldom before. There had been fears that a slip of the tongue or error of detail might risk a stock market run or an international incident. After the first three live conferences, however, the television trade press concluded that "television has proved about as hazardous for Kennedy as water for a fish" (Watson 1994: 74).

Kennedy's economical manner of speaking and conservative range of gesture seemed to strengthen the authority of his responses in the live televised setting. He looked "cool" and "at ease," in command. Given the novelty of the situation and the culture of deference still in place from wartime experiences of military service, viewers expected reporters to treat the president with deference and did not welcome casualness on their part or over-aggressive questioning. The viewers' identification with Kennedy was also bolstered by the fact that reporters' questions either came from a distance or even off camera, whereas Kennedy addressed the camera, delivering his answer to the television viewers rather than to the reporters in the auditorium. This reinforced the feeling that Kennedy spoke directly to the people, taking his message to them without the distortion of press coverage.

The live press conferences also showcased Kennedy's strengths as a communicator. His recall of factual detail was impressive and he had a dry, laconic wit that he used to good effect. Yet the press conferences' fame is disproportionate to their frequency. Kennedy held just sixty-four conferences, fewer than FDR, Truman, or Eisenhower, an acknowledgement that they were events that had to be orchestrated and that he did not want to devalue them by holding them too frequently. He likened them to final exams, but both he and Salinger really believed that the live transmission was worth it because previous presidents had suffered due to the selective reporting of press conferences. They worried especially because few of the main press outlets were likely to be sympathetic to a Democratic administration.

A by-product of the new practice of the live conference and the greater visibility of the White House press office was to reinforce a tendency, since FDR's time, to see the presidency as the real engine of governance, rather than Congress. This both strengthened the development of the so-called "imperial presidency" which the Cold War had set in train, and aggravated relations with Congress, who resented the relative lack of attention paid to them. At the same time, it made Americans harbor increasingly unrealistic expectations of their president, embedding his appearances into a popular culture that favored superheroic acts of miraculous rescue and redemption.

Since Kennedy, the so-called "honeymoon period" for American presidents has shortened, and public patience with their efforts has diminished. Even in the case of Kennedy, the first revisionist accounts of his presidency stressed that his positive reputation rested more on image than substance. At the same time, the persistence of JFK's popularity with the public has rested on a belief that, had he survived, the tragedies of Vietnam and the disorder and disillusionment of the late 1960s would have been avoided; a belief that flows from an emotional attachment to his posthumous image. In 1963, Kennedy's image among Americans was far more mixed than it would be in the wake of his assassination. White Southern segregationists were angered by his proposed civil rights reforms. Many businessmen recalled that in the midst of his clash with the nation's steel companies he had declared that he now believed his father, who had told him that all businessmen were "sons of bitches." They continued to harbor the suspicion that this rich man's son had never made a dime of his own or run a company.

Criticized for what he had done by 1963, he was equally faulted for what he had failed to do. Activists in civil rights circles doubted his sincerity and asked for proof that his recent declaration of moral support marked a real commitment. Still more ominously, in Cuban refugee communities in Florida and elsewhere, Kennedy's refusal to commit US troops to save anti-Castro forces in 1961 and his noninvasion agreement with Khrushchev at the time of the 1962 Missile Crisis added up to a betrayal of their cause. A similar sense that, despite his initial declarations, Kennedy had gone soft on Communism was prevalent among right-wing groups and some senior military and intelligence figures. But the image of Kennedy that has proved most enduring is of a smiling, youthful, and confident president, seated next to his lovely wife, waving to crowds on a sunny day in the moments before the shots rang out. Its predominance over other images has been the product of a large process of memorialization that continues even today.

Note

* Kennedy's speeches are most easily accessed via the American Presidency Project at the University of California Santa Barbara. See www.presidency.ucsb.edu.

9 Remembrance

LBJ's use of JFK

Understandably, the assassination has colored the process of remembrance. Most Americans in 1963 felt that the new president, Lyndon Johnson, handled the difficult transition well. His rallying call to Congress—"Let us continue"—deliberately echoed John F. Kennedy's opening statement to Congress—"Let us begin." To underline continuity, Johnson decided to retain most of Kennedy's Cabinet and used the powerful political leverage that the assassination provided to bolster support for his own, wider-ranging domestic political agenda. Thus, from the very start, remembrance was slanted for political advantage.

Johnson's "Great Society" program—which included landmark social welfare measures such as Medicare and Medicaid (health care for senior citizens and the poor), immigration reform, and legislation protecting African American civil rights, as well as ambitious efforts to fight poverty and expand the cultural work of the federal government—has been seen by Kennedy apologists as flowing directly from JFK's agenda for a second term. In key respects, however, it was much more the embodiment of Johnson's New Deal-style approach, of placing the federal government alongside the people to assist them. Certainly, the massive liberal legislative program passed between 1964 and 1966 dwarfed what Kennedy had achieved during his presidency. Nevertheless, the invocation of Kennedy that aided passage of such key measures as the 1964 Civil Rights Act in the face of conservative opposition helped to cement Kennedy's place in the pantheon of liberal heroes.

"Camelot"

The national shock and grief at the assassination also left the general public keen to remember their slain president in the most positive terms. The climate was conducive to acts of permanent commemoration. Less than two months after the assassination, Congress designated the planned National Cultural Center on the Potomac in Washington the Kennedy Center for the Performing Arts, thus reinforcing the perception that Kennedy had been a champion of the arts. This view of JFK rested largely on the artistic sensibilities of his wife, Jackie, and she continued to play a large role in shaping the nation's remembrance. She granted an interview to journalist Theodore White, which appeared in an early December 1963 edition of *Life* magazine. White dutifully reported her recollection of how JFK's childhood reading of history and its heroes had predisposed him to seek the same greatness and gallantry while in office. Quoting the concluding lines of the title song from the Alan Jay Lerner musical *Camelot* ("Don't let it be forgot / That once there was a spot / For one brief shining moment that was known / As Camelot"), Jackie urged White to ensure that the heroic quality of Kennedy's all-too-brief period in power should not be forgotten. White may have set the tone, but, as the next chapter indicates, it was Arthur Schlesinger's *A Thousand Days* and Theodore Sorensen's *Kennedy* that became the lyrical chronicles of Kennedy's Camelot.

Commemoration: Places, stamps, and coins

One of Kennedy's most memorable initiatives was his call for Americans to land a man on the Moon before the end of the decade. In memory of this, Cape Canaveral, from where the rockets were launched, was renamed Cape Kennedy. However, this renaming of a geographical feature rather than a human settlement or structure was not universally popular, particularly among local Floridians. A decade after Kennedy's death, at the instigation of state politicians, the name of the Cape itself reverted to Canaveral while the space center sited there retained the Kennedy name. New York City's Idlewild Airport was renamed for JFK in December 1963.

Far less controversial than renaming places was the speedy commemoration of Kennedy on stamps and coins. On May 29, 1964, the US Postal Service issued a commemorative stamp of JFK, which featured his image and the "eternal flame" that Jackie Kennedy had asked to be installed at his grave. A half-dollar silver coin featuring JFK had been in circulation since March 1964 and had proven extremely popular, not just with American but also with foreign collectors. By the time of the first anniversary of the president's death, 160 million coins had been issued, yet few appeared in circulation, suggesting that the coins had been acquired strictly as mementos. The silver content within the coins also added to their appeal, at a time when silver prices were rising. International fascination with Kennedy was reflected not just in overseas purchases of US stamps and coins but also in the production of commemorative stamps by many nations.

Kennedy had made two significant moves to improve the reputation of the United States across the developing world: the Alliance for Progress in Latin America specifically and the Peace Corps more broadly. While the latter was arguably far more successful and enduring, the extensive memorialization of Kennedy in South America confirmed that he had had a powerful impact there. Commemorative stamps were issued within a year of his death in Argentina, Brazil, Columbia, and Guatemala, and, at the same time, the work of the Peace Corps and of the Kennedy administration in support of newly independent African nations prompted commemorative stamps from nations such as Nigeria, the Central African Republic, and Dahomey. More predictably, Kennedy's death was marked by stamp commemoration in Germany, and Eyre Square in Galway, Ireland, which JFK visited on his whirlwind summer tour in 1963, was renamed in his honor. An elaborate memorial to JFK was opened in 1965 at Runnymede in England, in the presence of his widow and Queen Elizabeth II, and the square near the Berlin city hall where Kennedy gave his famous 1963 address was renamed "John F. Kennedy Platz."

The first year: Profound fascination

On the assassination's first anniversary, the *New York Times* noted that the American public's interest in their fallen president remained strong and visible (* see Note page 261). The design of the Kennedy burial site at Arlington had been adapted to take account of the large number of visitors it seemed likely to attract. The temporary grave had already been visited by 7.7 million visitors, requiring the planners to consider how best to accommodate peak flows of as many as 50,000 visitors a day. The same article noted the presence of a compilation volume, *The Kennedy Wit*, on the *Times* bestseller list for fifteen weeks, and the release of some two dozen audio records of Kennedy's speeches. This was a considerable turnaround from November 1963, when the top nonfiction seller in the US was Victor Lasky's vituperative *JFK: The Man and the Myth*, a journalistic attack by a writer who felt that Kennedy was a fraud.

As time passed, the anniversary became dominated more by doubts about the Warren Commission's findings than by grief for the nation's lost hero. No special ceremonies were held at Arlington for the first time in 1967, although visitor numbers to the grave remained high: 21 million since 1963. The number of schools, streets, and memorials in Kennedy's honor was still growing worldwide.

The impact of Kennedy's brothers, Bobby and Edward

The continuing political careers of Kennedy's brothers, Robert and Edward, complicated the task of memorialization, while at the same time keeping JFK's own legacy very much in the public gaze. The 1968 assassination of Bobby Kennedy in San Francisco, shortly after he had won the California presidential primary, intensified the public obsession with the Kennedys. At the outset of his presidential bid, Bobby Kennedy had faced criticism for his late announcement, which threatened to split the anti–Vietnam War movement that had previously given its support to Senator Eugene McCarthy. Some charged that Kennedy seemed to think he had an automatic right to be the party's nominee, and his longstanding mutual antipathy with President Lyndon Johnson ensured that Bobby was obliged to respond to leaked press reports about misuse of his powers as attorney general, including his involvement in plots to kill Fidel Castro. Bobby's murder underscored the poignancy of JFK's remembrance services in November 1968, where his as-yet-unmarked grave lay beside his brother's completed monument.

The tarnishing of the memory of Camelot by contemporary politics grew again after the 1969 Chappaquiddick incident, in which a young woman, Mary Jo Kopechne, died in a car accident involving Senator Edward Kennedy. Unanswered questions about Kennedy's role in the incident—specifically what the married senator was doing in an isolated spot with a young woman, and why he did not stay at the scene or make greater efforts to save Kopechne—forced him to abandon any presidential ambitions until he challenged incumbent Democrat Jimmy Carter in 1980. A decade after JFK's death, intimates like Sorensen and O'Donnell were eager in the *New York Times* to reburnish their leader's reputation by stressing how much was lost with his death. Reflecting on the past decade of "inflation, recession, riots, apathy, crimes both high and low," Sorensen told the National Press Club that he was convinced that these accumulated troubles flowed from the death of a leader poised on the edge of greatness.

Criticism of the "imperial presidency"

The 1970s brought Watergate and defeat in Vietnam, as well as a growing sense that American society had not fulfilled its 1960s promise. As we shall see in the next chapter, the revisionist approach to JFK was partly a reflection of this sharpened cynicism. Certainly, by 1973 there were those who saw Kennedy as a crucial figure in the emergence of an "imperial presidency" that could both surreptitiously escalate America's involvement in a foreign war and illegally attack the president's domestic enemies. Both Watergate and Vietnam, in this view, sprang directly from Kennedy's style of governance. His main point of difference with Johnson and Nixon was their clumsiness of practice, rather than a variance of substance. The shadow of contemporary events eclipsed the memory of Kennedy, to some extent, a decade after his death. On November 22, 1973, the *Washington Post,* for instance, was struck with how little attention the anniversary now drew in places like Ireland, or at the Kennedy Memorial in England.

Twenty years later

Despite the development of a revisionist scholarship that questioned Kennedy's status as a foreign policy leader or as a champion of liberal causes like civil rights, the regular pattern of anniversary remembrance gave JFK a continuing elegiac quality. Talking to visitors at the gravesite on the twentieth anniversary in 1983, the *Washington Post* recorded the comments of parents trying to convey the greatness and importance of Kennedy to their children who had been born long after his death. Reflecting on her efforts to instruct her eleven-year-old, one mother mused: "It's difficult. ... The facts don't account for much."

While underlining the respect accorded to JFK by one generation, the article also noted that it was increasingly hard to instill the same attitude in the next, some of whom on a school trip were playing, largely oblivious to where they were. Marking the anniversary, editorial pieces in the *New York Times* included one from the devoted Sorensen and another from Bobby Kennedy's speechwriter, Adam Walinsky, the former summarizing Kennedy's complexities but affirming his worth, and the latter expressing the hope that the period of debunking was now over. In a similar vein, in the *Los Angeles Times*, Robert J. Donovan reflected positively on the Kennedy legend, and (reflecting the Reagan era) he extolled the positive benefits of having a president that people saw in heroic and charismatic terms.

Although there were partisan reverberations in the twentieth anniversary memorials in 1983, the success of Republican Ronald Reagan (a president who survived an assassination attempt early in his term) in turning American political culture away from what was increasingly presented as the follies of the 1960s meant that, even in the election year of 1988, the quarter-century commemorations seemed to be as much about the significance of remembrance as about JFK himself. *New York Times* columnist Barbara Gamarekian wrote of the 150 film crews sent to Washington to capture the commemoration and the range of events, from religious services to public readings. Efforts by the Kennedy family to move commemoration to JFK's birthday (May 29) rather than the anniversary of his death seemed to have little impact.

The media self-referencing its memories

A refocusing on the processes of commemoration, noted in 1988, was still more evident by 1993, with columnists more impressed by the deluge of commemorative television specials than intrigued by JFK himself. Howard Kurtz of the *Washington Post* wrote of the cottage industry that remembering Kennedy had become. He noted more than a dozen special TV programs and magazine issues to mark the thirtieth anniversary and quoted Robert Kennedy biographer Evan Thomas's remark that "there's a soap opera quality to the Kennedys that never fails to sell." It was less a case of the vibrancy of memory than the obviousness of the merchandising opportunity. Thomas summarized the different narrative forms that could appeal to different segments of a mass audience. The Camelot eulogy of unmatched wit and courage played to the true keepers of the Kennedy flame. The tales of illicit sex titillated those of a more tabloid taste. Muscular confrontations with Soviet power appealed to "neocons" eager for unipolar assertiveness in foreign affairs, and for the many disenchanted who mistrusted officialdom and took pleasure in uncovering secrets there were the many tangled conspiracy theories. Historian Richard Reeves, whose new biography was selling well at the time of the thirtieth anniversary in 1993, remarked that the figure in the media commemorations was largely a fictional one created since 1963.

Forty years later

By the time of the fortieth anniversary, the gulf between the event and the nation had widened sufficiently for certain scars to heal amidst the forgetting. By that time two-thirds of the US population had not been born when Kennedy was killed. Dallas, a city branded by the assassination, had largely kept its commemoration of the notorious event to a minimum. Many of the participants in earlier commemorative ceremonies in Dallas had been out-of-town visitors. But in 2003, the city embraced the occasion with a concert, featuring Leonard Bernstein's "Mass," a work commissioned by Kennedy's widow for the opening of New York's Kennedy Center in 1971, and other events centered on Dealey Plaza. By 2003 the Texas Book Depository, considered for demolition by city fathers at one stage, housed a bustling museum space on its sixth floor. As a tourist destination, the Book Depository outstripped the appeal of the solemn, hollow white memorial cenotaph designed by Philip Johnson, which stands two blocks east of the assassination site. To the media, which had focused on remembrance in 1993, the theme for 2003 was forgetfulness. Columnist Frank Rich, in a December 7 *New York Times* review of Tony Kushner's musical play *Caroline or Change*, wondered aloud if this would be the fate of 9/11 in forty years' time: passing from memory to history like Pearl Harbor.

Television remembers

TV specials formed an important part of the remembrance of JFK over the years. In key respects, this act of remembering Kennedy acted as a form of celebrating journalism, particularly television journalism. The dominant message was that television had held the nation together through a national trauma. Normal programming had been suspended and all three major networks had devoted their airtime to the assassination and its aftermath until the funeral was over. This also meant that all the networks, and most of the major news magazines and newspapers, had abundant materials that made "anniversary journalism" a relatively inexpensive genre to maintain.

Twenty-five years after the assassination, networks and cable channels offered the American public no fewer than ten specials about JFK and his murder. Most of the specials focused on the theories surrounding the assassination and reminiscences as to where celebrities were when they first got the news, but equally prominent was the theme of how the journalists at the scene or in the TV studio responded to the unfolding drama of November 22. Many of these journalists—Walter Cronkite, Dan Rather, and Robert MacNeil, for instance—subsequently had, and continued to have, high-profile roles on television. Thus the 1988 CBS special featured both Cronkite and Rather and implicitly celebrated the quality of the network's news coverage. Similarly, the Arts & Entertainment cable channel used a compilation of NBC's coverage of the assassination for its six-hour special featuring MacNeil and David Brinkley. The NBC network itself supplemented archival footage with contemporary interviews with high-profile Kennedy administration veterans Ted Sorensen, McGeorge Bundy, and Dean Rusk (Zelizer 1992).

The miniseries

By 1988, there were also made-for-TV movies and miniseries, which could be premiered or replayed. An NBC miniseries *Kennedy*, featuring Martin Sheen as JFK, had premiered on the network in 1983 and was aired again on cable in 1988. The cumulative effect of this diet of documentary footage and dramatization was to ensure that most Americans, even those who were too young to recall the events of 1963 or the Kennedy presidency more generally, had the images of that time etched into their consciousness. Since this pattern was not present for other presidents—FDR or his successors—it served to reinforce the sense that JFK was exceptional. It also strengthened the focus on his death with a subgenre of docudramas devoted to theories about not just his death, but those of his brother Robert, and contemporaries Marilyn Monroe and Martin Luther King.

On the fortieth anniversary, in 2003, the same mix dominated television, with the emergence of cable channels allowing for longer, more specialist coverage. Thus, over two nights, the History Channel aired a three-hour special, *JFK: A Presidency Revealed*, using archival materials, documentary footage, and specially taped interviews. The result was generally held to mark a more balanced, historical appraisal, with figures such as Robert McNamara admitting that mistakes were made in relation to Cuba and Vietnam that had longlasting negative consequences. The extent of JFK's ill health was also candidly discussed. MSNBC commemorated the assassination with a program dedicated to the question: Where were you when you heard? which had a new poignancy for a generation affected by the 9/11 attacks. CNN ran a discussion with veteran journalists about their coverage of the assassination and PBS aired a documentary devoted to Jackie Kennedy Onassis, who had died in 1994. Her son, John F. Kennedy, Jr., had also died in an air crash off Martha's Vineyard in 1999. The succession of family tragedies experienced by the extended family and the intense media scrutiny given to their celebrity lifestyle also ensured that, despite the passage of time, the public fascination with the Kennedys remained a powerful cultural phenomenon that impacted on the evaluation of JFK as president.

When rumors began to circulate in the autumn of 1968 that JFK's widow was planning to marry Aristotle Onassis, a man with a lurid reputation relating to both his business tactics and philandering (most recently with Jackie's older sister Lee and the famed opera singer Maria Callas), Americans were incredulous. The Kennedy family, still reeling from Bobby's death, felt the move was likely to tarnish JFK's memory, and this was one reason why the October 20 marriage took place in Greece. Public reaction was largely hostile. The feeling was captured by a Stockholm newspaper headline: "Jackie How Could You?" (Bradford 2000: 454).

It was really only after Onassis's death in 1977 that Americans forgave the former first lady. Jackie's decision to work at the Viking publishing house in New York fascinated them. Her role at the Kennedy Library already ensured that she remained one of the chief guardians of the Kennedy legend, despite the family's fear that she had diminished it. A succession of writers—William Manchester, Ben Bradlee, and even Arthur Schlesinger—had been rebuked for revealing too much about the First Couple's private life. The revelations in 1976 about JFK's affair with Judith Exner, the mistress of mobster Sam Giancana, brought Jackie firmly back into the family fold to defend the Camelot myth. From her new base in New York City, Jackie remained eager to limit the damage of each succeeding revelation, and did so until her death in 1994.

In 2010, plans for a miniseries about the Kennedys, to be produced by Canadian company Shaw Media, became public, and a concerted wave of criticism was unleashed, based on the negative portrayal of key family members, including Jackie, evident in early script drafts. The series had originally been commissioned to air on the History Channel in the US, but in early 2011 the cable station responded to the furor by dropping it. The series' director and executive producers claimed that the decision was made because of strong Kennedy family pressure. The Kennedys could not prevent the series airing in other countries, and it soon became widely available in the US, where its focus on the family's sexual escapades and drug habits, as well as Jackie's drinking, offered a vision that was more soap opera than Camelot. In 2012, in a perhaps ill-advised bid to restore her mother's reputation, Caroline Kennedy rescinded the bar on publication of Jackie's 1964 oral history interview. It revealed a woman who was determined to present her late husband in the best possible light, while remaining eager to gossip about the weaknesses and vices of other men, including Martin Luther King.

Kennedy movies and Oliver Stone

The public fascination with JFK and the unanswered questions surrounding his death have ensured that filmmakers have been drawn repeatedly to the topic. Ten years after the assassination, the movie *Executive Action*, directed by David Miller and starring Burt Lancaster as one of the conspirators, was released to a barrage of hostile criticism that led to its rapid withdrawal from most theaters. With input from Warren Commission critic Mark Lane, the film depicted JFK as the victim of a plot largely funded by right-wing Texan business figures and presented Lee Harvey Oswald as a "fall guy" set up to take the blame. The alleged conspiracy is fueled in the movie by Kennedy's increasingly liberal policies on civil rights and nuclear disarmament, and is spurred into action decisively by his apparent decision to withdraw from Vietnam. The assassination is presented as an "executive action" taken by the real rulers of America.

Although it too faced caustic criticism for its depiction of the assassination as a conspiracy that Oswald served to conceal, Oliver Stone's 1991 movie *JFK* was much more positively received than was *Executive Action*. Stone centered his movie on the figure of New Orleans-based district attorney Jim Garrison, whose pursuit of several local figures, notably Clay Shaw, as conspirators in the Kennedy assassination had drawn headlines in the late 1960s. Garrison, played in the movie by Kevin Costner, reveals in a climactic court scene that Oswald could not be the sole assassin capable of hitting both Kennedy and Governor John Connally with a single "magic bullet" fired from the Book Depository.

The truth, as Stone sees it, has been revealed via the confessions of men like David Ferrie, who in the movie openly admit their CIA ties and the identity of the Cubans who murdered Kennedy.

Critics have repeatedly pointed out that in reality Ferrie denied being in the CIA, or having knowledge of a plot by anti-Castro Cubans to kill the president, orchestrated by Shaw on behalf of the agency. Garrison's suspicions of high government involvement are confirmed in the movie by a mysterious military official, known in the movie only as "X," played by Donald Sutherland. The details recounted by "X" elaborate the methods used to pursue the plot, and reinforce the impression that highly placed governmental officials were directly implicated in JFK's murder because of his readiness to withdraw from Vietnam.

Overall, the movie offered Americans a view of Kennedy that enhanced his historical significance, as a progressive figure intent on global peace and domestic social justice, and explained his death in terms that intensified the outrage felt over the human cost of Vietnam and the mendacity of government in relation to the American people. Stone's *JFK* was a critical success: it won a Golden Globe and was nominated for eight Academy Awards, winning two. It was not an immediate box office success, but its overall popularity, in terms of video or DVD sales, suggests that it was commercially profitable. Stone's vociferous call for a further investigation of the assassination and charges of a governmental cover-up certainly played a part in the passing of the 1992 Assassination Records Review Act, intended to ensure that all official documents were placed in the public domain as soon as possible.

While Stone's movie was inspired by his own conviction that Americans had been lied to in 1964, an academic study of audience members who attended showings of *JFK* argued that its psychological impact was not to mobilize individuals politically but to render them more apathetic (Butler, Koopman, and Zimbardo 1995). The movie's portrayal of government could be seen as reinforcing cynicism and a sense of hopelessness, rather than championing the possibility of popular revolt. Ironically, a recurrent theme of media eulogies to the lost promise of the Kennedy era is for the public to embrace the sense of possibility implicit in Kennedy's inaugural invocation for Americans to "ask not what your country can do for you—ask what you can do for your country." This view of the Kennedy assassination as a watershed that closed a period of optimism and began a period of disillusionment is held to explain why Kennedy is so positively assessed by Americans, decades after his death.

In addition to the many television programs and movies devoted to the Kennedys, to the assassination, and to the Kennedy presidency in general, there have also been some focused more narrowly on the Cuban Missile Crisis. A docudrama, *The Missiles of October*, aired in 1974, and was based on Bobby Kennedy's laudatory account of his brother's finest hour, *Thirteen Days*. Misleadingly, the 2000 movie *Thirteen Days*, starring Kevin Costner as Kennedy aide Kenny O'Donnell, is actually based on accounts of the Ex-Comm meetings by Ernest May and Philip Zelikow. Predictably, surviving members of Ex-Comm, like Robert McNamara, did not take kindly to the movie's enhancement of O'Donnell's role in national security matters. The award-winning account of McNamara's career, *The Fog of War* (2004), while focused on Vietnam, treats the Missile Crisis directly. More generally, whenever US television or moviemakers wish to depict the presidency in heroic terms, they draw upon Kennedy iconography, as in the highly successful and long-running series, *The West Wing* (1999–2006). In the recent, highly praised Steven Spielberg movie, *Lincoln* (2012), the famed president is depicted in a White House that resounds to the playful antics of his son Tad, in a manner highly reminiscent of JFK's time with John Junior. Thus, an allusion to Kennedy creates a sense of heightened sympathy with the more distant figure of Lincoln.

Kennedy in fiction

In the years since his death, Jack Kennedy has also featured in a wide variety of fiction, most of which, like the TV series and the films, have focused on his violent death. The trend was set even during his presidency, when in 1962 the British crime writer John Creasey, writing under the pseudonym J.J. Marric, published *Gideon's March*, in which his Inspector Gideon investigates a plot to murder the president in London. Also in 1962, two Washington-based journalists, Fletcher Knebel and Charles Bailey, published a political thriller, *Seven Days in May*, which depicts a military coup against an American president who is seeking nuclear disarmament and détente to the lethal fury of his generals. Kennedy is supposed to have read and approved of the novel, which in 1964 became a movie starring Fredric March as the president and Burt Lancaster as one of the plotting generals.

The most celebrated literary investigations of the Kennedy assassination have focused more on his supposed assassin than on the president himself. Don DeLillo's *Libra* (1991) centers itself on Oswald, an outsider who is manipulated by the CIA in a plot to force an invasion of Cuba, although not one necessarily requiring JFK's death. DeLillo is more interested in the process of piecing together meaning than in the goal of revealing historical truth. It is precisely the irresolvable character of the Kennedy assassination that attracts him. Oswald is also the subject of Norman Mailer's 1995 work *Oswald's Tale: An American Mystery*, written at a time when Mailer had turned from fiction to journalism, especially in the wake of his study of murderer Gary Gilmore, *The Executioner's Song*. Mailer also took advantage of new access to records of Oswald's time in Russia. He presents Oswald as a man who killed in order to affirm himself, and as a quintessential product of the Cold War, having lived in both systems.

Edwin Shrake's novel *Strange Peaches* (1972) is often commended for its vivid depiction of Dallas in 1963 as a city in which oil barons advocate assassination and Cubans and drug runners mix in strip clubs linked to the mob. This strangeness of Dallas in 1963, as a context for the assassination, is explored again by Brian Woolley in his novel *November 22* (1982). Stephen King also used the date *22.11.63* in his recent novel that takes as its premise the watershed character of the Kennedy assassination. Its plot centers on a time traveler journeying back to eliminate Oswald and thus save Kennedy, and consequently the lives of all those Americans killed in Vietnam after his death. King's character discovers that altering the past is difficult and has unexpected consequences. The many conspiracy theories that argue Oswald was not the lone gunman and/or that others killed Kennedy provide novelists and dramatists drawn to the "time travel" theme with many challenges and possibilities, as illustrated by treatment of the assassination in the 1990 movie *Running Against Time* and the 1992 TV series *Quantum Leap*. A common feature of such works is that saving Kennedy turns out to be the wrong thing to do.

Other media

Such is the pervasiveness of the Kennedy image across popular culture that it even extends into the video game market, with the 2004 game *JFK Reloaded*. This game places the player in the Book Depository with the challenge of killing JFK. Amidst outrage from the Kennedy family, the game's makers argued that they hoped to gather evidence as to whether the Warren Commission's account of Oswald's shooting from the Depository was technically feasible. A player's score is determined by his first three shots within a fixed time frame. A revised version of the game also allows players to take up positions at other sites, such as the grassy knoll, and compare their accuracy. Despite condemnation for its tastelessness, this game produced by a Scotland-based software company illustrates the place of the assassination within global popular culture, and the way in which JFK remains a historical figure with extraordinary popular significance. He does so almost solely because of his death.

In 2010, Gallup polled Americans to determine how they ranked past presidents of the modern era in terms of their performance in office. Kennedy ranked first, with 85 percent of those polled approving his performance. He has topped the poll ever since the question was first posed in 1990. Fifty years after the election of 1960, he easily outstripped his closest rival, Ronald Reagan, who polled 74 percent, and he trounced his 1960 challenger Richard Nixon, whose reputation remained so stained by the Watergate scandal, that only 29 percent approved his performance. A 2009 C-SPAN poll of 65 historians and what was termed "professional observers of the presidency," which gave presidents scores on different attributes, saw JFK ranked sixth out of all US presidents, up two places from his position in the 2000 poll. The top five presidents— Lincoln, Washington, FDR, Theodore Roosevelt, and Harry Truman—all had a longer period in office than JFK in which to prove themselves. Two of them—Lincoln and FDR—died in office, like Kennedy, but with more accomplishments behind them, and two of them—Theodore Roosevelt and Harry Truman—succeeded on the death of a president. This suggests that death colors the assessment in different ways. Nevertheless, Kennedy's high ranking is remarkable and continues to prompt debate.

In a strongly worded *New York Times* article (of November 27, 2011), Ross Douthat argued that JFK was the most overrated president, and complained that his standing was a product of the 1960s baby boom generation's need to perpetuate its own significance. Once that generation had passed, he averred, Kennedy's ranking would plummet. Douthat represents those who see JFK's standing as overwhelmingly a matter of image. He is not remembered for his deeds, but for what he represented. His most potent legacy is a nostalgic recollection of lost youth. Even during his lifetime, critics charged that JFK was more image than substance, and the accusation has shaped the scholarship that has unfolded since his death. The scale of that scholarship nevertheless testifies to Kennedy's status. His brief tenure should make him a historical topic on a par with Gerald Ford, yet he is explored with the alacrity shown for Lincoln. It is to this scholarly literature that we now turn, as we seek to assess his achievements.

Note

* References to newspaper content in this chapter can be followed up in the ProQuest online collections of archived American newspapers, at www.pro quest. com.

10 Bibliographical essay

Archival research on John F. Kennedy begins with the presidential library in Boston, which has now digitalized significant portions of its holdings (www.jfklibrary.org). There remain some restrictions on access to materials. Visitors to Boston may also wish to use the Nigel Hamilton Collection at the state historical society. Primary materials in published form begin with *Public Papers of the Presidents*, with three volumes for Kennedy (1962–64), matched by volumes related to his earlier Senate and House career (1964a). Kennedy is also listed as the author of four books: *Why England Slept* (1940); *As We Remember Joe* (1945); *Profiles in Courage* (1956); and the posthumous volume *A Nation of Immigrants* (1964b).

The biographical literature on JFK began to take shape with John Hersey's coverage of his heroics in the South Pacific, a very positive profile which was expanded by numerous magazine articles about the glamorous young senator in the 1950s. Even during his presidency, further accounts of the rescue of the *PT 109* crew appeared (Hersey 1944; Donovan 1962; Tregaskis 1962). James Macgregor Burns published a good campaign biography (1960) and historian Allan Nevins edited a collection of JFK's foreign policy speeches in 1960. The presentation of Kennedy in Theodore White's *The Making of the President* (1961) continued the process of boosting Kennedy's credentials, but already Victor Lasky was gathering material for his overtly hostile *JFK: The Man and the Myth* (1963).

Camelot

After Kennedy's assassination, early biographies came from journalists close to the president, such as Pierre Salinger (1966) and

Hugh Sidey (1964), but so-called Camelot scholarship began in earnest with the glorifying narratives of the Kennedy White House from former staffers Arthur Schlesinger (1965) and Theodore Sorensen (1965), Schlesinger being the more culpable of the two. Of all the presidents, Kennedy was, for Schlesinger, the wittiest and wisest. Even JFK's secretary Evelyn Lincoln, his longtime friend Paul Fay, and his children's nanny Maud Shaw joined in the eulogies (all 1966). Attention also turned to the larger family, with tributes to Jacqueline Kennedy (Langley Hall and Pinchot 1966) and a full-length biography of Joseph Kennedy (Whalen 1964). At this point controversy erupted over a pending study of the assassination by William Manchester, as the Kennedy family sought to have material retracted because it might harm the reputation of the former first lady and Bobby Kennedy and exacerbate the Kennedy–Johnson feud. *The Death of a President* eventually appeared in 1967 and remains a key account of the assassination period. By this stage, the initial acceptance of the Warren Commission Report (1964) had given way to forthright criticism, led most notably by Mark Lane's *Rush to Judgment* (1966). The assassination of both Robert Kennedy and Martin Luther King in 1968 intensified the growth of this assassination literature (see below). The many accounts that lament what was lost with JFK's death are the chief continuation of the Camelot tradition.

Revisionism

In the 1970s, the biographical treatment of JFK reversed its tone (Fairlie 1973; Miroff 1976; Paper 1975; Wills 1982). Although Kennedy's right-hand men, Ken O'Donnell and Dave Powers, published a laudatory memoir (1972), another intimate, journalist Ben Bradlee (1975), was less willing to overlook Jack's faults. Even the *PT 109* incident was scrutinized (Blair and Blair 1974). These more critical studies often stressed the Cold War orthodoxy that framed Kennedy's approach to foreign affairs and helped to make the early 1960s "the hour of maximum danger" that he claimed it to be (Walton 1972). It was Kennedy, they argued, who began to increase involvement in Vietnam and to plot against Castro, and who saw these conflicts as new fronts in the Cold War.

Despite his claim in speeches to understand the force of nationalism, Kennedy was seen by revisionists like Paterson's contributors
(1989) as still viewing local struggles through the prism of the
containment doctrine.

These critics also complained that he was ineffectual and
unprincipled in domestic matters, whether it was civil rights
reform or congressional relations more generally. Whereas early
insider accounts had praised JFK's willingness to give tasks to and
take advice from whichever staffer was close at hand, the revisionists complained that his White House was disorganized and so
Kennedy-centered that it lacked any collective sense of what it was
doing (Johnson 1974). Even apparent triumphs like the Cuban
Missile Crisis came to be seen as at best successful recoveries; since
the crisis was set in motion by Kennedy's own precipitous efforts
to topple Castro (Dinnerstein 1976). Episodes such as the dispute
with steel magnates and his brother's authorization of wiretapping
foreshadowed the later evils of the imperial presidency evident in
Watergate (Sherter 1977; Garrow 1981).

The culmination of this revisionism came in the 1990s with
studies by Thomas Reeves and Seymour Hersh. Reeves' *A Question
of Character* (1991) presents a critique of Kennedy that presents
him as a man of such deep-seated character flaws as to be an
unworthy icon. Journalist Seymour Hersh's *The Dark Side of
Camelot* (1997) is more tendentious, being a thorough debunking
exercise that stresses Kennedy's reckless sexual escapades, drug
use, and overall mendacity, the last trait being displayed by many
other Kennedys as well. Coinciding with the Lewinsky scandal
during the Clinton administration, these salacious portraits of
Kennedy marked the apogee of the hostile portraiture and they
have since given way to more balanced accounts. Like the assassination accounts that refer back to the Warren Commission even
after its official rejection, the debunkers have needed the Camelot
strand as a foil for their own position.

Postrevisionism

The postrevisionist writing does not deny the faults in Kennedy's
character but offers extenuation in terms of the difficult context

in which he operated. The trend began with Herbert Parmet's two-volume biography (1980, 1983), and continued with Richard Reeves's *President Kennedy: Profile of Power* (1993), James Burner's *John F. Kennedy and a New Generation* (1988), and James Giglio's *The Presidency of John F. Kennedy* (1991, second edition 2006). It reached its apogee in Robert Dallek's *An Unfinished Life* (2003). Dallek's unprecedented access to Kennedy's medical history fleshed out in graphic detail the physical suffering that was such an integral part of Kennedy's daily life, and thus made this fact a basic context for assessing his performance in a period of intense international and domestic pressure. Dallek forcefully restates that JFK was a man who grew towards greatness during his presidency. Kennedy was a better president in 1962 than in 1961, and showed still further promise in the summer of 1963, with the test ban treaty and the civil rights bill. Michael O'Brien's biography (2005) is comprehensive and balanced, and he has followed it with a shorter collection of essays (2010) and a study of Kennedy's women (2011). The postrevisionists accept that the Kennedy presidency was good rather than great, flawed rather than calamitous. Burner, for example, writes of an administration that was "so emphatic in its sense of energy and so unclear in the direction of that energy" (1988: 168). This mirrored JFK's own character, with his energetic pursuit of life and achievement matched by a somewhat amoral sense of what could be achieved. Kennedy embraced peace to avoid a nuclear holocaust but still clung to the need for victory as a political goal, and he sought reelection more ardently than he pursued racial justice or an end to poverty. He wanted to be president largely because he was confident that he could be president (just as his father wanted) and not because he yearned to do things that only a president could do.

The evolving literature has developed some new areas of scrutiny, notably how JFK embodied a particular style of Cold War masculinity (Dean 1998), how his policies internationally can be seen as extending the "soft power" of the United States through aid and propaganda (Haefele 2001), how he considered the domestic electoral implications of foreign policy (Meriwether 2008), and especially how he embraced modernization (Latham 2000).

The family

Kennedy's political success and our continuing fascination with him stem from his remarkable family. Doris Kearns Goodwin's book, *The Fitzgeralds and the Kennedys* (1987), offers the best ancestral overview. It can be supplemented by several works on JFK's father, Joseph Kennedy, Sr. (Whalen 1964; Schwartz 2003; Nasaw 2012) and mother, Rose (Cameron 1971; Higham 1995), and by Rose's memoir (1974). Laurence Leamer has penned separate volumes on the men (2001) and women (1996) of the Kennedy clan. Predictably, brother Robert has been most frequently studied (Newfield 1969; Schlesinger 1978; Schmitt 2010; Thomas 2002) followed by Edward (Cannelos 2010; Clymer 1999; Klein 2009; Macgregor Burns 1976). Jacqueline, too, remains a fascination (Bradford 2000).

Civil rights and domestic policy

John F. Kennedy's major focus was on foreign policy and it can be argued that his approach to domestic matters was governed largely by this preoccupation. Thus, civil rights gained his attention when it created international embarrassment, which it did frequently between 1960 and 1963. The role of the Cold War in propelling racial reform has been well documented by Dudziak (2002) and Borstelmann (2001).

Whereas early accounts of the Kennedy administration and civil rights (Brauer 1977) were largely laudatory, more recent ones have been critical, ranging from the expected emphasis on political calculation (Stern 1992) to the morally condemnatory (Bryant 2006; Niven 2003). For his critics, it is Jack's brother Robert rather than Jack himself who shows moral development in relation to the civil rights question. Admittedly, taped phone conversations related to civil rights crises in Alabama and Mississippi expose the readiness of both president and attorney general to cooperate with segregationist governors (Rosenberg and Karabell 2003), but the fall in JFK's popularity with the American public following his endorsement of civil rights reform provides a sobering reminder of why he was so hesitant to embrace the cause. Kennedy was a "guilty bystander," to use Bryant's term, but postrevisionism would give greater weight to the political forces working against him, especially in the congressional committees dominated by Southerners (Goduti 2012).

On other aspects of domestic policy, the trajectory of assessment has been largely upward. Early assessments stressed JFK's limits: he failed to secure federal aid for education, healthcare for seniors, or a reflationary tax cut. More recent works, notably Irving Bernstein's *Promises Kept* (1991) have presented the Kennedy years as the largely neglected launchpad for the War on Poverty. Measures such as the Equal Pay Act, the Manpower Development and Training Act, the Areas Redevelopment Act, and the Peace Corps were all important, in their own right and as the platform from which Johnson's Great Society measures flowed. This positive assessment is typically linked to the belief that, had JFK survived, then the tax cut, the civil rights bill, Medicare, and aid to education would have rapidly followed.

Ironically, given that the tax cut was seen to mark JFK's conversion to Keynesian economics, his policy has received its most acute attention in relation to Ronald Reagan's tax cuts, part of a Reagan revolution that was seen as marking the end of Big Government Keynesianism (Tobin and Weidenbaum 1989). JFK's ability to secure Medicare is also questioned by congressional insiders like Wilbur Mills, chair of the vital House Ways and Means Committee, who feels LBJ was crucial to this achievement (Blumenthal and Marone 2008: 111). Similarly, McAndrew (1991) stresses LBJ's clarity of vision and enhanced liberal majority in Congress as key elements in securing federal aid for education in 1965. Thus, the actual record of Kennedy domestically was relatively modest. His beginnings in terms of measures to protect women's rights in the workplace or to extend the range of foreign aid were important but only a start, and richer in rhetoric than in substance (Harrison 1988; Zelman 1982; Pearce 2001).

A good symbol of the interaction between Kennedy's domestic and foreign policies is the space program. Congress passed the appropriations for increased space exploration because in many cases they brought well-paid jobs into the emerging Sunbelt of new industries, but Kennedy promoted it also because he recognized its Cold War significance. Whether the millions spent were justified, given the other needs that might have been targeted, is still debated (McDougall 1985; Logsdon 2011; Scott and Leonov

2005). Related to this is the larger issue of defense spending, which Kennedy boosted considerably, largely by campaigning falsely that the US was falling behind and the Soviet bloc was becoming more powerful (Preble 2004). At the same time, Kennedy deserves credit for the steps he achieved towards disarmament (Oliver 1997).

Foreign policy

Documents can be accessed readily now through the State Department history website (http://history.state.gov). Studies of Kennedy's foreign policy can be broken down by country and topic, since there is a vast literature, but one can begin by noting the works relating to his key policy advisors on national security. McGeorge Bundy wrote a study of atomic diplomacy that reflected his position (1988), and both his influence and that of his brother at the State Department's Far East desk are the subject of Kai Bird's insightful dual biography (1998). Since Mac Bundy stayed on as National Security Advisor to Johnson and guided the Vietnam escalation, he has been the focus of critical studies (Goldstein 2009; Preston 2006). Bundy has remained a less contentious figure than Defense Secretary Robert McNamara, especially in the light of McNamara's reexamination of Vietnam in particular (McNamara and Vandemark 1995; McNamara 2000; Blight and Lang 2004). His recantation has angered veterans of the conflict. Other hawks and doves from the Kennedy days have had their say. Leading the hawks is veteran diplomat George Kennan (Kennan 1972; Lukacs 2007; Thompson 2009; Gaddis 2012). Alongside him most would place Secretary of State Dean Rusk (Rusk 1990; Cohen 1980; Schoenbaum 1988; Zeiler 1999), as well as Walter Rostow (Rostow 1972; Milne 2009), Paul Nitze (Nitze 1989; Callahan 1990), and Roger Hilsman (1967).

To these hawks, one can add the Chiefs of the Armed Services, although Kennedy conferred with them less directly than had Eisenhower. Curtis LeMay at the Air Force was the most hawkish, followed by George Anderson at the Navy. Kennedy's replacement of the Army's Lyman Lemnitzer by General Maxwell Taylor as head of the Joint Chiefs marked his attempt to secure greater control (Keeney 2012; McMaster 1998; Binder 1997; Taylor 2002). Doves were less prominently placed in terms of office and less numerous, but some, like Ted Sorenson and Arthur Schlesinger, have recorded their interventions, and Kennedy listened to them. Among the leading doves were George Ball on Vietnam (1982) and Charles Bohlen on Cuba (1973). Ambassador to India and famed economist J.K. Galbraith (1969, 1981, 1998) was a regular advocate of diplomacy rather than military intervention. Other doves were less appreciated by Kennedy, notably Chester Bowles (Bowles 1971; Schaffer 1993) and Adlai Stevenson (Martin 1977).

For an excellent overview of foreign policy, one can begin with Stephen Rabe's recent *John F. Kennedy: World Leader* (2010) and Lawrence Freedman's *Kennedy's Wars* (2000) as representative of the postrevisionist interpretation of JFK's international stance. Still instructive is the harsher, revisionist collection edited by Thomas Paterson (1989). For US–Soviet relations more specifically, Michael Beschloss links the several crises expertly (1991) and several works provide valuable information on the Soviet side (Leffler 2007; Fursenko and Naftali 1997). For Kennedy's efforts to lead his European allies, the best recent study is by Brinkley and Griffiths (1999). This can be supplemented by works that look more specifically at the so-called "special relationship" between the US and Great Britain, seemingly embodied in the warm relationship between Kennedy and Macmillan (Priest 2006; Baylis 1984; Dumbrell 2006).

Berlin

Although Kennedy faced failure in Cuba and challenges in Africa and Southeast Asia before Khrushchev confronted him over Berlin in the summer of 1961, the Berlin crisis was his first direct superpower confrontation. At the time, there was general pressure for JFK to take a firm stance (Mander 1962), and what is striking is the persistence of the charge that Kennedy erred in accepting a summit with Khrushchev that in any way implied a willingness to negotiate on Berlin, and erred again when he gave indications that he accepted that East Berlin was already in the Soviet sphere and so access rights would not be defended. In this view, he gave a green light for the Wall (Kempe 2011). The most positive assessment of Kennedy's role in the crisis comes from Honoré Catudel (1980). As with many other crises, reinterpretation has often rested on fresh revelations about the other players: the pressure on Khrushchev from hardliners and the East German leader, and the role of German leader Adenauer, French president de Gaulle and British premier Macmillan (Granieri 2004; Mahan 2002). By revealing US strategic superiority in terms of missiles in late 1961, Kennedy aggravated Khrushchev's problems and, increasingly frustrated with European disunity, he was unwilling to fight a war for East Berlin; the Wall was welcome in this sense (Schick 1971; Wyden 1989).

Cuba

Kennedy may have inherited the CIA's plan for a US-backed invasion by anti-Castro dissidents, but, as he acknowledged, he had to take responsibility for the Bay of Pigs fiasco (Jones 2008). At quarter-century intervals, writers vie with each other in terms of titles that capture the full extent of the debacle: Rasenberger's *The Brilliant Disaster* (2011) builds on Higgins' *The Perfect Failure* (1989). Kennedy's refusal to commit US forces to save the embattled Cuban Brigade still incenses the Brigade's survivors and its CIA sponsors (Lynch 2000). The full postmortem on the incident has been declassified (Kornbluh 1998).

While the balance of opinion supports Kennedy's conduct during the Bay of Pigs, it is more critical of his authorization of subsequent efforts to topple Castro, although existing documentation does not contain evidence of his direct involvement (Bohning 2006). More clearly implicated is Bobby Kennedy, within the so-called Special Group Augmented (US Department of State, Office of the Historian 1997). The vendetta between the Kennedy brothers and Castro fuels a major strand of the assassination literature (see below) but it also provides the essential prelude for the Cuban Missile Crisis.

The Missile Crisis itself is one of the most closely studied incidents of the Cold War. The highly positive assessment of Kennedy's performance was established as orthodoxy by Schlesinger (1965) and other insiders (Kennedy 1968). Lavish praise continued through to Allison's widely cited analysis of the decision making in Ex-Comm (Allison 1971). Since then, the release of transcripts of the taped meetings and availability of Russian and Cuban materials has created a richer account, from which JFK continues to emerge well, if less heroically. Sheldon Stern, in particular, has shown how others in Ex-Comm, notably Bundy and McNamara, on occasion pressed the president for military action and that Bobby Kennedy was less influential than his own account implied (May and Zelikow 1997; Fursenko and Naftali 1997; Frankel 2004; Stern 2012). Michael Dobbs' *One Minute to Midnight* (2009) nicely captures the scale of the military escalation and the reality that none of the leaders were completely in control of events. Coleman's *The Fourteenth Day* (2012) demonstrates that the crisis took longer to resolve than is popularly assumed, and while JFK's reputation was enhanced, the nation's self-confidence was dented (George 2003). Underlining the range of players involved in the crisis, Nash (1997) explores the vexed question of the Turkish Jupiter missiles, which formed a key part of the secret bargain.

Latin America

The best overview of Kennedy's policy towards Latin America remains Stephen Rabe's *The Most Dangerous Area in the World* (1999), which can be amplified by relevant sections of Michael Latham's *Modernization as Ideology* (2000). Rabe has also provided a detailed treatment of Kennedy's intervention against the left-leaning government in British Guiana (2009). Central to Kennedy's policies in the region was the Alliance for Progress, which is assessed by Jeffrey Taffet (2007). Critics have long charged that the Alliance's pursuit of Cold War priorities explains its failings as an aid program (Levinson and de Onis 1972; Blazier 1976). Its proponents within the administration, including Schlesinger, Dillon, and Rostow, continued to defend it decades later (Scheman 1988). The periodical literature allows students to probe policies towards several countries in South and Central America: Brazil (Leacock 1979; Weis 2001); Guatemala (Streeter 2006); Peru (Le Roy 2002) and Venezuela (Zeiler 1990). The consensus is that there was a gulf between the idealistic rhetoric of the Alliance and the sometimes crudely anti-Communist policies actually pursued.

Africa

The same Cold War concerns amidst a wave of decolonization obliged Kennedy to pay attention to Africa. The standard study remains Mahoney's 1983 work, which inevitably dwells on the Congo crisis that formed the basis for Kalb's 1982 study of the Katangan secession. This, like the Algerian situation, was a problem inherited from the Eisenhower administration. As a senator, Kennedy had spoken in favor of Algerian independence, and as president he made a concerted effort to court African nationalist leaders (Muehlenbeck 2012).There was an obvious interaction between the emerging nations of Africa and the rising civil rights protest movement inside the United States, and Kennedy wanted to court both with rhetoric and symbolic gestures. The substance of his commitment in both cases remains debatable (Nwaubani 2003; Meriwether 2008).

The Middle East

Given the importance of North Africa to Middle Eastern politics, there was an inevitable overlap of issues for Kennedy, in terms of the impact of his policies on European allies, oil, and domestic politics, especially in relation to Israel (Gardner 2009; Fain 2002; Bass 2003). Kennedy had been a champion of Algerian independence but wanted to placate Gaullist France in relation to his overall Grand Strategy in Europe (Lefebvre 1999). He tried to induce Nasser to move away from the pro-Soviet tilt that followed the Suez Crisis (Little 1988). At the same time, he had to rein in Israel's nuclear ambitions while reassuring its security concerns by approving arms sales (Ben-Zvi 2002). As in Latin America and Asia, Kennedy wanted to nurture modernization in the Middle East along Western rather than Soviet lines. This strengthened ties more readily with new regimes in Iraq, Syria, and Egypt and aroused misgivings in the kingdoms of Jordan and Saudi Arabia. Overall, Kennedy seemed to leave US policy in the region no better than he found it, but postrevisionists would point to the conflicting pressures he faced (Matthews 2011; Cohen 2009; Miller 2007).

China

The growing tension between Mao's China and the USSR has been seen as an opportunity that JFK failed to exploit. This was due partly to the strength of the virulently anti-Communist China lobby within the US that tied itself to the Chiang Kai-shek regime in Taiwan, and partly to Kennedy's own perception that his practical options in relation to China were limited and that China's imminent acquisition of nuclear weapons represented the gravest threat to world peace (Chang 1988; Kochavi 2002; Maddock 2010). The debate over China policy often occurred in relation to US involvement in Southeast Asia, since China's intervention had been pivotal to the stalemate in Korea, but in 1962 it also complicated US relations with India and Pakistan due to military conflict on the Indo–Chinese border (Devereaux 2009; Brecher 1979–80).

Indochina (Laos and Vietnam)

When Kennedy came to power, US foreign policy was already committed to the "domino theory" that any loss in Southeast Asia was likely to be catastrophic. The situation was especially unstable in Laos in 1961, and it was one of the few achievements of the Vienna summit that Khrushchev seemed prepared to accept a neutralization agreement in Laos (Wehrle 1998; Stevenson 1972; Jacobs 2012). The solution was unsatisfactory and continuing instability in Laos helped to limit the range of realistic options in relation to neighboring Vietnam. But JFK's refusal to commit troops, as recommended by his military advisors, is seen by his supporters as evidence of how the Bay of Pigs experience reinforced his caution and as a sign of how he would have resisted escalation in future.

Kennedy's main challenge was to determine whether the US should continue to support the Diem regime in Vietnam as a bastion against Communist expansion. Given the controversy that swirls around US involvement in Vietnam it is important that students give some time to the primary sources. The *Foreign Relations of the United States* collections available for Vietnam deliberations during the Kennedy years (volumes 1–4) are accessible from the State Department history website (www.history.state.gov).

The revisionist tide in Kennedy studies was powerfully linked to the question: Why was America fighting in Vietnam? While both damned the Johnson administration for lying, the leaked official report, *The Pentagon Papers* (Sheehan 1971), and journalist David Halberstam's scathing *The Best and the Brightest* (1972) also refocused attention on the policies that Kennedy launched and the people he selected. Vietnam, in this view, was the price paid for the arrogance of the Kennedy men. JFK may have been less guilty than McNamara, but his marriage of caution and hubris led the celebrated rationalist president, in Halberstam's words, to "continue the most irrational of all major foreign policies, the policy towards ... Asia" (Halberstam 1972: 102). Halberstam reissued his journalistic pieces on the unviability and corruption of the Diem regime with a revised critique in 1992 (Halberstam and Singal 2007). As an apparent Cold War hardliner, Kennedy had declared in his inaugural address that the nation was prepared "to pay any price," and the rising body count from Vietnam was the measure of that cost. In retrospect, even Schlesinger became embarrassed by Kennedy's inflated rhetoric, which seemed to foreshadow Vietnam (Schlesinger 1978).

Throughout a long life, Schlesinger remained a consistent defender of Kennedy over Vietnam, arguing that, at the time of his death, JFK had already set limits to the scale of US intervention and was seeking to reduce rather than increase that commitment once his re-election had been achieved. The Harvard historian nonetheless had to concede that Kennedy's private intention was accompanied by public declarations that South Vietnam was a key US security interest that must be defended. Other proponents of the view that Kennedy would have responded to the deepening crisis in Vietnam differently than Johnson have labored the distinction between advisors and combat troops. They have also stressed the deep divisions of opinion inside the administration, especially in relation to whether or not to topple the Diem regime (Newman 1992; Kaiser 2000; Jones 2003; Rust 1985). Particularly controversial is Mark Moyar, who argues that if the US had backed Diem and taken more forceful action to intercept movements along the Ho Chi Minh trail, the mission would have been vindicated by victory. Moyar is especially animated by the biases of liberal and New Left historians, and this has triggered a heated debate (Moyar 2006; Wiest and Doidge 2010).

An early advocate that JFK wanted counterinsurgency to be a flexible response that would not lead to full-scale intervention is

R.B. Smith (1986). The same stress on Kennedy's repeated veto-ing of combat troops is evident in *Virtual Kennedy*, an ambitious attempt at counterfactual history that tries to consider what Kennedy would have done if he had survived. The same study, however, makes evident that the assassination made it even more difficult for Johnson to withdraw rather than escalate (Blight, Lang, and Welch 2010). The window of opportunity, in terms of avoiding an escalating conflict, was far more evident in the summer and early autumn of 1963 than in the spring of 1965, and American withdrawal was more politically possible before the Diem coup than after it (Logevall 2001). Thus, the disarray evident in Kennedy's policy in relation to the coup remains a blot upon his record.

The media

The recurrent theme of image within Kennedy scholarship springs partly from the fact that Kennedy became president at a time when television was becoming the dominant medium (Watson 1994). This coincidence worked largely in JFK's favor and his skillful use of television has made him the paradigm for pre-sidential communications strategy for the last fifty years (Berry 1987). To place Kennedy in the more general history of TV's evolution, see Erik Barnouw (1970). Specific episodes have received extended treatment, notably the 1960 election debates (Kraus 1977), and scholars have pondered the broader pattern, notably in relation to foreign crises (Kern, Levering, and Levering 1983). Although innovations like the live televised news con-ferences sharpened the political importance of television, the print media remained important players and Kennedy's relations paral-leled those of other presidents. Scholars have detected three phases: an initial alliance between president and reporters, increased competition to get a different story, and finally a growing detachment in order to signal press independence (Grossman and Kumar 1979).

The assassination

It is impossible to summarize the range of writing on the assassi-nation, since it spans so many conspiracy theories and genres.

Students should be aware that the Warren Commission Report (1964) has already been discarded by subsequent official investigations. Materials are now conveniently available via the National Archives website (www.archives.gov), as required by the John F. Kennedy Assassination Records Review Act of 1992. The House Select Committee (US HSCA 1979) concluded that there was strong circumstantial evidence of a conspiracy but was partially misled to this conclusion by scientific analysis of acoustic evidence which suggested there had been a fourth shot, and thus a second gunman. This evidence has since been challenged. The Assassination Records Review has led to the release of additional records, including some declassified by the CIA in 2006. None of these records provide a definitive answer to the question of a larger conspiracy.

One of the most popular of the many works that see Kennedy as the victim of a coup by malevolent forces within the military–industrial complex is *JFK and the Unspeakable* (Douglas 2008), which also illustrates how the event and the extraordinarily tangled web of connections around it can be used to link the crime to a larger cause—world peace. The House Committee came close to believing that they had evidence of an organized crime link, and this view is expounded in several books (Scheim 1988; Davis 1989, 1993). The most forceful presentation of the case against Lee Harvey Oswald remains Gerald Posner's *Case Closed* (1993), and the same position is evident in Dale Myers's *With Malice* (1998), which deals with the Tippit killing. But Oswald's involvement does not preclude a conspiracy, as Kaiser's *Road to Dallas* (2008) makes clear. The fundamental failings of the initial investigation, in terms of management of the crime scene and the autopsy on the president's body, are well summarized by Kurtz (2006).

The approach of the fiftieth anniversary has prompted fresh theories or refurbished old ones. At the time of the Warren Commission there were grave fears that the assassination might be plausibly linked to a foreign power, probably the USSR or Cuba. The fact that the Warren Commission was a cover-up in large part because it feared a superpower confrontation has not deterred conspiracy theorists from using its failure to investigate key leads as proof that it was part of an attempt to spark a military showdown. Robert Holmes argues that rogue elements within the

KGB used Oswald to kill Kennedy to salve the dishonor they felt over the Cuban Missile Crisis (Holmes 2012). Similarly, former CIA agent Brian Latell argues that there is evidence of Castro's foreknowledge of an assassination attempt on November 22, 1963 (Latell 2012). The list of suspects remains a lengthy one: for Philip Nelson (2011), Lyndon Johnson is the guilty man; for Harrison Livingstone (2006), it was a consortium of well-financed right-wing groups; and there was a flurry among conspiracy theorists across the internet when it was revealed that Kennedy had asked for more information about UFO sightings ten days before his death. The inaccurate information that circulated at the time of the assassination and the basic failings of the forensic teams who examined the crime scene and the body ensure that there will continue to be theories rather than demonstrable facts.

Memorialization

The shock of the assassination is well remembered (Gillon 2009; Hvalich and Payne 1996) and has become part of the academic study of collective memory (Olick et al. 2011; Neal 2006). Barbara Zelizer (1992) offers an interesting discussion of the role of the media in the days after the murder and subsequently in the repackaging of the event for commemorative purposes. An even more wide-ranging discussion, of the role of the assassination in the larger iconography of American popular culture, is offered by David Lubin (2003). The Zapruder film footage and its questioned authenticity have prompted several studies (Wrone 2003; Fetzer 2003; Trask 2005; Vagnes 2011). Peter Knight (2007), who has written extensively on American conspiracy culture, provides a useful summary of the assassination's cultural impact, as does Alice George (2012).

The literary reflections and treatments of the Kennedy assassination have tended to succeed best when they have told the story from the point of view of protagonists other than JFK, notably Oswald (Mailer 1995; DeLillo 1991). Cinematic treatments, epitomized by Oliver Stone's *JFK*, have succeeded best as genre films rather than historical documentaries. TV dramatizations have similarly edged towards "soap opera," which partly explains why the History Channel backed out of showing the Canadian-produced

The Kennedys (2011), although the vociferous complaints against the project by Kennedy sympathizers illustrates how the family continues to exert influence over the process of remembering. Dismayed by the portrait of her mother Jackie in the series, Caroline Kennedy authorized the release of her mother's oral history interview, which Jackie herself had wanted to have limited circulation (Kennedy and Beschloss 2011). Around the same time, a documentary about Ethel Kennedy, Bobby Kennedy's widow, rekindled rumors that Jackie and Bobby had become lovers as they mourned JFK's death. The process of memorialization continues therefore to mix objective reflection with gossip and other forms of cultural telling. In combination, they help to make Kennedy the most famous modern president.

Conclusion

In death, JFK became a liberal icon, but we misjudge both him
and his times if we see him as automatically the chief standard
bearer for an American social democratic tradition associated with
FDR's New Deal reforms. This is apparent from the start of his
political career. As a congressman and a senator, Kennedy was
more clearly an embodiment of his father's skepticism towards the
New Deal than one of its staunch defenders. At the end of the 1940s,
he was a politician whose limited liberal aspirations were tailored
to his election needs in Massachusetts, and whose more expansive
foreign policy views were geared to securing higher office. Even in
the Senate, his domestic policy goals seemed circumspect compared to those of outright liberals like Hubert Humphrey, and his
foreign policy statements, although they did contain an awareness
of the importance of nationalist sentiment in areas affected by
decolonization, were still largely compatible with the containment
doctrine.

Fighting Communism was a large plank in the platform of
Kennedy's political career, and while this would ultimately lead
him towards the internationalism that FDR had inherited from
Woodrow Wilson it also made him a critic of labor unionism and
a champion of heightened military preparedness. To understand
the Kennedy candidacy and the beginnings of his presidency, one
needs to appreciate that the political consensus of the 1950s was
more assuredly anti-Communist than it was liberal. In short,
instead of seeing Kennedy as an icon of the liberal 1960s, one
should see him as a product of the conservative 1950s. Arguably it

is the posthumous Kennedy who is his most liberal incarnation. In life, he was averse to the label.

While the media during his brief time in office tended to present Kennedy positively and applaud his mastery of issues and detailed knowledge, subsequently scholars have raised important questions about his presidential style. In some respects, his abandonment of Eisenhower's consultative practices for a more informal "kitchen cabinet" approach provided a poor precedent. His successor Lyndon Johnson proved less able to use this unstructured approach, particularly in relation to foreign policy, and might have been better served if JFK had preserved Eisenhower's committee structure. Kennedy held few full Cabinet meetings and liked to keep most policy initiatives firmly in his own hands. This reliance on a relatively small circle of trusted intimates and on policies that were pursued by ad hoc teams rather than formally accountable agencies became characteristic of the so-called imperial presidency that culminated in the Watergate scandal under Nixon. There was a decided tendency to give tasks to staff members whom JFK favored, and to avoid formal Cabinet meetings and full National Security Council meetings. This reinforced the secrecy that the Cold War context already fostered, producing actions of dubious legality—phone tapping of domestic suspects by the FBI and CIA, and aggressive actions against foreign governments, including assassination attempts, in the case of Castro—that later official investigations have condemned. The Kennedy White House may have seemed "cool" and tough, but policy-making was possibly less careful than in Eisenhower's committees.

To this charge, Kennedy apologists can counter that committees do not guarantee sound policy or success. They would point to the dubious activities of the CIA under Eisenhower, the deteriorating US–Soviet relations at the end of the 1950s, and the recession from 1957 onwards. Kennedy was not the first to use questionable means, and the scandals of Watergate under Nixon, Iran–Contra under Reagan, and the dubious rationale for the 2003 invasion of Iraq illustrate how the tendency of power to corrupt high officials persists, despite measures taken to restrain executive action since Kennedy's time. Nevertheless, for those who wish to portray Kennedy as the victim of forces in the military, the FBI, the CIA, and government more broadly, it is important to acknowledge that JFK was eager to topple Castro, that he saw Martin Luther King as a problem rather than an ally, and that he authorized actions by US advisors in Vietnam and elsewhere that entailed civilian casualties and blurred the distinction between combat troops and advisors. The nostalgia for the Kennedy years needs to be tempered, despite the clear sense of loss his death evoked.

There can be no last word on the Kennedy assassination, largely because the evidence needed to provide a definitive answer is not available. The emphasis here is not on a massive, wide-ranging conspiracy that concealed the truth in order to protect the guilty, but on the powerful tendency of institutions to respond to catastrophe in ways shaped primarily by immediate self-interest. If the CIA, FBI, and Secret Service were less than open in the investigation it was not because they were the agents behind the killing but because they feared a torrent of public criticism, because they had failed to prevent it. In Lyndon Johnson's case, taped conversations of his meetings with several members of the Warren Commission detail precisely that he wants them to solve the crime in ways that avoid a dangerous escalation of international tensions that could culminate in nuclear annihilation. Evidence that led to Cuba and the Soviet Union was sought less eagerly than evidence that Oswald was the shooter and that his murderer Jack Ruby was simply an outraged citizen in a city rife with guns.

In the decades since his death, the iconography of Kennedy has ensured that he can be symbolically deployed as part of a larger discourse of distrust and delegitimation. Reinforced by the faults of his presidential successors and the traumas that America has experienced since 1963, the images of the Kennedy era have become a form of visual shorthand for a nostalgic impulse that serves to critique the present, and to express a popular mood that is reluctant to accept the claims of ordained authorities. By 1992, the tide of alienation was high enough to allow one in five Americans to vote for a third-party candidate, Ross Perot, who was endorsed by lobby group THRO (Throw the Hypocritical Rascals Out).

Successive presidents have had special prosecutors appointed to investigate alleged crimes and misdemeanors, and when Bill Clinton declared on camera: "I did not have sex with that woman," he was speaking to a nation largely divided into those

...believe him and were outraged, and those who didn't
...m and didn't care. The office of the presidency had
...firmly associated with the idea of deception or spin, and
...rocess began with John F. Kennedy and was bolstered by
...subsequent revelations about the lies that even his adminis-
...tion perpetrated. Paradoxically, Kennedy is invoked as a symbol
of the age of innocence that in key respects he himself was
implicated in destroying, through his media manipulation and
effective concealment of his personal weaknesses, both medical and
moral.

In noting the mood of disillusionment that invokes the Kennedy
memory, it is important to note that the strength of this reaction
has swelled because the immediate response was its opposite.
In the aftermath of the assassination, shocked Americans placed an
enormous amount of faith in government. The liberal impulse,
while present in US politics before that event, became briefly its
vital center, enabling President Johnson to pass key measures
whose fate was uncertain at the time of Kennedy's death. Even
before Johnson's landslide victory over conservative Republican
Barry Goldwater in 1964, he had maneuvered both the Kennedy
tax cut and the civil rights bill through a Congress that had previously shown every sign of remaining in the grip of its conservative elements. In victory, Johnson was able to pass the Great
Society and War on Poverty legislation that marked the high-
water mark of liberalism, and he did so by invoking the Kennedy
name. Thus, the arc of Kennedy's presidency led towards the
apogee of liberalism. At the time of his nomination in 1960, JFK
had been a suspect figure for many liberals (as the son of a discredited father, in the eyes of the followers of Eleanor Roosevelt
and Adlai Stevenson). By 1963, he had charmed many of these
liberals, and in death they embraced him.

The disenchantment with New Deal liberalism that marked
political culture in the subsequent decades has entailed a recurrent
engagement with Kennedy memories. The disillusionment with
the Warren Commission's rush to judgment and its corollary, a
willingness to believe that malign forces plotted Kennedy's death,
are symptomatic of a shift away from a New Deal belief that
government can protect the people and give them greater security,
to the Reagan stance that government is not the solution,

government is the problem. Thus the chief political consequence of the Kennedy years was, first, the triumph of liberalism, but equally, and more enduringly, its defeat. This conservative resurgence had many causes, with elements in train even as Kennedy was emerging as a presidential contender in the 1950s, and other factors becoming more salient in the 1980s, as the social welfare policies adopted in the 1960s were systematically critiqued.

Kennedy won the 1960 election over Richard Nixon by promising to be more vigorous in the fight against Communism, not by offering voters détente and disarmament as his policy goals. His early actions—backing the Bay of Pigs operation, securing a neutral government in Laos, increasing support for the Diem regime in Vietnam, resisting Soviet attempts to overturn the settlement with regard to the status of Berlin, rallying Congress and the people to the need for greater defense spending—were those of a Cold Warrior. At the same time, the chastening failure in Cuba, the ambitious goals of the Alliance for Progress and Peace Corps, and his growing recognition that nuclear weapons were of limited practical use in dealing with problems like the Berlin crisis marked stages in the rapid education and refinement of Kennedy as a foreign policy leader.

The perils he confronted over the Cuban Missile Crisis in October 1962 remained those of a Cold War politician. He had to respond to what was perceived as a challenge to the US or risk acute political damage at home or abroad. He could not accept McNamara's assessment that the new missiles did not alter the strategic balance of power, nor could he willingly enter publicly into horse-trading in terms of the Jupiter missiles in Turkey. The politics of the situation necessitated an open confrontation and this risked a cycle of escalation culminating in nuclear war.

Praise for Kennedy must be limited to his management of the confrontation itself, and most especially his resistance to the many insistent voices calling for air raids and the invasion of Cuba. He cannot be praised for his prior actions giving Castro ample grounds to fear an imminent invasion, and thus providing grounds for Soviet military protection. He cannot be praised for his administration's military build-up and the lack of appreciation he showed for Khrushchev's position in relation to Maoist criticism and hostility from hawks inside the Kremlin. Few scholars today would speak of brinkmanship glowingly. Khrushchev's decision to offer to withdraw the missiles in return for a public disavowal of plans to invade Cuba and a private commitment to withdraw missiles from Turkey seems less supine than sagacious. But if Kennedy cannot be praised in every respect, in the key decision not to move rapidly to military action and risk escalation the praise should be lavish, since it was a powerful and fateful choice. If he had not stood firm, the consequences could have been literally earth shattering.

Kennedy also deserves praise for the 1963 test ban treaty. It confirms that in office he came to recognize that nuclear weapons represented a threat to US national security rather than its surest safeguard. The test ban was only a first step, but it was a step, and one that achieved Senate ratification despite the strongly anti-Communist posture of the key figures in that Chamber. The test ban, alongside Kennedy's "Peace" address at the American University in June 1963, also supports the view that Kennedy was better able to perceive that peaceful coexistence with Communism required him to be mindful of not just what was possible in American politics but what was possible in the internal politics of the Communist bloc, which were more complex than American propaganda had previously suggested. In this respect, too, readers are entitled to feel the loss that the November gunfire brought to international relations.

Evaluating Kennedy as a statesman in the final three months of his life nevertheless requires us to acknowledge that he remained a politician seeking reelection in a nation still wedded to anti-Communism and the containment doctrine. His 1963 speech in Berlin, with its denunciation of Communism's failures, was a reflection of this electoral imperative, as well as of the need to reassure Berliners, and Europeans more generally, that US support was unwavering. Similarly, his vacillations in relation to the Diem regime in Vietnam capture the extent to which he remained committed to containing Communism and yet recognized that local conflicts can only be resolved locally. If Kennedy had believed that the Laotian settlement provided a model for disengagement in Vietnam, and if he had been committed to that policy in the summer of 1963, the Buddhist uprising and associated loss of credibility for the Diem regime gave him the opportunity to step back. Instead, he backed the coup which produced the political instability inside South Vietnam that largely precluded the option of withdrawal thereafter.

Ultimately, while those who argue that Kennedy, had he lived, would have responded differently to the deteriorating situation in Vietnam can make a case, the argument that he was set on withdrawing troops before he died is tendentious. It fails to give adequate weight to his political considerations: namely, he was not prepared to do so if it jeopardized his reelection. Communist victories were still seen by Americans generally as American defeats, and Kennedy knew that he would be reelected only if most Americans saw him as a president who could fight Communism effectively.

Combined with this overarching political concern that the nation's international strength should not be in doubt heading into the 1964 election was Kennedy's enduring concern with the sluggish economy. The persistent balance of payments problem and an unemployment rate which remained obdurately above 5 percent could readily fuel electoral retaliation. Kennedy did not want to be left, as Jimmy Carter was in his losing contest with Ronald Reagan in 1980, squirming before an opponent who asked: Are you better off than you were four years ago? Similarly entangled with foreign policy, the civil rights question was something into which Kennedy's privileged, lily-white life gave him limited insight (in marked contrast to Lyndon Johnson). Only the forces of the civil rights movement pushed Kennedy reluctantly along the path of justice, compelling him in June 1963 to try to use the so-called "bully pulpit" of the presidency to educate Americans on the need to ensure racial equality in their democracy. Racial reform may have appealed to him for Cold War reasons abroad, but it also did so because African American insurgency seemed to threaten civil war at home.

Here, too, the praise awarded Kennedy by supporters for his moves towards Keynesian-style reflation and for his belated championing of civil rights needs to be tempered by a proper appreciation of the political context. The US Congress remained a body the majority of whose members had a limited knowledge of economic theory, and a strong sense of the need to protect their own authority. They had blocked most of Kennedy's economic proposals, limiting the boost to the economy largely to defense spending and corporate tax depreciation allowances. Kennedy was more likely to face an election in which he was fighting for tax cuts than one in which he was pointing to the economic revival that tax cuts had wrought.

It seems likely that in November 1963 Kennedy remained more persuaded of the political advantages of securing economic recovery than of the merits of comprehensive civil rights legislation, notwithstanding the eloquence of his June speech portraying racial equality as a moral challenge to which the nation must rise. His muted reaction to the Birmingham church bombings in September even suggests that he may have seen the gravest threat to law and order as coming from inflamed white segregationist opinion, and hoped to persuade African American leaders to limit any actions that might trigger violence. Overall, favorable poll ratings among African Americans and a sharp awareness of the difficulties that seeking civil rights legislation entailed in Congress would have made him far less of a champion of the civil rights cause than Lyndon Johnson proved to be in 1964. No serious student of Kennedy's position on civil rights can fail to acknowledge its overriding pragmatism, and the gulf between this fact and the high esteem he enjoys among African Americans still puzzles.

Kennedy's inaugural address and subsequent early rhetoric were firmly in the tradition of appeals for national solidarity and fortitude in the face of the enemy. His principal image was that of a man of energetic action. Yet what marked his successes in foreign policy were two traits: the practice of compromise and the exercise of caution. Repeatedly, he rejected calls to commit US combat troops: in support of the Cuban Brigade at the Bay of Pigs, in Laos, and in Vietnam. While embracing components of a flexible response in defense strategy, he also stood firm against those military chiefs who believed in a "winnable" nuclear war. As a result, his greatest foreign policy success—the Missile Crisis—was less about embracing the brink than respecting it. Conversely, his failings—the covert actions against Castro and the coup against Diem—flowed from the absence of caution and an inability to see compromise as politically feasible.

As the bibliographical essay in Chapter 10 makes clear, the postrevisionist literature on Kennedy develops its critique by stressing the limited range of real options available and the complexities of the problems JFK faced. Critics may charge that his judgment that the Berlin Wall was better than a war was a betrayal of the hopes of many Berliners, but can they persuasively argue that access rights between East and West could have been maintained if Kennedy had been more resolute? Apologists can similarly insist that at the time of his death JFK had decided to withdraw from Vietnam, reducing rather than increasing US military involvement and hoping for a Laos-style neutral solution. But can they maintain that, if confronted by conservative charges of vacillating in the face of Communist expansionism, he would have done anything prior to the 1964 election? And is it credible that he would have wished to begin a second term with a possible defeat in South Vietnam graver than the one on Cuban beaches in 1961?

Ironically, perhaps, the qualities that marked success in foreign policy limited Kennedy's achievements domestically. With a Congress whose committees were dominated by a conservative Southern Democrat and Midwestern Republican coalition, he was too eager to compromise, and in general too cautious in his pursuit of legislation. The contrast between what Kennedy struggled to achieve and what Johnson passed is too sharp to be ignored.

However, here too the critical elements were not simply biographical—Kennedy's lack of rapport with his former congressional colleagues and LBJ's fabled ability to "arm-twist." It was contextual as well. Kennedy was a president elected with barely any mandate in terms of his margin of victory and his leverage with the conservative coalition on matters other than defense was meager. Johnson, on the other hand, had the assassination and maneuvered to ensure that opposition to his proposals was seen as being against the slain president and as affronts to a stricken people. How could the party of Lincoln (the Republicans) fail to back the civil rights bill? Why should the nation's needs be held hostage by representatives of the South, the section that had bred assassins?

Kennedy's presidential tenure was tragically short. Of the single-term presidents of the postwar era, none of the others—Ford, Carter, Bush Senior—would excite any great public demand that they be given a second chance. When asked, however, Americans commonly name JFK as the president they would most like to see back in the White House. A part of this study seeks to explain this appeal and finds its answer not just in the man and the leader that Kennedy was, but in the shock and the memory that his violent death created. In November 1963 Kennedy's approval rating was one of his lowest in office, and within the FBI, the CIA, and the senior echelons of the armed forces, not to mention among anti-Castro Cubans, radical conservatives, and organized crime figures, there was a sense of anger, betrayal, and ultimately hatred. A biography of one of America's best-loved presidents must explain that he was far from universally admired.

JFK was a great person to have in charge in a crisis and a flawed politician in terms of overseeing policy consistently and shaping it towards the best ideals. By this measure, he had international successes, but cannot be seen as a reliable ally of minorities at home or the dispossessed of the world. Certain aspects of his success—the importance of wealth in the launching of his career and of media strategy or public relations in his rise to the presidency—may be seen as pernicious trends that hamper democracy and exploit its deficiencies. The excitement for his staff that he brought to the task of government was less beneficial to the institution of the presidency as an instrument of government than was the rather staid formality of Eisenhower's committee structure. Trying to match the glamor of his wife and children remains a burden borne by each First Family since. In these ways, Kennedy left the presidency a more difficult office to hold.

The perception that JFK stood "eyeball to eyeball" with Khrushchev, on the brink of nuclear war, is perhaps the most dangerous part of his legacy, partly mitigated by the reality that Kennedy himself was more impressed by the dangers he had confronted than press plaudits. The idea of solving problems through both violence and the threat of violence continues to influence American political culture to an alarming degree. Allied to this aspect of the Kennedy legend and equally damaging is the level of expectation placed upon the president. To an outsider it appears as if, in choosing and appraising their presidents, many Americans blur the line between the world as it is and the fantasy world of superheroes within their popular culture. Candidates must feed this hope and struggle with the subsequent disillusionment.

Another aspect of the Kennedy style was the elaboration of the threat to the nation, which has persisted more recently in the context of the so-called War on Terror. Overall, the impact of Kennedy on the presidency and politics more generally is hard to celebrate.

Nevertheless, a study of John F. Kennedy does have traits to celebrate. Politics is the richer if its practitioners have charm, and Kennedy's self-deprecation, coolness, eloquence, and intellectual interests properly continue to excite admiration and inspire emulation. Even more so when one learns that he exhibited these traits while in daily pain. While many political offices can be safely entrusted to people who persevere with the detail, high executive office may require figures like Kennedy who display their exceptional talents in critical moments. A president who can foresee the ramifications of military action and stand firm against strong efforts to induce him to authorize such action is preferable to one who sees only the immediate threat and is swallowed up by the chorus. Kennedy will forever rank ahead of Johnson and George W. Bush in this respect.

Perhaps the only subsequent president to excite the same fond remembrance as Kennedy is Ronald Reagan. Both have been seen as great communicators and the parallel may be extended in terms of their impact on the public mood. This intangible should not be lightly dismissed by historians. Scholars may see the damage that the Reagan years did to the long-term solvency of the United States, just as some of them perceive the Kennedy years as leaving the Cold War dangerously poised in Southeast Asia. The US–Soviet détente signaled by the test ban treaty did not mark a thoroughgoing revision of containment and the emergent commitments to counterinsurgency and flexible response proved a formula for the descent into the Vietnamese quagmire. But, for Americans at the time, Reagan appeared to have taken a despondent nation lacking in confidence, and given it the ability to move on. Kennedy, similarly, boosted the nation's faith in itself.

The Kennedy portrayed in these pages is a president of promise: a figure who changed the nation's mood and at times directed its energies towards its noblest goals, as with the Peace Corps. He is also an ambivalent figure, a president whose political style is privately cautious and publicly firm, just as his public image was one of the healthy Catholic family man whereas privately he was ill, promiscuous, reckless, and profane. Some noted that JFK lived a compartmentalized life, able to live comfortably with his own contradictions, apt to proceed on contradictory paths, postponing the moments of final decision. There is a truth here.

Bibliography

Allison, G.T. (1971) *Essence of Decision: Explaining the Cuban Missile Crisis*, Boston: Little, Brown.

ARRB (Assassination Records Review Board), (1998) *The Assassination Records Review Board: Final Report*, Washington DC: US Government Printing Office.

Ball, G. (1982) *The Past Has Another Pattern*, New York: Norton.

Barkun, L. (2003) *A Culture of Conspiracy: Apocalyptic Visions in Contemporary America*, Berkeley: University of California Press.

Barnouw, E. (1970) *A History of Broadcasting in the United States: The Image Empire, Volume 3: From 1953*, New York: Oxford University Press.

Bass, W. (2003) *Support Any Friend: JFK's Middle East and the Making of the U.S.-Israel Alliance*, New York: Oxford University Press.

Baylis, J. (1984) *Anglo-American Defence Relations, 1939–1984*, London: Macmillan.

Ben-Zvi, A. (2002) *John F. Kennedy and the Politics of Arms Sales to Israel*, New York: Routledge.

Bernstein, I. (1991) *Promises Kept: John F. Kennedy's New Frontier*, New York: Oxford University Press.

Berry, J.P. (1987) *John F. Kennedy and the Media*, Lanham, MD: University Press of America.

Beschloss, M. (1991) *The Crisis Years: Kennedy and Khrushchev, 1960–1963*, New York: HarperCollins.

Binder, L.J. (1997) *Lemnitzer: A Soldier for his Time*, Washington DC: Brassey Inc.

Bird, K. (1998) *The Color of Truth: McGeorge Bundy and William Bundy: Brothers in Arms*, New York: Simon & Schuster.

Blair, J. and Blair, C. (1974) *The Search for JFK*, New York: Putnam.

Blazier, C. (1976) *The Hovering Giant: US Responses to Revolutionary Changes in Latin America*, Pittsburgh: University of Pittsburgh Press.

Blight, J.G. and Lang, J.M. (2004) *The Fog of War: Lessons from the Life of Robert S. McNamara*, Lanham, MD: Rowman & Littlefield.

Blight, J.G. and Welch, D.A. (1989) *On the Brink: Americans and Soviets Re-examine the Cuban Missile Crisis*, New York: Hill and Wang.

Blight, J.G., Lang, J.M, and Welch, D.A. (2010) *Virtual Kennedy: Vietnam if Kennedy had Lived*, Lanham, MD: Rowman & Littlefield.

Blumenthal, D. and Marone, J.A., eds. (2008) *The Heart of Power: Health and Politics in the Oval Office*, Berkeley: University of California Press.

Bohlen, C.E. (1973) *Witness to History, 1929–1969*, New York: W.W. Norton.

Bohning, D. (2006) *The Castro Obsession: U.S. Covert Operations in Cuba, 1959–1965*, Washington, DC: Potomac Books.

Borstelmann, T. (2001) *The Cold War and the Color Line: America's Race Relations in the Global Arena*, Cambridge, MA: Harvard University Press.

Bowles, C. (1971) *Promises to Keep: My Years in Public Life, 1941–1969*, New York: Harper & Row.

Bradford, S. (2000) *America's Queen: The Life of Jacqueline Kennedy Onassis*, New York: Viking Penguin.

Bradlee, B. (1975) *Conversations with Kennedy*, New York: Norton.

Brauer, C.M. (1977) *John F. Kennedy and the Second Reconstruction*, New York: Columbia University Press.

Brecher, M. (1979–80) "Non-alignment under Stress: The West and the India–China Border War," *Pacific Affairs,* vol. 52, no. 4: 612–30.

Brinkley, D. and Griffiths, T. (1999) *John F. Kennedy and Europe*, Baton Rouge: Louisiana State University Press.

Bryant, N. (2006) *The Bystander: John F. Kennedy and the Struggle for Black Equality*, New York: Basic Books.

Bugliosi, V. (2007) *Four Days in November: The Assassination of President John F. Kennedy*, New York: W.W. Norton.

Bundy, M. (1988) *Danger and Survival: Choice about the Bomb in the First Fifty Years*, New York: Random House.

Burner, D. (1988) *John F. Kennedy and a New Generation*, Glenview IL: Scott Foresman.

Butler, L., Koopman, C., and Zimbardo, P.G. (1995) "The Psychological Impact of Viewing the Film *JFK*: Emotions, Beliefs, and Political Behavioral Intentions," *Political Psychology*, vol. 16, no. 2: 237–57.

Callahan, D. (1990) *Dangerous Capabilities: Paul Nitze and the Cold War*, New York: HarperCollins.

Cameron, G. (1971) *Rose: A Biography of Rose Fitzgerald Kennedy*, New York: Putnam.

Cannelos, P.S. (2010) *The Last Lion: The Fall and Rise of Ted Kennedy*, New York: Simon & Schuster.

Caro, R.T. (2012) *The Passage of Power*, volume 4 of *The Years of Lyndon Johnson*, London: Bodley Head.

Catudel, H.M. (1980) *Kennedy and the Berlin Crisis: A Case Study in U.S. Decision Making*, Berlin: Berlin-Verlag.

Chang, G.H. (1988) "JFK, China and the Bomb," *Journal of American History*, vol 74, no.4: 1287–1310.

Clymer, A. (1999) *Edward M. Kennedy: A Biography*, New York: Harper.

Cohen, S.P. (2009) *Beyond America's Grasp: A Century of Failed Diplomacy in the Middle East*, New York: Farrar, Strauss, Giroux.

Cohen, W.I. (1980) *Dean Rusk*, Totawa, NJ: Cooper Square Publishing.

Coleman, D.G. (2012) *The Fourteenth Day: JFK and the Aftermath of the Cuban Missile Crisis*, New York: W.W. Norton.

Connally, N and Herskowitz, M. (2003) *From Love Field: Our Final Hours with President John F. Kennedy*, New York: Rugged Land Books.

Dallek, R. (2003) *An Unfinished Life: John F. Kennedy, 1917–1963*, Boston: Little, Brown and Company.

Davis, J.H. (1989) *Mafia Kingfish: Carlos Marcello and the Assassination of John F. Kennedy*, New York: Signet Books.

Davis, J.H. (1993) *The Kennedy Contract: The Mafia Plot to Assassinate the President*, New York: Harper Collins.

Dean, R.D. (1998) "Masculinity as Ideology: John F. Kennedy and the Domestic Politics of Foreign Policy," *Diplomatic History*, vol. 22, no. 1 (winter): 29–62.

DeLillo, D. (1991) *Libra*, New York: Viking Penguin.

Devereaux, D.R. (2009) "The Sino-Indian War of 1962 in Anglo-American Relations," *Journal of Contemporary History*, vol. 44, no. 1: 71–87.

Dinnerstein, H.S. (1976) *The Making of the Missile Crisis: October 1962*, Baltimore, MD: Johns Hopkins University Press.

Dobbs, M. (2009) *One Minute to Midnight: Kennedy, Khrushchev and Castro on the Brink of Nuclear War*, London: Arrow.

Donaldson, G.A. (2007) *The First Modern Campaign: Kennedy, Nixon, and the Election of 1960*, Lanham, MD: Rowman & Littlefield.

Donovan, R.J (1962) *PT-109: John F. Kennedy in World War II*, Greenwich, CT: Crest Books.

Douglas, J.W. (2008) *JFK and the Unspeakable: Why He Died and Why It Matters*, Maryknoll, NY: Orbis Books.

Druks, H. (2005) *John F. Kennedy and Israel*, New York: Praeger.

Dudziak, M. (2002) *Cold War Civil Rights: Race and the Image of American Democracy*, Princeton, NJ: Princeton University Press.

Dumbrell, J. (2006) *A Special Relationship: Anglo-American Relations from the Cold War to Iraq*, London: Palgrave Macmillan.

Fain, W.T. (2002) "John F. Kennedy and Harold Macmillan: Managing the 'Special Relationship' in the Persian Gulf Region," *Middle Eastern Studies*, vol. 38, no. 4: 95–122.

Fairlie, H. (1973) *The Kennedy Promise*, Garden City, NY: Doubleday.

Fay, P. (1966) *The Pleasure of His Company*, New York: Harper & Row.

Fetzer, J. (1989) "Clinging to Containment: China Policy" in Paterson, T.G., ed., *Kennedy's Question for Victory: American Foreign Policy, 1961–1963*, New York: Oxford University Press: 178–97.

Fetzer, J.H. (2003) *The Great Zapruder Film Hoax: Deceit and Deception in the Death of JFK*, Chicago: Catfleet Press.

Frankel, M. (2004) *High Noon in the Cold War: Kennedy, Khrushchev, and the Cuban Missile Crisis*, New York: Ballantine

Freedman, L. (2000) *Kennedy's Wars: Berlin, Cuba, Laos and Vietnam*, New York: Oxford University Press.

Fursenko, A. and Naftali, T. (1997) *"One Hell of A Gamble": Khrushchev, Castro and Kennedy, 1958–1964*, New York: W.W. Norton.

Gaddis, J.W. (2012) *George F. Kennan: An American Life*, New York: Viking Penguin.

Galbraith, J.K. (1969) *Ambassador's Journal: A Personal Account of the Kennedy Years*, Boston: Houghton Mifflin.

Galbraith, J.K. (1981) *A Life in Our Times*, Boston: Houghton Mifflin.

Galbraith, J.K., ed. Goodman, J. (1998) *Letters to Kennedy*, Cambridge: Harvard University Press.

Gardner, L.C. (2009) *Three Kings: The Rise of an American Empire in the Middle East*, New York: The New Press.

Garrow, D.J. (1981) *The FBI and Martin Luther King*, New York: Norton.

George, A.L. (2003) *Awaiting Armageddon: How Americans Faced the Cuban Missile Crisis*, Chapel Hill: University of North Carolina Press.

George, A.L. (2012) *The Assassination of John F. Kennedy*, New York: Routledge.

Giglio, J.N. (2006) *The Presidency of John F. Kennedy*, 2nd ed., Lawrence: University of Kansas Press.

Gillon, S.M. (2009) *The Kennedy Assassination: 24 Hours After*, New York: Basic Books.

Goduti, P.A. (2012) *Robert F. Kennedy and the Shaping of Civil Rights, 1960–1964*, Jefferson, NC: McFarland and Co.

Goldstein, G.M. (2009) *Lessons in Disaster: McGeorge Bundy and the Path to War in Vietnam*, New York: Henry Holt and Co.

Goodwin, R. (1988) *Remembering America*, Boston: Little, Brown.

Granieri, R.J. (2004) *The Ambivalent Alliance: Konrad Adenauer, the CDU/CSU and the West, 1949–1966*, New York: Berghahn.

Grossman, M.B. and Kumar, M.J. (1979) "The White House and the News Media: The Phases of their Relationship," *Political Science Quarterly*, vol. 94 (spring): 37–53.

Haefele, M. (2001) "John F. Kennedy, USIA and World Public Opinion," *Diplomatic History*, vol. 25, no. 1 (winter): 63–84.

Halberstam, D. (1972) *The Best and the Brightest*, New York: Random House.

Halberstam, D. and Singal, D. (2007) *The Making of a Quagmire: America and Vietnam in the Kennedy Era*, Lanham, MD: Rowman and Littlefield.

Hamilton, N. (1992) *JFK: Reckless Youth*, New York: Random House.

Harrison, C. (1988) *On Account of Sex: The Politics of Women's Issues, 1945–1968*, Berkeley: University of California Press.

Hersey, J. (1944) "Survival" [A Reporter at Large], *New Yorker*, June 17.

Hersh, S. (1997) *The Dark Side of Camelot*, Boston: Little, Brown.

Heymann, C.D. (1998) *RFK: A Candid Biography*, New York: E.P. Dutton.

Higgins, T. (1989) *The Perfect Failure: Kennedy, Eisenhower, and the CIA at the Bay of Pigs*, New York: W.W. Norton.

Higham, C. (1995) *Rose: The Life and Times of Rose Fitzgerald Kennedy*, New York: Pocket Books.

Hilsman, R. (1967) *To Move a Nation: The Politics of Foreign Policy in the Administration of John F. Kennedy*, Garden City, NY: Doubleday.

Holmes, R. (2012) *A Spy Like No Other: The Cuban Missile Crisis and the KGB Links to the Kennedy Assassination*, London: Biteback Publishing.

Hvalich, L. and Payne, D. (1996) *Reporting the Kennedy Assassination: Journalists Who Were there Recall their Experiences*, Dallas, TX: Three Forks Press.

Jacobs, S. (2012) *The Universe Unraveling: American Foreign Policy in Cold War Laos*, Ithaca, NY: Cornell University Press.

Johnson, R.T. (1974) *Managing the White House: An Intimate Study of Three Presidents*, New York: Harper and Row.

Jones, H. (2003) *Death of a Generation: How the Assassinations of Diem and JFK Prolonged the Vietnam War*, New York: Oxford University Press.

Jones, H. (2008) *The Bay of Pigs*, New York: Oxford University Press.

Joynt Kumar, M. (2006) *Managing the President's Message: The White House Communications Operation*, Baltimore, MD: Johns Hopkins University Press.

Kaiser, D. (2000) *American Tragedy: Kennedy, Johnson and the Origins of the Vietnam War*, Cambridge, MA: Harvard University Press.

Kaiser, D.E. (2008) *The Road to Dallas: The Assassination of John F. Kennedy*, Cambridge, MA: Harvard University Press.

Kalb, M.G. (1982) *The Congo Cables: The Cold War in Africa—From Eisenhower to Kennedy*, New York: Macmillan.

Kallina, E.F. (2010) *Kennedy v. Nixon: The Election of 1960*, Gainesville: University of Florida Press.

Kearns Goodwin, D. (1987) *The Fitzgeralds and the Kennedys*, New York: Simon & Schuster.

Keeney, L.D. (2012) *15 Minutes: General Curtis LeMay and the Countdown to Nuclear Annihilation*, New York: St Martin's.

Kempe, F. (2011) *Berlin 1961: Kennedy, Khrushchev and the Most Dangerous Place on Earth*, New York: Berkley Trade (Penguin).

Kennan, G.F. (1972) *Memoirs, 1950–1963*, Boston: Little, Brown.

Kennedy, C. and Beschloss, M. (2011) *Jacqueline Kennedy: Historic Conversations on Life with John F. Kennedy*, New York: Hyperion.

Kennedy, J.F. (1940) *Why England Slept*, New York: Wilfred Funk.

Kennedy, J.F., ed. (1945) *As We Remember Joe*, privately printed 1945.

Kennedy, J.F. (1956) *Profiles in Courage*, New York: Harper.

Kennedy, J.F. (1962–64) *Public Papers of the Presidents: John F. Kennedy, 1961–1963*, Washington DC: US Government Printing Office.

Kennedy, J.F. (1964a) *John Fitzgerald Kennedy: A Compilation of Statements and Speeches Made During His Service in the United States Senate and House of Representatives*, Washington DC: US Government Printing Office.

Kennedy, J.F. (1964b) *A Nation of Immigrants*, London: Hamish Hamilton.

Kennedy, R.F. (1968) *Thirteen Days: A Memoir of the Cuban Missile Crisis*, New York: Norton.

Kennedy, R. (1974) *Times to Remember*, Garden City, NY: Doubleday.

Kern, M., Levering, P.W., and Levering, R.B. (1983) *The Kennedy Crises: The Press, the Presidency, and Foreign Policy*, Chapel Hill: University of North Carolina Press.

King, S. (2011) *11.22.63*, New York: Simon & Schuster.

Klein, E. (1996) *All Too Human: The Love Story of Jack and Jackie Kennedy*, New York: Pocket Books.

Klein, E. (2009) *Ted Kennedy: The Dream that Never Died*, New York: Crown.

Knight, P. (2007) *The Kennedy Assassination*, Edinburgh: Edinburgh University Press.

Kochavi, N. (2002) *A Conflict Perpetuated: China Policy During the Kennedy Years*, New York: Praeger.

Kornbluh, P., ed. (1998) *Bay of Pigs Declassified: The Secret CIA Report on the Invasion of Cuba*, New York: Free Press.

Kraus, S. (1977) *The Great Debates: Kennedy versus Nixon, 1960*, Bloomington, IN: University of Indiana Press.

Kurtz, M. (2006) *The JFK Assassination Debates: Lone Gunman versus Conspiracy*, Lawrence: University of Kansas Press.

Lane, M. (1966) *Rush to Judgment: A Critique of the Warren Commission's Inquiry into the Murders of President John F, Kennedy, Officer J.D. Tippit and Lee Harvey Oswald*, New York: Rinehart & Winston

Langley Hall, G. and Pinchot, A. (1966) *Jacqueline Kennedy: A Biography*, New York: Signet.

Lasky, V. (1963) *JFK: The Man and the Myth*, New York: Macmillan.

Latham, M.E. (2000) *Modernization as Ideology: American Social Science and "Nation Building" in the Kennedy Era*, Chapel Hill: University of North Carolina Press.

Latell, B. (2012) *Castro's Secrets: The CIA and the Cuba's Intelligence Machine*, New York: Palgrave-Macmillan.

Le Roy, F. (2002) "Mirages over the Andes: Peru, France, the United States and Military Jet Procurement in the 1960s," *Pacific Historical Review,* vol. 71, no. 2: 269–300.

Leacock, R. (1979) "JFK, Business and Brazil," *Hispanic American Historical Review*, vol. 59, no. 4: 636–73.

Leamer, L. (1996) *The Kennedy Women: The Saga of an American Family*, New York: Ballantine Books.

Leamer, L. (2001) *The Kennedy Men, 1901–1963*, New York: William Morrow.

Lefebvre, J.A. (1999) "Kennedy's Algerian Dilemma: Containment, Alliance Politics and the 'Rebel Dialogue,'" *Middle Eastern Studies*, vol. 35, no. 2: 61–82.

Leffler, M.P. (2007) *For the Soul of Mankind: The United States, the Soviet Union, and the Cold War*, New York: Hill and Wang.

Levinson, J. and de Onis, J. (1972) *The Alliance that Lost its Way: A Critical Report on the Alliance for Progress*, New York: Quadrangle.

Liebovich, L. (2001) *The Press and the Modern Presidency*, Westport, CT: Praeger.

Lincoln, E. (1966) *My Twelve Years with John F. Kennedy*, New York: David McKay.

Little, D. (1988) "The New Frontier on the Nile: JFK, Nasser, and Arab Nationalism," *Journal of American History*, vol .75, no. 2: 501–27.

Livingstone, H. (2006) *The Radical Right and the Murder of John F. Kennedy*, Bloomington, IN: Trafford Publishing.

Logevall, F. (2001) *Choosing War: The Last Chance for Peace and the Escalation of War in Vietnam*, Berkeley: University of California Press.

Logsdon, J.M. (2011) *The Decision to Go to the Moon: Project Apollo and the National Interest*, Cambridge, MA: MIT Press.

Lubin, D.M. (2003) *Shooting Kennedy: JFK and the Culture of Images*, Berkeley: University of California Press.

Lukacs, J. (2007) *George F. Kennan: A Study of Character*, New Haven, CT: Yale University Press.

Lynch, T. (2000) *Decision for Disaster: Betrayal at the Bay of Pigs*, Washington, DC: Potomac Books.

McAndrew, L.J. (1991) "Beyond Appearances: Kennedy, Congress, Religion and Federal Aid to Education," *Presidential Studies Quarterly*, vol. 21, no. 3 (summer): 545–557.

McCarthy, J. (1951, June 14) *Congressional Record*, vol. 97, no. 5: 6556.

McDougall, W.A. (1985) *The Heavens and the Earth: A Political History of the Space Age*, New York: Basic Books.

Macgregor Burns, J. (1960) *John Kennedy*, New York: Harcourt Brace.

Macgregor Burns, J. (1976) *Edward Kennedy and the Kennedy Legacy*, New York: W.W. Norton.

McMaster, H.R. (1998) *Dereliction of Duty: Johnson, McNamara and the Joint Chiefs of Staff and the Lies that Led to Vietnam*, New York: HarperCollins.

McNamara, R.S. (2000) *Argument without End: In Search of Answers to the Vietnam Tragedy*, New York: Perseus Books.

McNamara, R.S. and Vandemark, B. (1995) *In Retrospect: The Tragedy and Lessons of Vietnam*, New York: Times Book.

Maddock, S.J. (2010) *Nuclear Apartheid: The Quest for American Atomic Supremacy from World War II to the Present*, Chapel Hill: University of North Carolina Press.

Mahan, E.R. (2002) *Kennedy, de Gaulle and Western Europe*, New York: Palgrave.

Mahoney, R.D. (1983) *JFK: Ordeal in Africa*, New York: Oxford University Press.

Mailer, N. (1995) *Oswald's Tale: An American Mystery*, Boston: Little, Brown.

Manchester, W. (1967) *The Death of a President*, New York: Harper & Row, 1972.

Mander, J. (1962) *Hostage for the West*, Harmondsworth: Penguin.

Martin, J.B. (1977) *Adlai Stevenson of Illinois*, Garden City, NY: Doubleday.

Matthew, C. (1996) *Kennedy and Nixon*, New York: Simon and Schuster.

Matthews, W.C. (2011) "The Kennedy Administration, Counterinsurgency and Iraq's First Ba'thist Regime," *Middle Eastern Studies*, vol. 43., no. 4: 635–653.

May, E.R. and Zelikow, P.D (1997) *The Kennedy Tapes: Inside the White House during the Cuban Missile Crisis*, Cambridge MA: Harvard University Press.

Meriwether, J.H. (2008) "'Worth a Lot of Negro Votes': Black Voters, Africa and the 1960 Presidential Campaign," *Journal of American History*, vol. 95, no. 3: 737–63.

Miller, B. (2007) *States, Nations and the Great Powers: the Source of Regional Peace and War*, New York: Cambridge University Press.

Milne, D. (2009) *America's Rasputin: Walt Rostow and the Vietnam War*, New York: Hill and Wang.

Miroff, B. (1976) *Pragmatic Illusions: The Presidential Politics of John F. Kennedy*, New York: David McKay.

Moyar, M. (2006) *Triumph Forsaken: The Vietnam War, 1954–1965*, New York: Cambridge University Press.

Muehlenbeck, P. (2012) *Betting on the Africans: John F. Kennedy's Courtship of African Nationalist Leaders*, New York: Oxford University Press.

Myers, D.K. (1998) *With Malice: Lee Harvey Oswald and the Murder of Officer J.D. Tippit*, Milford MI: Oak Cliff Press,

Naftali, T., ed. (2001) *The Presidential Recordings: John F. Kennedy: The Great Crises, vol. 1: July 30 – August 1962*, New York: Norton.

Naftali, T. and Zelikow, P.D. (2001) *The Presidential Recordings: John F. Kennedy: The Great Crises, vol. 2: September – October 21, 1962*, New York: Norton.

Nasaw, D. (2012) *The Patriarch: The Remarkable Life and Turbulent Times of Joseph P. Kennedy*, New York: Penguin.

Nash, P. (1997) *The Other Missiles of October: Eisenhower, Kennedy and the Jupiters, 1957–1963*, Chapel Hill: University of North Carolina Press.

Neal, A.G. (2006) *National Trauma and Collective Memory*, Armonk, NY: M.E. Sharpe.

Nechiporenko, O.M. (1993) *Passport to Assassination: The Never-Before-Told Story of Lee Harvey Oswald by the KGB Colonel Who Knew Him*, Ann Arbor, MI: Birch Lane Press.

Nelson, P.F. (2011) *LBJ: The Mastermind of the JFK Assassination*, New York: Skyhorse Publishing.

Nevins, A., ed. (1960) *The Strategy for Peace*, New York: Harper & Row.

Newfield, J. (1969) *Robert Kennedy: A Memoir*, New York: E.P. Dutton.

Newman, J.M. (1992) *JFK and Vietnam*, New York: Warner.

Nitze, P. (1989) *From Hiroshima to Glasnost: At the Center of Decision*, New York: Weidenfeld and Nicolson.

Niven, D. (2003) *The Politics of Injustice: The Kennedys, the Freedom Rides and the Electoral Consequences of a Moral Compromise*, Knoxville: University of Tennessee Press.

Nixon, R.M. (1978) *The Memoirs of Richard M. Nixon*, New York: Viking Penguin.

Nwaubani, E. (2003) "The United States and the Liquidation of European Colonial Rule in Tropical Africa, 1941–1963," *Cahiers d'Etudes Africaines*, vol. 43: 505–52.

O'Brien, L. (1974) *No Final Victories*, Garden City, NY: Doubleday.

O'Brien, M. (2005) *John F. Kennedy*, New York: St. Martin's Press.

O'Brien, M. (2010) *Re-thinking Kennedy: An Interpretive Biography*, Chicago: Ivan R. Dee.

O'Brien, M. (2011) *John F. Kennedy's Women: The Story of an Obsession*, Chicago: Now and Then Publishing.

O'Donnell, K.P. and Powers, D.F. (1972) *"Johnny, We Hardly Knew Ye,"* Boston: Little, Brown.

Olick, J.K., Vinitzky-Seroussi, V., and Levy, D., eds. (2011) *The Collective Memory Reader*, New York: Oxford University Press.

Oliver, K. (1997) *Kennedy, Macmillan and the Test-ban Debate*, Basingstoke: Palgrave-Macmillan.

Paper, L.J. (1975) *The Promise and the Performance: The Leadership of John F. Kennedy*, New York: Crown.

Paterson, T.G., ed. (1989) *Kennedy's Quest for Victory: American Foreign Policy, 1961–1963*, New York: Oxford University Press.

Parmet, H. (1980) *Jack: The Struggles of John F. Kennedy*, New York: Dial.

Parmet, H. (1983) *JFK: The Presidency of John F. Kennedy*, New York: Penguin.

Pearce, K.C. (2001) *Rostow, Kennedy and the Rhetoric of Foreign Aid*, Kalamazoo, MI: Michigan State University Press.

Posner, G. (1993) *Case Closed: Lee Harvey Oswald and the Assassination of JFK*, New York: Random House.

Preble, C.A. (2004) *John F. Kennedy and the Missile Gap*, Dekalb, IL: University of Northern Illinois Press.

Preston, A. (2006) *The War Council: McGeorge Bundy, the NSC and Vietnam*, Cambridge, MA: Harvard University Press.

Priest, A. (2006) *Kennedy, Johnson and NATO: Britain, America and the Dynamics of Alliance, 1962–1968*, New York: Routledge.

Rabe, S. (1999) *The Most Dangerous Area in the World: John F. Kennedy Confronts Communist Revolution in Latin America*, Chapel Hill: University of North Carolina Press.

Rabe, S. (2009) *US Intervention in British Guiana: A Cold War Story*, Chapel Hill: University of North Carolina Press.

Rabe, S. (2010) *John F. Kennedy: World Leader*, Washington, DC: Potomac Press.

Rasenberger, J. (2011) *The Brilliant Disaster: JFK, Castro, and America's Doomed Invasion of Cuba's Bay of Pigs*, New York: Scribners.

Reeves, R. (1993) *President Kennedy: Profile of Power*, New York: Simon and Schuster.

Reeves, T.C. (1991) *A Question of Character: A Life of John F. Kennedy*, New York: Macmillan.

Rorabaugh, W.J. (2009) *The Real Making of the President: Kennedy, Nixon and the 1960 Election*, Lawrence: University of Kansas Press.

Rosenberg, J. and Karabell, Z. (2003) *Kennedy, Johnson and the Quest for Justice: The Civil Rights Tapes*, New York: W.W. Norton.

Rostow, W.W. (1972) *The Diffusion of Power: An Essay in Recent History*, New York: Macmillan.

Rusk, D. (1990) *As I Saw It*, New York: Norton.

Rust, W.J. (1985) *Kennedy in Vietnam*, New York: Scribner.

Salinger, P. (1966) *With Kennedy*, Garden City, NY: Doubleday.

Schaffer, H. (1993) *Chester Bowles: New Dealer in the Cold War*, Cambridge, MA: Harvard University Press.

Scheim, D.E. (1988) *Contract on America: The Mafia Murder of President John F. Kennedy*, New York: Shapolsky Publishers.

Scheman, L.R. (1988) *The Alliance for Progress: A Retrospective*, New York: Praeger.

Schick, J.M. (1971) *The Berlin Crisis 1958–1962*, Philadelphia: Temple University Press.

Schlesinger, A., Jr. (1965) *A Thousand Days*, Boston: Houghton Mifflin.

Schlesinger, A., Jr. (1978) *Robert Kennedy and His Times*, Boston: Houghton Mifflin.

Schmitt, E.R. (2010) *President of the Other America: Robert Kennedy and the Politics of Poverty*, Amherst: University of Massachusetts Press.

Schoenbaum, T. (1988) *Dean Rusk: Waging Peace and War*, New York: Simon & Schuster.

Schwartz, T. (2003) *Joseph P. Kennedy*, Hoboken, NJ: John Wiley and Son.

Scott, D. and Leonov, A. (2005) *Two Sides of the Moon: Our Story of the Cold War Space Race*, NewYork: Pocket Books.

Shaw, M. (1966) *White House Nanny: My Years with Carolina and John Kennedy Jr.*, New York: New American Library.

Sheehan, N., ed. (1971) *The Pentagon Papers*, New York: Quadrangle Press.

Sherter, S. (1977) *Steel and the Presidency—1962: The Public Interest or Abuse of Power?* Boston: John F. Kennedy Library.

Shrake, E. (1972) *Strange Peaches*, Dallas: Texas Monthly Press.

Sidey, H. (1964) *John F. Kennedy, President*, New York: Atheneum.

Smith, R.B. (1986) *An International History of the Vietnam War: The Struggle for South-east Asia, 1961–1965*, vol. 2, London: Palgrave Macmillan.

Sorensen, T. (1965) *Kennedy*, New York: Harper Row.

Sorensen, T. (2008) *Counsellor: A Life at the Edge of History*, New York: Harper Collins.

Stern, M. (1992) *Calculating Visions: Kennedy, Johnson and Civil Rights*, New Brunswick: Rutgers University Press.

Stern, S. (2012) *The Cuban Missile Crisis in American Memory: Myths versus Reality*, Palo Alto: Stanford University Press.

Stevenson, C.A. (1972) *The End of Nowhere: American Policy towards Laos*, Boston: Beacon Press.

Streeter, S.M. (2006) "Nation-building in the Land of Eternal Counter-insurgency: Guatemala and the Contradictions of the Alliance for Progress," *Third World Quarterly*, vol. 27, no. 1: 57–68.

Taffet, J.F. (2007) *Foreign Aid as Foreign Policy*, New York: Routledge.

Taylor, J.M. (2002) *An American Soldier: The Wars of General Maxwell Taylor*, Washington DC: Presidio Press.

Taylor, M.D. (1972) *Swords and Ploughshares*, New York: Norton.

Thomas, E. (2002) *Robert Kennedy: His Life*, New York: Simon & Schuster.

Thompson, N. (2009) *The Hawk and the Dove: Paul Nitze, George Kennan and the History of the Cold War*, New York: Henry Holt & Co.

Tobin, J. and Weidenbaum, M., eds. (1989) *Two Revolutions in Economic Policy*, Cambridge, MA: MIT Press.

Trask, R. (2005) *National Nightmare on Six Feet of Film*, Danvers, MA: Yeomans Press.

Tregaskis, R. (1962) *John F. Kennedy and PT-109*, New York: Random House.

Tubridy, R. (2010) *JFK in Ireland: Fours Days that Changed a President*, New York: Harper Collins.

US Department of State (1997) *Foreign Relations of the United States 1961–1963, volume X, Cuba, January 1961–September 1962*, Washington DC: Government Printing Office.

US Government Printing Office (1964) *The Warren Commission Report*, Washington, DC: US Government Printing Office.

US HSCA (House Select Committee on Assassinations) (1979) Vol. 9: *The Salerno Report*, Washington DC: USGPO.

US Senate Select Committee on Intelligence Activities (1975) *Interim Report: Alleged Assassination Plots involving Foreign Leaders*, Washington DC: US Government Printing Office.

Vagnes, O. (2011) *Zaprudered: The Kennedy Assassination Film in Visual Culture*, Austen: University of Texas Press.

Walton, R.J. (1972) *Cold War and Counter-revolution: The Foreign Policy of John F. Kennedy*, New York: Viking Press.

Watson, M.A. (1994) *The Expanding Vista: Television in the Kennedy Years*, New York: Oxford University Press.

Wehrle, E.F. (1998) "'A Good, Bad Deal': John F. Kennedy, W. Averell Harriman, and the Neutralization of Laos, 1961–62," *Pacific Historic Review*, vol. 67, no. 3: 349–77.

Weis, W.M. (2001) "The Twilight of Pan-Americanism: The Alliance for Progress, Neo-colonialism and Non Alignment in Brazil, 1961–64," *International History Review*, vol. 23, no. 2: 322–44.

Whalen, R.J. (1964) *The Founding Father: The Story of Joseph Kennedy*, New York: Signet.

Whalen, T.J. (2000) *Kennedy versus Lodge*, Boston: Northeastern University Press.

White, M.J. (1997) *Missiles in Cuba: Kennedy, Khrushchev, Castro and the 1962 Crisis*, Chicago: Ivan R. Dee.

White, T. (1961) *The Making of the President 1960*, New York: Atheneum.

Wiest, A. and Doidge, M. (2010) *Triumph Revisited: Historians Battle Over the Vietnam War*, London: Routledge.

Wills, G. (1982) *The Kennedy Imprisonment: A Meditation on Power*, Boston: Little, Brown.

Woolley, B. (1982) *November 22*, Berkley: Mass Market Publishing.

Wrone, D.R. (2003) *The Zapruder Film: Reframing JFK's Assassination*, Lawrence: University of Kansas Press.

Wyden, P. (1979) *The Bay of Pigs: The Untold Story*, New York: Simon & Schuster.

Wyden, P. (1989) *Wall: The Inside Story of Divided Berlin*, New York: Simon & Schuster.

Young, M. (1991) *The Vietnam Wars 1945–1990*, New York: Harper Collins.

Zeiler, T.W. (1990) "Kennedy, Oil Imports and the Fair Trade Doctrine," *Business History Review*, vol. 64, no. 2: 286–310.

Zeiler, T.W. (1999) *Dean Rusk: Defending the American Mission Abroad*, Washington DC: Scholarly Resources Inc.

Zelikow, P. and May, E., eds. (2001) *The Presidential Recordings: John F. Kennedy: The Great Crises, vol. 3: October 22–28, 1962*, New York: Norton.

Zelizer, B. (1992) *Covering the Body: The Kennedy Assassination, the Media, and the Shaping of Collective Memory*, Chicago: University of Chicago Press.

Zelman, P.G. (1982) *Women, Work and National Policy: The Kennedy–Johnson Years*, Ann Arbor, MI: UMI Research Press.

Index